"What do the epistles of James, Peter, John, and Jude have in common... ~, either neglected or cherry-picked for a few key themes, like faith and works (James) or God is love (1 John). Darian Lockett, an accomplished researcher in this field of study, removes these letters from the shadows by combining patristic evidence, the best of contemporary scholarship, and his own keen reading. His concise, direct, and sometimes passionate style results in a remarkably full historical introduction and canonical exposition of all seven Catholic letters in under three hundred pages. Pastors, students, and other serious Bible readers will find here fresh insight and understanding based on solid learning and due reverence for the treasures these letters contain."

Robert W. Yarbrough, professor of New Testament at Covenant Theological Seminary

"Darian Lockett knows the books of James through Jude well, having written about them extensively. This helpful primer on the Catholic Epistles, which takes a canonical-collection approach, will help readers think carefully about the meaning of these letters and their relevance for today. Here also is a reminder why we need all of Scripture."

Brandon D. Crowe, professor of New Testament at Westminster Theological Seminary and book review editor for the *Westminster Theological Journal*

"All introductions to the Catholic Epistles offer helpful guidance for understanding the context and the content of each of the seven letters individually. Lockett's *Letters for the Church* does this exceptionally well and is worth reading for this reason alone. With this book, however, what Lockett uniquely brings to the table is a sustained reflection on how these seven letters relate to one another, and how they together give us insight into the theology and practice of the early church. Readers will find this approach to be fruitful and illuminating."

Kelly D. Liebengood, dean of the school of theology and vocation, professor of biblical studies and theology, LeTourneau University

"Darian Lockett has provided a richly needed resource on the Catholic Epistles collection for the church and the academy. He introduces the need to read the letters of James through Jude *as a collection*, and deftly draws connections between the letters even as he guides the reader through each text. For those of us who love these letters for their wealth of practical wisdom, this book is a gift. For those who have not spent extensive time in these letters, this book is a necessity."

Mariam Kamell Kovalishyn, assistant professor of New Testament at Regent College, Vancouver

"Darian Lockett provides a helpful and lucid reading of the letters by James, Peter, John, and Jude as a coherent collection of writings that address common concerns in the life of the church. His analysis shows, however, that these documents do not simply agree with each other but are part of an organic whole that provides a deeper understanding of each document, the life of the early church, and the balance of the New Testament canon."

Félix H. Cortez, associate professor of New Testament literature at Andrews University

Letters for the Church

**READING JAMES, 1-2 PETER,
1-3 JOHN, AND JUDE AS CANON**

DARIAN R. LOCKETT

Academic

An imprint of InterVarsity Press
Downers Grove, Illinois

InterVarsity Press
P.O. Box 1400, Downers Grove, IL 60515-1426
ivpress.com
email@ivpress.com

InterVarsity Press® is the book-publishing division of InterVarsity Christian Fellowship/USA®, a movement of students and faculty active on campus at hundreds of universities, colleges, and schools of nursing in the United States of America, and a member movement of the International Fellowship of Evangelical Students. For information about local and regional activities, visit intervarsity.org.

Scripture quotations, unless otherwise noted, are from the Christian Standard Bible®, Copyright © 2017 by Holman Bible Publishers. Used by permission. Christian Standard Bible® and CSB® are federally registered trademarks of Holman Bible Publishers.

Extracts from An Introduction to the Catholic Epistles *by Darian Lockett (T&T Clark, 2012) reprinted by kind permission of T&T Clark, an imprint of Bloomsbury Publishing plc.*

Cover design and image composite: David Fassett
Interior design: Daniel van Loon
Images: St. James: © A. Dagli Orti / De Agostini Picture Library / Bridgeman
     blank white postage stamp: © troyek / E+ / Getty Images

ISBN 978-0-8308-5089-1 (print)
ISBN 978-0-8308-5090-7 (digital)

Printed in the United States of America ♾

InterVarsity Press is committed to ecological stewardship and to the conservation of natural resources in all our operations. This book was printed using sustainably sourced paper.

Library of Congress Cataloging-in-Publication Data
A catalog record for this book is available from the Library of Congress.

P	25	24	23	22	21	20	19	18	17	16	15	14	13	12	11	10	9	8	7	6	5	4	3	2	1
Y	42	41	40	39	38	37	36	35	34	33	32	31	30	29	28	27	26	25	24	23	22	21

For Maddie, Evan, and Aidan

"Now to him who is able to protect you from stumbling and to make you stand in the presence of his glory, without blemish and with great joy" (Jude 24).

Contents

Acknowledgments

IT IS SAID THAT THOUGH research and writing is often a solitary task, it is seldom accomplished without the aid of others. This book is no exception. I'm grateful that nearly every semester I am able to study the Catholic Epistles with Biola University students. Many of the insights and particular features of this book are a direct result of ideas and suggestions from students over the years. The particular shape of this book was conceived during a conversation with Dan Reid in my office in winter 2015. Dan's genuine enthusiasm for a project on the Catholic Epistles that both introduced the letters and stressed their canonical shape and significance was very encouraging. Our conversation took place in the middle of my work on a project that directly influences this one. My monograph *Letters from the Pillar Apostles: The Formation of the Catholic Epistles as a Canonical Collection* provides the evidential basis for the claims regarding canonical connections between the Catholic Epistles made in this book. Upon Dan's retirement, I am grateful that I was entrusted to the capable hands of Anna Gissing of IVP Academic.

Most of this book was written during a research leave in spring 2018 generously given by Talbot School of Theology. I'm grateful to Clint Arnold and Scott Rae for granting and to Doug Huffman, Matt Williams, and the undergraduate New Testament faculty for facilitating my research leave. Matt Williams deserves special thanks as he tirelessly encouraged me to take the leave and to seek the necessary funding. Several individuals gave generously along with Talbot School of Theology in order for me to secure the leave. I am deeply humbled and grateful for the generosity of Robbie Castleman, Iron and Grace Kim, Steve Williams,

Nathan and Abby Goodman, Ron and Barb Goodman, Teresa Swagerty, Jim and Anne Ryun, James and Grace Kim, Trinity Presbyterian Church OC, and, especially, Joyce Lockett. My deepest thanks to you all.

Several colleagues and former students read and commented on all or sections of the work. Thanks are due to Zach Seals, Hannah Grady, and Micah Hogan for reading sections of the text and suggesting improvements. I'm especially grateful to Joyce Lockett, who read the entire manuscript more than once for style and clarity. The work is vastly improved because of her careful eye. In the fall and spring of 2019–2020 the Ekklesia Community used a draft of the book for their study of the Catholic Epistles. I'm grateful for their enthusiastic and warm welcome extended to my wife and me, and especially for Elijah Fan, Laura Poochigian, and Joanne Jung for offering their careful and detailed comments on the work. I also owe a debt of gratitude to Sean Christensen. Sean read the entire manuscript, offering comments on the substance of the entire work. Yet more, Sean has been a conversation partner on the Catholic Epistles over the years, and I have benefited greatly from his insights and, more, his friendship.

My deepest joy and greatest achievement has been being dad to Maddie, Evan, and Aidan. I gratefully dedicate this book to my three children.

Abbreviations

PRIMARY SOURCES

Ant.	Josephus, *Jewish Antiquities*
Haer.	Irenaeus, *Adversus haereses*
Hist. eccl.	Eusebius, *Historia ecclesiastica*
Ign. *Phld.*	Ignatius, *To the Philadelphians*
Ign. *Rom.*	Ignatius, *To the Romans*
Ign. *Smyrn.*	Ignatius, *To the Smyrnaeans*
LXX	Septuagint (Greek Old Testament)

SECONDARY SOURCES

AB	Anchor Bible
BECNT	Baker Exegetical Commentary on the New Testament
CBQ	Catholic Biblical Quarterly
CSB	Christian Standard Bible
ESV	English Standard Version
HCSB	Holman Christian Standard Bible
ICC	International Critical Commentary
KJV	King James Version
LCL	Loeb Classical Library
MNTC	Moffatt New Testament Commentary
NASB	New American Standard Bible
NCBC	New Century Bible Commentaries
NET	New English Translation

NICNT	New International Commentary on the New Testament
NIV	New International Version
NIVAC	New International Version Application Commentary
NPNF2	*Nicene and Post-Nicene Fathers.* Series 2. Translated by Ernest Cushing Richardson. Edited by Philip Schaff and Henry Wace. New York: Christian Literature Company, 1892
NRSV	New Revised Standard Version
NTT	New Testament Theology
PNTC	Pillar New Testament Commentaries
RSV	Revised Standard Version
SBL	Society of Biblical Literature
THNTC	Two Horizons New Testament Commentary
TNTC	Tyndale New Testament Commentaries
WBC	Word Biblical Commentary
WUNT	Wissenschaftliche Untersuchungen zum Neuen Testament

Introduction

THE CATHOLIC EPISTLES give us a unique window into early Christian theology and practice. These letters highlight the centrality of love for not only fellow believers (1 Peter and 1 John) but the neighbor in general (James). They explore the inevitability of trials and testing in life that are ultimately from God and therefore strengthen faith (James and 1 Peter). Throughout these letters one finds the pervasive contrast between allegiances to God and this world as incompatible loyalties (James and 1 John) along with an emphasis on the reality that true faith is always accompanied by a transformed life—a faith united with works (especially Jas 2:14-26). Finally, the concern for correct doctrine both in the face of false teaching (2 Peter and 1 John) and the influence of immoral living (Jude) surfaces again and again.

Though other New Testament letters are also concerned with the connection between orthodox teaching and moral living, the Catholic Epistles are especially focused on this connection. James focuses on hearing and doing, having faith and works integrated together, and 1 Peter encourages Jesus followers to live out their new identity in Christ among a watching, nonbelieving world. First John specifically connects an orthodox confession of Jesus with the moral duty of loving other believers and keeping God's commands. Both Jude and 2 Peter address threats facing the early church. Jude confronts those who deny right doctrine through their immoral and lawless lifestyles, while 2 Peter counters false claims regarding the prophets and Christian expectation for Christ's return as cleverly invented myths. These are some of the particular ways the Catholic Epistles enrich the life of the church by focusing on the connection between faith and works.

Yet despite these theological and practical riches, the Catholic Epistles have not traditionally received the attention they deserve, somewhat standing in the shadow of the Gospels and Paul's letters. This book is an attempt to introduce (or reintroduce) readers to these important Christian letters at the end of the New Testament and to suggest how they might be read together as a canonical collection.

WHAT ARE THE CATHOLIC EPISTLES?

Before moving any further, I should answer the basic question: What are the Catholic Epistles? Some describe these letters as the non-Pauline epistles—thus, the letters not written by the apostle Paul. Others describe them as "concluding letters" or "the end of the New Testament," where the Catholic Epistles are lumped together with Hebrews and Revelation. Some scholars wonder what to do with these leftover letters of the New Testament. Even in the church, the Catholic Epistles are rarely treated as a coherent collection (unlike the Gospels and Paul's letters).

What letters are we talking about? Generally, scholars organize the New Testament documents into groups such as the Gospels and Paul's letters. The term *Catholic Epistles* (or *General Letters*) labels another group of New Testament texts; however, the question is: What letters belong in this group? The Catholic Epistles are variously counted as nine (Hebrews through Revelation) or six (Hebrews through Revelation without the letters of John). Or, perhaps most often, they are grouped together as a list of eight texts (Hebrews through Jude). This last association is so common that when colleges and seminaries do offer classes on non-Pauline letters of the New Testament, it is usually a class focusing on

Hebrews through Jude. This grouping, however, was not known in the early church.

This book will argue that the Catholic Epistles are made up of the letters of James, 1–2 Peter, 1–3 John, and Jude. Such a conclusion is based on evidence from the early church. For example, Eusebius, when discussing the death of James, the Lord's brother, notes: "Such is the story of James, whose is said to be the first of the Epistles called Catholic . . . as is also the case with the Epistle called Jude's, which is itself one of the seven called Catholic" (*Hist. eccl.* 2.23.24–25).[1] In this passage, written sometime around AD 300, Eusebius indicates that there was a collection of seven Christian letters called "Catholic," of which James was first (and perhaps Jude was last).

The makeup of the Catholic Epistles becomes even more clear just after the time of Eusebius. In several lists or comments, the Catholic Epistles are limited to these seven letters and are most always found in the order James, Peter, John, and Jude. About fifty years after Eusebius, Cyril of Jerusalem (ca. 350) recorded a canon list that states, "Receive . . . these the seven Catholic Epistles of James, Peter, John, and Jude" (*Catechesis* 4.36).[2] In the Synod of Laodicea (363), each of the Catholic Epistles were listed by name and placed after the four Gospels and Acts and before the Pauline letters. Athanasius's Easter Letter (367) lists the "Acts of the Apostles and seven letters, called Catholic . . . one by James, two by Peter, then three by John, and after these, one by Jude" (*Festal Letters* 39.5).[3] Though the ordering of the seven letters varies at times, it is only ever the letters of James, Peter, John, and Jude that are called Catholic Epistles.[4]

What do we call these letters? Traditionally, the Catholic Epistles and General Letters have been used as interchangeable titles for these New

[1] All translations of Eusebius are from Lake K. Oulton and J. E. L. Oulton, *Ecclesiastical History*, 2 vols., LCL (Cambridge, MA: Harvard University Press, 1926–1932).
[2] E. L. Gallagher and J. D. Meade, *The Biblical Canon Lists from Early Christianity: Texts and Analysis* (Oxford: Oxford University Press, 2017), 115.
[3] Gallagher and Mead, *Biblical Canon*, 123.
[4] In the majority of the early manuscripts, Hebrews circulated in the Pauline corpus.

Testament books. It should be said that these are Catholic letters not because they are somehow especially connected to the Roman Catholic Church but rather because the term *catholic* means universal. In this sense, the term *catholic* or *general* is a genre distinction. That is, a catholic or general letter is a letter written to a nonspecific or general audience. For example, James is written "To the twelve tribes dispersed abroad" (Jas 1:1), and 2 Peter is written "To those who have received a faith equal to ours" (2 Pet 1:1), and again, Jude writes "To those who are called, loved by God the Father and kept for Jesus Christ" (Jude 1).

Though some of the Catholic Epistles address general audiences, not all of them do so. Both 2 and 3 John are personal letters sent from "the elder" to specific audiences: to the "elect lady" (2 Jn 1) or to "Gaius" (3 Jn 1). Furthermore, both Jude and 1 John address specific situations where either intruders have infiltrated (Jude) or a group of schismatics have left (1 John) a specific church. Thus, technically neither should be called a general letter. These observations should caution against overgeneralizing these letters as uniformly written to general audiences.

Therefore, rather than primarily noting a genre distinction—marking a specific kind of letter—the label "Catholic Epistles" should be understood as a title given to a specific group of early Christian letters. This specific title was not given by the early church as a way to differentiate specific kinds of letters (genre) but rather as a way to identify a specific collection or group of letters (not unlike Paul's letters). In other words, the term *Catholic* is not an adjective (describing a kind of letter) but a proper noun—it is a title given to a specific collection of New Testament letters.[5]

This insight connects to the larger discussion regarding how the New Testament canon was formed. Rather than individual books, such as Matthew or 1 Corinthians, coming into the New Testament canon individually, the early development of the New Testament was characterized by groups of books being received as authoritative. Early on the four

---

[5]For a full argument for this perspective, see chap. 3 in Darian R. Lockett, *Letters from the Pillar Apostles: The Formation of the Catholic Epistles as a Canonical Collection* (Eugene, OR: Pickwick, 2017).

Gospels began circulating among Christian communities as a fourfold collection. Not long after that, a collection of Paul's letters was read by Christians as far as Pontus and Bithynia and was received as Scripture (2 Pet 3:15-16). The central point is that we should not think of the New Testament as developing book by book but rather collection by collection. One of those important collections was the group of letters called the Catholic Epistles.

WHY ARE THE CATHOLIC EPISTLES IMPORTANT?

Now that we understand what letters we are talking about and what to call them, why focus an entire book on them? Christians have received these books as part of Holy Scripture from the beginning, and this is the first reason to focus on them. These letters make up part of the New Testament witness to the gospel of Jesus Christ. As such, they offer a complementary, non-Pauline witness to Christian practice and belief.

A second reason to focus on the Catholic Epistles is that the early church thought they were written in order to defend orthodox faith and morals against the rising challenge of heretics. John's letters are interested in combating false teaching by citing agreed-on apostolic confessions of high Christology—"Who is the liar, if not the one who denies that Jesus is the Christ?" (1 Jn 2:22) and "Many deceivers have gone out into the world; they do not confess the coming of Jesus Christ in the flesh" (2 Jn 7). Likewise, both Jude and 2 Peter are clearly focused on defending the once-for-all entrusted faith by combating false teaching (2 Peter) and false living (Jude).

Finally, the Catholic Epistles are important because they make it clear that Christian faith is a matter of practice as well as of formal belief. James, Peter, and John are all agreed on the assumption that faith without works is dead. The works spoken of in these letters are not those of the Mosaic law but those deeds that spring naturally from faith in Jesus Christ—most importantly, deeds of charity or love. The early church summarized these works as self-sacrifice, generosity, humility, and love. The emphasis on such deeds meant that Christians must be prepared to live their lives and give their lives for the faith. The patient endurance of suffering here and now, living out Christian faith in the midst of a hostile world, is a preparation for giving witness for the gospel even to the point of death, as the example of Jesus' earthly life bears witness. This is why the Catholic Epistles are so important.

HOW TO USE THIS BOOK

The purpose of this book is to introduce the context and content of the Catholic Epistles while, at the same time, emphasizing how all seven letters are connected to each other as they stand in the New Testament canon. While there are other books that introduce these letters, they usually include more than just the Catholic Epistles (typically also treating Hebrews and sometimes Revelation). Furthermore, other introductions do not focus on how the Catholic Epistles were received as a coherent collection in this particular order. This misses a key theological concern, namely, that these letters are not merely one-off writings to disconnected communities, but rather they are a coherent collection of Christian texts that have a unified vision of God and his work in the world through Jesus Christ. Therefore, while introducing the context and content of each of these letters, I will also suggest ways these letters were connected via shared themes and canonical connections.

The book is designed to complement one's own reading of the Catholic Epistles. This text will work best if readers have both this book and the Bible open at the same time. Each chapter will focus on one of the letters (with the exception of chapter five, which will consider 2–3 John together) and will follow the same basic structure. Each chapter opens with an introduction suggesting connections with the previous letter, stressing a canonical connection with neighboring texts. Then a section called "Occasion and Setting" gives a brief outline of the context of the letter, including discussion of author, audience, and genre. The next section describes the overall structure of the letter and outlines the flow of thought in the form of a section-by-section commentary. Rather than giving exhaustive comments about each word or verse, the commentary section focuses on tracing the flow of thought of the entire book. The strength of this approach is that it helps readers actually read through the text with insight into how the theological argument of the letter progresses to its main point.

Throughout these chapters, readers will find two kinds of text boxes offering further insights. First, readers will find "Going Deeper" sections focusing on background issues that help illuminate aspects of the letter. Second, sprinkled through the commentary section, readers will find boxes that highlight themes or theological issues that connect the Catholic Epistles together. These latter boxes are designed to remind readers that these letters were collected together because the early church understood them to be interrelated. The themes highlighted in these text boxes are fleshed out in the concluding chapter of the book. Thus, when reading through the commentary section and coming on a thematic reminder, readers can always refer to the final chapter for further information regarding how that theme is developed through the Catholic Epistles as a whole.

Finally, each chapter concludes with a section for further reading, where important commentaries and monographs are suggested for further research.

My hope in writing this book is that you will discover the rich theological and practical insights woven into these early Christian letters. I am convinced that these treasures are hidden in plain sight not only in the text of each letter but also in viewing these seven letters together as a coherent witness to early faith in Jesus Christ.

FURTHER READING

Chester, Andrew, and Ralph P. Martin. *The Theology of the Letters of James, Peter, and Jude*. NTT. Cambridge: Cambridge University Press, 1994.

Davids, Peter. *A Theology of James, Peter, and Jude: Living in the Light of the Coming King*. Grand Rapids, MI: Zondervan, 2014.

Jobes, Karen. *Letters to the Church: A Survey of Hebrews and the General Letters*. Grand Rapids, MI: Zondervan, 2011.

Lockett, Darian R. *Introduction to the Catholic Epistles*. T&T Clark Approaches to Biblical Studies. London: T&T Clark, 2012.

———. *Letters from the Pillar Apostles: The Formation of the Catholic Epistles as a Canonical Collection*. Eugene, OR: Pickwick, 2017.

Nienhuis, David R. *Not by Paul Alone: The Formation of the Catholic Epistle Collection and the Christian Canon*. Waco, TX: Baylor University Press, 2007.

Nienhuis, David R., and Robert W. Wall. *Reading the Epistles of James, Peter, John and Jude as Scripture: The Shaping and Shape of a Canonical Collection*. Grand Rapids, MI: Eerdmans, 2013.

CHAPTER ONE

The Letter of James

THE LETTER OF JAMES is the first of the Catholic Epistles and one of two letters we have from the brothers of Jesus (Jude is the other). James's placement as the first Catholic Epistle and its connection to Jude within this collection was noted in the ancient church. Eusebius, the church historian, records: "Such is the story of James, whose is said to be the first of the Epistles called Catholic . . . as is also the case with the Epistle called Jude's, which is itself one of the seven called Catholic" (*Hist. eccl.* 2.23.24–25). Reflecting on this passage, John Painter concludes, "James and Jude, the brothers of Jesus, form . . . the bookends of this collection."[1]

James and Jude show signs of connection both at the beginning and ending of their letters. The letter opening of Jude identifies the author as "Jude, a servant of Jesus Christ and a brother of James" (Jude 1). The reference to James not only draws a connection between James and Jude as brothers but also suggests an association between the two letters as well. Also, rather than draw on the family relationship with Jesus to support their authority, both James and Jude call themselves servants of Jesus Christ (Jas 1:1; Jude 1). These connections at the beginning of each letter are accompanied by an interesting connection between the ending of the

---

[1]John Painter, "The Johannine Epistles as Catholic Epistles," in *The Catholic Epistles and Apostolic Tradition*, ed. K.-W. Niebuhr and R. W. Wall (Waco, TX: Baylor University Press, 2009), 458n11.

letters. The final exhortation of James, situated just after a discussion of prayer, brings the letter to an abrupt end and instructs believers to recover a fellow brother or sister from "the error of his way" (Jas 5:20), and the final exhortation of Jude calls for believers to have mercy on those who waver or dispute. Both letters end with a command for restoration. These connections reinforce the relationship between James and Jude, which in turn functions like a bracket defining the boundaries of the Catholic Epistle collection.[2]

OCCASION AND SETTING

Authorship. Unlike several of the other letters in the New Testament (for example the letters of Paul), James does not contain many concrete hints regarding the letter's original occasion or historical situation. Looking at the letter itself, the text claims to have been written by "James, a servant of God and of the Lord Jesus Christ" (Jas 1:1). The name "James" (Hebrew, *Ya‘ăqōb*; Greek, *Iakōbos*) was a very common name in the first century, and it is likely that a well-known James must be in view because the letter contains no further description of the author's identity. If this is accurate, two questions arise: First, what well-known individual named James is in view, and, second, after identifying this James, is this individual the actual or historical author of the letter?

Taking up the first question, though in the New Testament there are several individuals named James, only two are clear possibilities who could have authored the letter. First, James the son of Zebedee, who was the brother of John and one of the Twelve (Mk 1:19; 5:37; 9:2; 10:35; 14:33) and acted as a prominent member within the circle of Jesus' disciples. Yet he was put to death by Herod Agrippa I in AD 44 and thus much too early to author this letter (see Acts 12:2). Second is James, "the Lord's brother" (Gal 1:19). Though he was not one of the twelve disciples or a follower of Jesus during his ministry, James, the Lord's brother, was well

---

[2]For more on this connection between James and Jude see Darian R. Lockett, "James and Jude as Bookends to the Catholic Epistles Collection," in *The Identity of Israel's God in Christian Scripture*, ed. Don Collett et al., Resources for Biblical Study 96 (Atlanta: SBL Press, 2020), 353-66.

known due to his relationship to Jesus. After Jesus' resurrection, he became a disciple (Jn 7:5; Acts 1:14) and influential leader of the Jerusalem church (Acts 12:17; 15:13; 21:18), where he served until his death in AD 62. James, the brother of Jesus, was widely known and respected as the leader of the church in Jerusalem and therefore is likely the James referred to in this letter.

Though scholarship is virtually unanimous in concluding that James, the Lord's brother, is the James referenced in James 1:1, there is little to no consensus regarding whether he was the actual author of the letter. For much of the modern era scholars have argued that this letter was composed between AD 80 and 120 by an unknown author. Due to its lack of coherence, Martin Dibelius concluded that James must have been drawn together from several sources and could never have been sent as a real letter.[3] Further, the letter was relatively slow to receive acceptance into the New Testament canon, and it seems unlikely that the flowing style of the Greek and Hellenistic concepts used in the text could have been produced by a Jewish carpenter in Galilee. These objections have largely been addressed in recent scholarship.[4]

The first clear reference to James as both authored by the Lord's brother and fully canonical appears in Origen some time before 253.[5] Jerome states that James only gained recognition in the church "little by little" (Jerome [ca. 393], *Lives of Illustrious Men* 2). In the end, James was fully accepted in the Western church at the Synod of Hippo (ca. 393) and the Third Council of Carthage (ca. 397).

A number of scholars have argued that James, the brother of Jesus, was the actual historical author.[6] For these scholars, three factors strengthen this conclusion: first, the similarities in the Greek between the letter and

---

[3]Martin Dibelius and Heinrich Greevan, *James*, trans. Michael A. Williams (Philadelphia: Fortress, 1976), 2.

[4]See especially Luke Timothy Johnson, *The Letter of James*, AB (New York: Doubleday, 1995), 221; Todd C. Penner, *The Epistle of James and Eschatology: Re-reading an Ancient Christian Letter*, Journal for the Study of the New Testament Supplemental Series 121 (Sheffield, UK: Sheffield Academic Press, 1996).

[5]Though there could be allusions to James much earlier; see *1 Clement* and *Shepherd of Hermas*.

[6]Richard Bauckham, *James: Wisdom of James, Disciple of Jesus the Sage* (London: Routledge, 1999), 25.

James's speech in Acts 15:13-21; second, the way in which the author loosely alludes to Jesus' sayings, which would be less likely after such traditions were written down in the Gospels; and third, lack of any reference to the destruction of the Jewish temple. Rather than appealing to his family relationship with Jesus, the author only mentions his position as a "servant" (*doulos*, "slave," Jas 1:1) of God and the Lord Jesus Christ. For some, the author leaving out reference to his familial relationship with Jesus reinforces the authenticity of authorship.[7]

If James, the brother of Jesus, wrote the letter, the composition date would be roughly between AD 46 and 62. The upper limit is fixed because about the year 62, when the procurator Festus died, the high priest, Ananus II, had James stoned to death—at least according to Eusebius (*Hist. eccl.* 3.23.3-17; see also Josephus, *Ant.* 20.200). Those who argue the letter was produced by an unknown individual writing under the pseudonym of James, however, insist on a date between AD 80 and 120.

Audience. As with the historical author, the letter contains very little information about the identity of the audience. Typically, identifying the audience rests on how one understands the phrase "to the twelve tribes dispersed abroad" (Jas 1:1). There are two prevailing interpretations: first, some argue that the address to the twelve tribes is a metaphorical reference to the Christian church. Rather than indicating anything about the readers' geography or ethnicity, this reference describes the audience as the "true Israel" who are exiled (on the earth) from their proper home (heaven). There are, however, some difficulties with this view. For example, the New Testament never records an instance where the tribal constitution of Israel ("the twelve tribes") is used to refer to the church. Though Paul famously refers to the church as the "Israel of God" (Gal 6:16), there are no references to the church as "the twelve tribes." A second view understands the address to the twelve tribes as a reference to Christians of Jewish heritage. On this view, the title "twelve tribes"

---

[7]Bauckham, *James*, 17, 25.

alludes to the twelve sons of Jacob, who became the leaders of the twelve tribes of Israel. Likewise, the term *diaspora* (translated in the CSB as "dispersed abroad") was used to denote Jews living outside Palestine (see Jn 7:35). More than just a term to convey Jewish exile, *diaspora* also communicated God's displeasure and punishment of his people for their sins. In the New Testament, the term *diaspora* usually does not refer to the church (yet note the prominent exception in 1 Pet 1:1), which might be another indication that the recipients of the letter were Christian Jews living in either Rome or Syria, or perhaps in various locations throughout the Mediterranean world.[8]

The identification of the recipients as Christian Jews may be further strengthened by several features of the text: the free use and expectation that the readers would understand the Old Testament (Jas 1:25; 2:8-13), the reference to their meeting place as a *synagōgē* (Jas 2:2), their faith in the Lord Jesus as "Christ" or "Messiah" (Jas 2:1), and the use of Old Testament and Jewish metaphors. Furthermore, there has been a lively discussion as to whether the audience was poor (Jas 1:9-11; 5:1-6) or a mix of rich and poor members. This has been notoriously difficult to determine with confidence, yet one should note that James addresses his readers as neither rich nor poor in James 2:1-13. Regardless of their social and financial standing, it is clear that the audience was experiencing hardships (Jas 1:2-4; 5:7-11) and that such external pressure created tensions within the audience (Jas 4:1-2, 11-12).

If James, the brother of Jesus, is the author of the letter, it is then likely that he wrote from Jerusalem within the time frame that James was a leader there. The Palestinian setting of the letter's composition is strengthened by internal factors: merchants seeking profits (Jas 4:13-17), absentee landlords defrauding a poor and landless labor force (Jas 5:1-6), and social and legal repression of the economically disadvantaged (Jas 2:5-7).[9]

---

[8]Bauckham, *James*, 14.
[9]See D. A. Carson, Douglas J. Moo, and Leon Morris, *An Introduction to the New Testament* (Grand Rapids, MI: Zondervan, 1992), 414-15.

Genre. Many of the historical conclusions regarding James have been profoundly influenced by the work of Martin Dibelius. Dibelius argued that James belongs to a type of writing called *paraenesis*, a collection of unoriginal maxims or proverbs designed to give moral instruction.

Paraenesis is characterized by a loose collection of moral sayings and essays held together by catchwords (repeated words or related terms that connect otherwise unrelated material). There are clear examples of moral sayings or proverbs (Jas 2:13, 26; 3:12, 18; etc.), essays (Jas 2:1-13, 14-26; 3:1-12; 3:13–4:10), and catchwords (greeting/joy, Jas 1:1-2; lacking/lacking, Jas 1:4-5; etc.) in James. And clearly both paraenesis and James contain many imperatives. Dibelius argued that such literature generally lacks literary coherence, theological content, and social location, yet a majority of scholars have questioned each of these conclusions regarding paraenesis in general and as applied to James specifically.

That the text opens with the form of a letter challenges the conclusion that James lacks any social location. James 1:1 contains a stereotypical form of letter opening, consisting of the formula of parties ("person *x* to person/group *y*") and a salutation ("greetings") typical of most ancient Greek letters. The other two typical elements of a first-century letter are a letter body and a salutation. James clearly contains a text body (Jas 1:2–5:6, or all the way to Jas 5:20); it does not, however, end with the typical letter salutation. Many have noted that James does not contain any personal greetings, requests, or specific information, some of which would be expected in a typical letter. These conspicuous omissions have led many to deny James as a real letter at all and thus maintain that the loose letter form in James is fictional. Others, notably Richard Bauckham, claim that the crucial point is that the letter opening makes James formally a letter whether it was ever sent or not.[10]

While James seems to have been a real letter, many have noted that the letter body closely resembles Jewish Wisdom literature. James, like Jewish Wisdom literature, characteristically gives commands, instructions, and

---

[10]Bauckham, *James*, 12.

specific examples (namely, contrasts between the wise and foolish), all of which direct the readers on the path of discipleship. The letter contains several brief, direct, and practical admonitions and bears a specific concern for wisdom in the lives of the readers (Jas 1:5; 3:13-17). Many have noted that James most closely resembles the Old Testament book of Proverbs and the apocryphal book of Sirach, books that communicate practical insight and instruction in the conduct of life. While the body of James bears all the characteristics of Wisdom literature, the opening frames the text as a letter. Thus, thematically and structurally James belongs to the tradition of Jewish Wisdom literature, though it was fashioned (and probably sent) as a letter.[11]

GOING DEEPER: TWO WAYS IN JAMES

Because James sharply contrasts life versus death and the humble versus the proud, the letter has been compared to the "two ways" motif. The two ways was a typical motif that appeared in Jewish Wisdom literature. It uses the imagery of a road or path in order to contrast positive and negative actions, all to illustrate the stark difference between the path of the righteous and the path of the wicked. In Jewish tradition, the two ways motif finds its origins in the blessings and curses associated with the covenant, especially found in the Pentateuch (Lev 26:1-39; Deut 28; 30:15-20) and in Hebrew Wisdom literature (Ps 1). The motif draws on the image of ways, roads, or paths, which in turn are used as metaphors contrasting the life of righteousness or unrighteousness, life or death, or wisdom or foolishness (and, in Greco-Roman literature, virtue or vice).

A typical characteristic of the two ways is that it highlights not only the path or way but also the ultimate end or goal of a particular path or way of living. The fact that at the end of the path is reward or punishment finds illustration in Deuteronomy 30:15: "See, today I have set before you life and prosperity, death and adversity." Growing out of Jewish wisdom tradition, the two ways motif developed from the blessings

---

[11]Bauckham, *James*, 15.

and curses derived from a this-worldly covenantal context to a way of talking about eschatological blessing and punishment.

James contains several elements of the two ways motif. First, the terms *way* and *life* appear in James. The opening section of the letter (Jas 1:2-8) contains an implicit contrast between the one who is perfect and the "double-minded," and it is the double-minded who is "unstable in all his ways" (Jas 1:8). James also uses *way* and *life* language to describe the peril of the double-minded in James 1:11; 4:14; 5:5, 19. For James, these two ways ultimately have very different ends. The final destination or ultimate end of the two ways of living simply is either death (Jas 1:15; 5:20) or life (Jas 1:12, 18). Second, as in the traditional motif, James indicates that there are guides or principles that lead an individual along either of the two paths. On the path of life, one is guided by the word (Jas 1:18, 21, 22, 23; 3:2), the law (Jas 1:25; 2:8, 9, 10, 11, 12; 4:11), and wisdom (Jas 1:5; 3:13, 15, 17); but those on the path of death are led along by desire (Jas 1:14, 15; 4:2). Finally, James contains several examples of positive and negative ethical statements (e.g., positive and negative commands regarding ethical conduct). On one hand, he uses negative commands, warnings *against* a particular action, and on the other, positive commands, exhortations *to adopt* a particular action (Jas 1:19-20; 4:8, 10; 5:9, 12, 16). Often these positive and negative commands are accompanied by an additional clause or rhetorical question giving motivation to continue living in keeping with a particular ethical framework or worldview.

Identifying the thematic use of the two ways in James helps in discerning both coherence and purpose in the letter. When people came into a new relationship with God through "faith in our glorious Lord Jesus Christ" (Jas 2:1), they needed to reorient themselves to a new way of life and a new way of viewing the world. The two ways strategy was used to help new converts adopt new behaviors, habits, and affections by offering them two clearly opposed ways of life. James takes up this strategy in order to challenge his readers to a new way of living and being in the world.

STRUCTURE

As the commentary section will focus on tracing the flow of thought through the text, it will be helpful first to make a few comments about the overall structure of the letter. James can be divided into three unequal parts: the letter opening or prescript (Jas 1:1), the introduction to the letter's themes (Jas 1:2-27), and the development or exposition of those themes in James 2–5.

The first chapter loosely functions as a preface (or table of contents) that gives a brief introduction to the majority of themes developed further in the rest of the letter. Each of these topics is presented through James 1 in quick succession, with very few links between them. More developed connections exist between the topics introduced in James 1 and the corresponding sections in James 2–5. For example, the ideas introduced in James 1:2-8 are developed further in James 3:13-18 (wisdom), James 5:7-11 (patient endurance), and James 5:13-18 (effectiveness of prayer). The various connections between themes in James 1 and their development in James 2–5 will be highlighted in the commentary section.

OUTLINE

I. Letter opening (Jas 1:1)

II. Introduction of themes (Jas 1:2-27)

   1. "Wholeness" and "double-mindedness" (Jas 1:2-8)

   2. The lowly brother and the rich (Jas 1:9-11)

   3. The path of "desire–sin–death" versus the way of life (Jas 1:12-18)

   4. Human anger and God's righteousness (Jas 1:19-21)

   5. Doing versus merely hearing the word (Jas 1:22-25)

   6. True versus false religion (Jas 1:26-27)

III. Exposition of themes (Jas 2:1–5:20)

   1. Partiality and the law of love (Jas 2:1-13)

   2. Faith and works (Jas 2:14-26)

3. The tongue (Jas 3:1-12)

4. True and false wisdom (Jas 3:13-18)

5. A call to the double-minded to repent (Jas 4:1-10)

6. Against judging one another (Jas 4:11-12)

7. Denunciation of merchants (Jas 4:13-17)

8. Denunciation of landowners (Jas 5:1-6)

9. Holding out until the coming of Christ (Jas 5:7-11)

10. Speaking the whole truth (Jas 5:12)

11. Prayer (Jas 5:13-18)

12. Reclaiming those who err (Jas 5:19-20)[12]

COMMENTARY | LETTER OPENING | JAMES 1:1

The opening statement in James 1:1 is enough to classify James as a letter. The author addresses the letter to the "twelve tribes dispersed abroad." As mentioned above, it is relatively clear that the letter is addressed to ethnic Jews who now are followers of Jesus living outside the land of Israel.

The letter is written by James, or in Greek *Iakōbos* (Jas 1:1; Hebrew *Yaăqōb*). A letter from *Yaăqōb* to "the twelve tribes" would evoke the larger story of Israel, where Jacob's twelve sons become the leaders of the twelve tribes of Israel. This is all the more striking when one realizes that at the time the letter was written, the twelve tribes no longer existed. The ten (or nine and a half) tribes of the north were snuffed out in the Assyrian invasion of 722 BC. Though the phrase "twelve tribes dispersed abroad" most certainly refers to the tribal membership and geographical context of his Jewish-Christian readers, at the same time it evoked "the lively first-century Jewish hope of the return of the exiles of all twelve tribes to the land of Israel. It incorporates the addressees in the messianic programme of redemption which Jesus had initiated by appointing twelve apostles," as Richard Bauckham writes.[13] James

---

[12]This outline is lightly adjusted from Bauckham, *James*, 62-64.

[13]Richard Bauckham, "James, 1 Peter, Jude and 2 Peter," in *A Vision for the Church: Studies in Early Christian Ecclesiology in Honor of J. P. M. Sweet*, ed. M. Bockmuehl and M. B. Thompson (Edinburgh: T&T Clark, 1997), 154.

clearly understands that the coming of Jesus has initiated this reconstitution of God's people, which now includes Gentiles into the eschatological people of God.

COMMENTARY | INTRODUCTION OF THEMES | JAMES 1:2-27

The remainder of the first chapter introduces the major themes of the letter in quick and somewhat disconnected succession and thus reads like a collection of wisdom sayings or proverbs. The concerns voiced in this introductory chapter resurface in later sections of the letter in expanded form, yet not in the same sequence. Throughout the commentary section addressing James 2–5, many of these connections will be highlighted.

"Wholeness" and "double-mindedness" (James 1:2-8). The opening section contrasts the one who is "mature and complete,

Diaspora in James and I Peter

The term *diaspora* only appears three times in the New Testament: John 7:35; James 1:1; and 1 Peter 1:1. Of all the letters in the New Testament, only James and 1 Peter describe their audience as in the diaspora. Whereas James likely assumes a geographic diaspora, 1 Peter envisions a temporal diaspora, where "during your time living as strangers" (1 Pet 1:17) describes Christians living in a kind of exile from their ultimate home in heaven. The key term *diaspora* draws the two letters together theologically by marking their readers as those living in some kind of exile.

lacking in nothing" (Jas 1:2) and the one who "lacks wisdom" (Jas 1:5), is a "doubter" (Jas 1:6), and ultimately is "double-minded" (*dipsychos*, Jas 1:8). In James 1:4, the key word *teleios* (translated either as "mature" or "perfect") announces a major (perhaps unifying) theme on display throughout the letter. For James, the word *perfect* entails wholehearted or single-minded devotion to God. The key term *teleios* appears several times throughout the letter either as a noun or verb (Jas 1:4 [2×], 15, 17, 25; 2:8, 22; 3:2; 5:11). The road to being perfect runs through various trials such that the testing or proving of faith leads to endurance and ultimately maturity, lacking nothing—perfection or wholeness, which is the ultimate goal of James.

It is important to ask whether James considers perfection as something attainable now or only in the future. A few observations are worth considering: first, the key terms "trials" (*peirasmois*) and "endurance" (*hypomonēn*) are often used in an eschatological context in Jewish and Christian writings; second, New Testament texts that are considered parallel passages to James 1:2-4 (1 Pet 1:7; Rom 5:3-4) are set within an eschatological context; and finally, James associates the overcoming of trials with receiving "the crown of life" (Jas 1:12; often understood as a reference to eternal life). These observations suggest that the goal of being perfect or attaining wholeness has a future orientation. Throughout the letter, however, James expects this characteristic to be developing or at least initiated in the life of his readers now.

In contrast to perfection, the one who is lacking (specifically wisdom) is to "ask God" (Jas 1:5). Yet, such asking must be done in faith, not doubting. Failing to ask in faith is tantamount to second-guessing or vacillating irresolutely between two choices. This person is halfhearted and divided in loyalty toward God—this is what it means to ask while doubting (Jas 1:5) and ultimately reveals the character of the double-minded (Jas 1:8). This is the one who, even when asking, should not expect to receive anything from God (Jas 1:7). Furthermore, James says the double-minded person is "unstable [*akatastatos*] in all his ways," an idea that conveys the sense of being unsettled or unstable in one's way of life. This opening section introduces the major theme of perfection or wholeness (wholehearted devotion to God, *teleios*) and its opposite, double-mindedness. Throughout the rest of the letter, James offers examples of both wholeness and double-mindedness.

The lowly brother and the rich (James 1:9-11). The next unit is a reversal statement where James contrasts the "lowly [*tapeinos*] brother" (my translation) with the "rich" (*plousios*). The lowly one is commanded to "boast" (*kauchasthō*) in his "exaltation" or his high position (Jas 1:9), while the rich one is to boast in his humiliation (*tapeinōsei*). The noun *humiliation* is related to the noun *lowly* and thus highlights the ironic reversal of status and position of the "rich" person.

Two observations are in line: first, whereas the text is very clear that the lowly one is a brother in James 1:9, it is unclear whether the rich one in

James 1:10 is also a brother. Though the term *brother* is missing from James 1:10, some argue that because it was common for some terms to drop out of the second of two phrases, one could reasonably assume the term in the second phrase. However, others object to seeing the rich as a fellow believer in Christ because of the sharp denunciation of the rich in James 5:1-6. A second observation is that James has used the term "lowly" (*tapeinos*) rather than the word typically used to describe the poor (the term *ptōchos*). The lowly not only are materially poor (as *ptōchos* alone would indicate) but also are humble or completely dependent on others for their needs. Perhaps the lowly are an example of those who are completely or wholeheartedly devoted to God—by contrast, later in the letter the rich are associated with the arrogant (Jas 4:13-17) and proud (Jas 4:6; 5:1-6).

This second observation is not intended to downplay the fact of material poverty among the first Christians, as though one could elevate the attitude of poverty ("spiritual poverty" or humility) and thus actually be materially wealthy and at the same time spiritually "poor." Though James draws attention to the attitude and disposition of the lowly, an attitude that either the materially well-off or disadvantaged can take up, he is clearly influenced by the traditional concern for the weak, vulnerable, and materially poor throughout his letter (Jas 1:27; 2:5, 14-17; 4:6). Here it is merely important to note that the categories of lowly and rich are first representative of larger groups of people and associated with characteristic attitudes (that is, the humble one wholly dependent on God versus the arrogance of the proud).

The path of "desire-sin-death" versus the way of life (James 1:12-18). Using several terms that connect back to James 1:2-4, this section pronounces a blessing on the one "who endures trials" (*hypomenei peirasmon* in Jas 1:12; compare with *peirasmois* in Jas 1:2 and *hypomonē* in Jas 1:4) through having "stood the test" (*dokimos* in Jas 1:12; compare with *dokimion* in Jas 1:3). This is one who, like the "mature and complete" individual in James 1:2-4, endures trials and as a result receives the "crown of life." The sequences of events in James 1:2-4 and James 1:12 are strikingly similar:

the "testing–endurance–perfect" sequence in James 1:2-4 is mirrored by the "testing–endurance–crown of life" sequence in James 1:12. The one who is wholly devoted to God or the one who has life moves through the experience of trial and endurance, which results in approval.

Though expressed by the same word in Greek (*peirasmos* in both cases), there is a clear distinction between testing and temptation in James 1:12-13. Whereas implicitly it is God who is in control of testing (which leads to endurance and maturity; Jas 1:2-4, 12), James is very clear that God is never the source of temptation ("No one undergoing a trial should say, 'I am being tempted by God,'" Jas 1:13). Rather, temptation originates from one's "own evil desire," which does the work of luring away and enticing (Jas 1:14). The sequence of events begins with being enticed by one's own evil desire, the result of which "gives birth [*tiktei*] to sin," and finally, when "sin is fully grown, it gives birth [*apokuei*] to death." It is helpful to note that the previously repeated sequence of "testing–endurance–perfect/crown of life" (found in Jas 1:2-4, 12) is now replaced by the opposing sequence of "desire–sin–death" in James 1:13-15. These two antithetical sequences should be seen as diametrically opposed ways of living, one leading to wholeness and life, the other leading to double-mindedness and death.

Not only does the sequence of desire–sin–death stand in opposition to what precedes, but it also stands in contrast to what comes next. In James 1:18, God's own purpose is announced: "Because of his own choice he gave us birth [*apekuēsen*] by the word of truth" (my translation). The repetition of the verb *apokueō* ("gives birth to death" in Jas 1:15, and "gave us birth" in Jas 1:18) helps draw attention to the contrast between one's own evil desire giving birth to death and God's will or choice to bring to life by the word of truth. Evil desire involves sin, which leads to death, but, by contrast, God's will enlists the word of truth to bring about birth. So here the desire–sin–death sequence stands in opposition to the "God's choice–by the word–life" sequence.[14] Next, the misconception of God's

---

[14]Scot McKnight notes: "The contrast could not be clearer: as desire leads to sin and sin gives birth to death, so God 'gives birth' to 'us' through his word (1:18)." See McKnight, *The Letter of James*, NICNT (Grand Rapids, MI: Eerdmans, 2011), 124.

responsibility for the evil of temptation (which Jas 1:13 warns against) is replaced by the correct understanding of God in James 1:17. Rather than tempting with evil, God is the giver of all good gifts.

Human anger and God's righteousness (James 1:19-21). Because anger does not reflect God's righteousness, James exhorts his readers to put off the old way of living and to receive the implanted word. Just before the contrast between human anger and God's righteousness, James instructs his readers to be quick to hear, yet slow to speak and slow to anger.

The contrast between God's righteousness (to which James's readers must "be quick to listen," Jas 1:19) and human anger (to which his readers must be slow) is further illustrated in the inferential conclusion in James 1:21: "Therefore, ridding yourselves of all moral filth and the evil that is so prevalent, humbly receive the implanted word, which is able to save your souls." Here James first states the negative aspect of accomplishing righteousness, namely, taking off impurity or metaphorically stripping off the pre-Christian lifestyle (see the similar phrase in 1 Pet 2:1). Second, he states the positive aspect of the same: "humbly receive the implanted word," which accomplishes God's righteousness, "able to save your souls" (Jas 1:21).

Much has been made of the phrase "implanted word" (*emphytos logos*). The word *emphytos* appears only here in the New Testament and can mean either "innate" or "implanted." Some argue the term means "innate" as in an innate moral character or virtue. If that is the case, then the phrase "the word of truth" in James 1:18 must refer to creation rather than to the message of the gospel. If one follows these two points, then the innate word refers to "the original capacity involved in the Creation in God's image which makes it possible for a man to apprehend a revelation at all."[15] This, however, does not explain how something innate is actually received. The term *emphytos* does not appear often in biblical literature, but the Greek version of the Old Testament consistently uses the related verb "plant" (*kataphyteuō*) in the context of Israel's restoration to the land (Ex 15:17). The use of

---

[15]F. J. A. Hort, *The Epistle of St. James* (London: Macmillan, 1909), 37.

"plant" (*kataphyteuō*) in Jeremiah 31:27-28 is especially helpful: "'The days are coming,' declares the LORD, 'when I will plant the kingdoms of Israel and Judah with the offspring of people and of animals. Just as I watched over them to uproot and tear down, and to overthrow, destroy and bring disaster, so I will watch over them to build and to plant [*kataphyteuein*],' declares the LORD" (NIV).

This passage is an example of the Old Testament using the plant metaphor to refer to God's work of restoration. One interpretation of James's implanted word is that it is an allusion to Jeremiah's prophecy of this promised internalized Torah planted within the hearts of the people of God.[16] Thus, it is likely that James is referring to God's instruction—now completely revealed in Jesus—which is implanted or written on the heart of the believer. Thus, God's implanted word is able "to save your souls."

Doing versus merely hearing the word (James 1:22-25). The contrast between being a doer and a mere hearer is the focus of James 1:22-25. The section opens with the instruction, "Be doers of the word, and not hearers only, deceiving yourselves," and is stated in the reverse in what follows: "Because if anyone is a hearer of the word and not a doer." James likens the one who only hears to someone who glances at her natural face in a mirror, only to go away and forget what she saw—an image that suggests the viewer forgets what kind of person she was. The moment of looking should have been an opportunity for self-examination, yet in James's example, it has become a superficial moment to check one's hair or makeup, a moment only to be forgotten, which fails to make any lasting difference.

Here we see another contrast, this time between the doer and the mere hearer of the word. In contrast to the mere hearer, who fails to examine himself, the doer of the word is "one who looks intently into the perfect law of freedom" (Jas 1:25). Why would there be such an abrupt change from the word (in Jas 1:18, 21, 22-23) to law (in Jas 1:25)?

---

[16]Douglas Moo argues that "James' description of the law as 'planted in' the believer almost certainly alludes to the famous 'new covenant' prophecy of Jer. 31:31-34." See Moo, *The Letter of James*, PNTC (Grand Rapids, MI: Eerdmans, 2000), 32.

There is good reason to think that *word* and *law* are referring to the same thing.[17] Thus, the word is the means of initial rebirth in James 1:18, and, though implanted by God in James 1:21, it must also be received in meekness. Then, in James 1:22-25 it is clear that true believers must know and do "the perfect law of freedom." The perfect law is none other than the implanted word in the hearts of responsive believers. Thus, for James the word and law, though distinct, are closely related. This word/law gives birth (Jas 1:18) and is able to save (Jas 1:21). The word/law is likely the fulfillment of Jeremiah's promise of God's law written on the heart. This word of truth and implanted word thus is a new character, a new heart's disposition created in the believer. It must be received (Jas 1:21), and, as the "law of freedom," it must be obeyed (Jas 1:22-25). Finally, the one who looks intently and is a doer receives a blessing in what he does (Jas 1:25)—which connects back to the blessing announced on the one who endures trials (Jas 1:12).[18]

True versus false religion (James 1:26-27). The overarching contrast posed in the last two verses of James 1 is between true and false "religion" (or perhaps better "piety," the actions springing from religious conviction). James argues that claiming devotion to God while failing to control one's speech leads to self-deception (Jas 1:26). Whereas James has warned of deception already in James 1:16-17, there he was concerned with the wrong understanding of God's good giving. Here, the one who thinks of himself as religious or pious while not controlling his tongue is actually worthless.

---

[17]Bauckham argues: "It is difficult to be sure what James means by the unparalleled term 'law of freedom' (1:25; 2:12), but in a context of Jewish thought the reference is presumably to the freedom to serve God, freedom from sin, freedom from the evil inclination which otherwise succumbs to temptation and produces sin and death (1:14-15). In that case, it should probably be related to 'birth by the word of truth' (1:18) and 'the implanted word' (1:21), which give the ability to overcome the evil inclination and set one free to serve God in obedience to his law. Behind these ideas would seem to lie Jeremiah's prophecy of the new covenant (31[LXX 38]: 31-34). The prophecy is not of a new law, but of *the* law, God's law, put within one and written on one's heart (Jer. 31:33)" (*James*, 146, emphasis original).

[18]Several ideas in this paragraph are from Mariam J. Kamell, "Soteriology of James in Light of Earlier Jewish Wisdom Literature and the Gospel of Matthew" (PhD diss., University of St Andrews, 2010), 137.

By contrast, the one who visits "orphans and widows" and keeps "unstained from the world" displays what James calls, "pure and undefiled religion" (Jas 1:27). Thus, true religion or piety includes both social action and pure doctrine or theology. Visiting widows and orphans was a common concern in the Old Testament. It was considered a covenantal obligation emphasized both in the Torah (Ex 22:20-21; 23:9; Lev 19:9-10, 33; 23:22; Deut 10:17-19; 14:28-29; 16:9-15; 24:17-18; 26:15) and the prophets (Amos 2:6-8; 3:2; Hos 12:8-9; Mic 3:1-4; Zeph 1:9; Zech 7:8-10). Throughout the Old Testament the usual examples of poor and vulnerable in the land were widows, orphans, sojourners (resident aliens), and day laborers. These particular groups were vulnerable to exploitation at the hands of the rich and powerful because either they could not work or they did not own land.[19] The notion of the verb "to visit" (*episkeptesthai*) orphans and widows conveys the idea of visiting with the intent to help, and in the Greek Old Testament God himself is often the subject of verbs such as these (Gen 21:1; 50:24-25; Ex 3:16; 4:31). Thus, the command to give aid to the vulnerable is a command not only to obey God but also to reflect God's own actions and character.

Along with visiting orphans and widows, the one who demonstrates genuine religion or piety must keep himself "unstained from the world" (Jas 1:27). This could be understood purely in a doctrinal sense—keep pure doctrine; do not believe what the world believes. Yet in James, the notion of keeping oneself unstained from the world also stresses one's actions. For James, keeping unstained from the world means wholehearted devotion to God; it entails doing, not just hearing; it requires caring for the vulnerable and controlling the angry tongue; it means, as we will see, being motivated by God's mercy rather than judgment, having faith that works, and being animated by wisdom from above.

In summary, it is significant that the introductory chapter is bookended with concern for wholeness, seen in the word *perfect* or *mature* (Jas 1:2-4) and *purity* (Jas 1:26-27). Though distinct ideas, the terms

---

[19]Bauckham, *James*, 146-47.

perfect (or *wholeness*) and *purity* overlap and express the related concern for exclusive devotion to God—wholehearted, rather than double-minded, devotion to God (*perfect*) and devotion to God expressed in a degree of separation from the world (*purity*). Throughout the letter, James expresses various ways individuals lack wholeness because of the inability to separate from the worldview of the world (for example, in the treatment of the poor, failing to maintain faith and works, failure to control the tongue, etc.). This association between *perfect* (or wholeness) and *purity* is worth keeping in mind as one reads through the letter.

COMMENTARY | EXPOSITION OF THEMES | JAMES 2:1-5:20

Partiality and the law of love (James 2:1-13). James 2:1-13 should be viewed as a unit, with the key contrast between partiality (Jas 2:1-7) and keeping the love command (Jas 2:8-13) running through it. James 2:1 contains the thesis statement of the entire passage, which is conveyed as a command: "My brothers and sisters, do not show favoritism as you hold on to the faith." The rest of the passage unpacks this central idea. The word "favoritism" or "partiality" (*prosōpolēmpsia*) is a rare Greek word (appearing only four times in the New Testament), and it seems to be a word coined in the Greek translation of Leviticus 19:15.[20] Because James goes on to quote Leviticus 19:18 in James 2:8, it seems that the author had themes and ideas from Leviticus 19 in mind.

After announcing the thesis in James 2:1, the letter goes on to illustrate the incongruity of partiality and faith in Christ. The evil of partiality is illustrated by the different treatment of the rich and poor in the community (Jas 2:2-4). The episode is set in a typical gathering (*synagōgēn*, Jas 2:2) where two very different people enter. First, a rich man enters wearing "a gold ring and dressed in fine clothes." The clothing and jewelry tell of his wealth and social standing (the gold ring

---

[20]Luke Timothy Johnson states: "The term *prosōpolēmpsiais* is a Christian neologism, based upon the Hebrew *naśa panim*, translated in the LXX by *labanein prosōpon*, literally 'to lift up the face/ appearance' (see Lev 19:15 and, similarly, Mal 1:8), in the sense of 'respecting persons' or showing favoritism (see Lk 20:21; Gal 2:6; also *Did* 4:3; *Barn.* 19:4)" (*Letter of James*, 221).

The Use of Leviticus in James and I Peter

Leviticus 19 and the command to love stands behind much of James 2. James quotes Leviticus 19:18 in James 2:8, and the reference to partiality in James 2:9 echoes Leviticus 19:15 as well. Similarly, 1 Peter also quotes from Leviticus 19:2 in 1 Peter 1:16 and then alludes to Leviticus 19:15 in the reference to the impartial Father in 1 Peter 1:17. Finally, it is likely that 1 Peter 1:22 is an allusion to the love command in Leviticus 19:18 as well. Along with the other striking similarities between James and 1 Peter, their dependence on and interpretation of Leviticus 19 is significant because both letters call their readers to love without partiality, relying on Leviticus 19 as authoritative grounds.

often marked one as from the equestrian class, which was one of the highest in the Roman aristocracy). By contrast, the other man, labeled as "poor" (*ptōchos*), enters the gathering wearing filthy clothes. The special treatment of the wealthy man, who is offered a prime seat in the gathering place, and the dismissive treatment of the poor man, who is relegated to either stand at the back or sit near one's footstool, is indicative of their difference in social status. Especially the command to sit down by one's footstool suggests submission or disgrace.[21] The point is that the judgment or prejudice against the poor exhibited in the congregation is a result of double-mindedness toward God. It manifests a "What can the rich give me?" attitude and fails to hear the instruction already outlined in James 1:27, where genuine piety is expressed in visiting orphans and widows, the kind of poor James has in mind here.

Second, after the illustration, James poses several rhetorical questions that further expose the injustice of showing partiality toward the rich (Jas 2:5-7). God's choice of those who, by the world's standards, are poor (Jas 2:5) is in direct opposition to the community's rejection of those same poor people: "Yet you have dishonored the poor" (Jas 2:6). This stands in tension with what James has indicated

---

[21]The term "footstool" or "feet" (*hypopodion*) is used elsewhere in biblical Greek, always of God's divine seat (LXX Ps 110:1). This may be an implicit reference to individuals usurping God's authority in judgment.

previously, namely, that the rich should boast in their humiliation and the lowly in their exaltation (Jas 1:9). Showing favoritism toward the wealthy in the assembly is an implicit claim to stand in judgment over other people—something only God has the right to do. Such favoritism is not compatible with faith in the glorious Lord Jesus. Rather than using God's standard of measure (that is, God's framework of judgment), James's readers are using the world's standard of measure, which favors the rich over the poor. This, of course, is radically inconsistent for those claiming to "hold on to the faith in our glorious Lord Jesus Christ." Rather than loving the neighbor (Jas 2:8), the congregation has chosen the rich at the expense of the poor. This is a failure to keep God's law— the law of love of neighbor.

Finally, James demonstrates the incongruity of partiality and faith in Christ by means of the authority of the Old Testament (Jas 2:8-13). Instead of using the world's measurement system to disqualify the vulnerable poor, James reminds his readers of God's standard. So, what is God's standard of judgment? It is his Torah, God's gracious law. The specific standard from the Torah that demonstrates the incompatibility between favoritism and faith in Christ is the love command, "Love your neighbor as yourself," which James calls the royal law. Yet the Torah is such that one cannot claim to have kept one part of it while ignoring others—the law is whole and must be kept as a whole (perhaps like a balloon, it does not matter whether it is popped from the left or the right; either way, the whole is broken). This point is illustrated by another appeal to the Old Testament, this time with reference to two of the Ten Commandments in James 2:11. It does no good to claim to have kept one law while at the same time breaking another—thus, if one "stumbles at one point," one is "guilty of breaking it all" (Jas 2:10).

James is saying: you might congratulate yourselves that you have not committed adultery or murder, but in your self-righteousness, you have broken the law of love of neighbor because you have shown partiality toward the unrighteous rich, thinking that they might benefit you and your community. In light of this James challenges his readers to speak and act as "those who are to be judged by the law of freedom." Addressing both speaking and acting is a way of saying in all of life to behave as those submitted to God's standards or Torah. Here, through appealing to the love command, James stresses that God's primary requirement is to show mercy to others. Jesus himself described the unforgiving slave who, after receiving mercy, failed to show it to others (Mt 18:21-35). Doug Moo argues: "The 'mercy' that James has been referring to in this context is human mercy, not God's (v. 12). We therefore think it more likely that he is making a point about the way in which the mercy we show toward others shows our desire to obey the law of the kingdom and, indirectly therefore, of a heart made right by the work of God's grace."[22] The one who has received and understood mercy shows it to others and thus, "mercy triumphs over judgment" (Jas 2:13).

Faith and works (James 2:14-26). This passage has become one of the most studied in James because of its apparent contradiction of Paul's teaching about salvation by faith alone. Though the relationship with Paul's teaching on justification by faith alone is important, in order to understand James's argument, we must come to this text on its own terms and only after that consider its relation to Paul. Rather than pitting faith against works, this section contrasts two antithetical kinds of faith: faith with works and a so-called faith without works—an idea already announced in the contrast between the mere hearer and the one who both hears and does in James 1:22-25. The section opens with two rhetorical questions, where the second refers back to the first. When James asks, "Can *such* faith save him?" or "Can *that* faith save him?" the faith that James has in mind, according to the context, is a faith that has no works. James draws the conclusion that faith without works is no faith at all and therefore, of course, cannot save.

This opening distinction between faith with and without works is at once supported by a negative example showing that "faith, if it doesn't have works, is dead by itself" (Jas 2:17), which is followed by an argument (specifically a diatribe) ending with the rhetorical question that again

---

[22]Moo, *Letter of James*, 118.

asserts, "faith without works is useless" (Jas 2:20). As common in James, he offers a vivid illustration and here the example is of a fellow believer seeking the basic needs of clothing and food (Jas 2:15-17). Lacking clothing means the fellow believer could merely be underdressed (only in undergarments) or actually naked—either way, he is not prepared for the current conditions. Along with clothing, the fellow believer lacks food for the day, which could suggest that rather than months' worth of groceries, he just needs a meal. It is worth noting that the verb "lacking" (*leipomenoi*) repeats the same verb from James 1:5, where if any lacks wisdom they should ask from God. It is interesting that these people are asking from other believers, and the expectation, as we saw in James 1:27, is that believers are called to care for the vulnerable just as God himself cares for them. Yet, rather than giving the material things needed, the believer in need is only given words. But this is an empty offer of words in the face of real, immediate human need. The example in James 2:14-15 illustrates how words without actions are useless, and, by extension, claiming to have faith without works—that is, claiming to have faith without any deeds of love, mercy, or charity—is useless. Thus, the summary in James 2:17 insists that faith is "dead by itself."

James 2:18-20 introduces an imaginary opponent whose wrong position is refuted for the sake of instructing his audience. But what does James's opponent actually say? In order to answer this question, we must first determine the limit of the quotation, which has proven quite difficult. Most modern translations confine the quote to James 2:18: "You have faith, and I have works." However, one prominent exception is the NASB, which extends the quotation to the end of the verse: "But someone may well say, 'You have faith, and I have works; show me your faith without the works, and I will show you my faith by my works.'" For several reasons, the longer quotation is unlikely. If the phrase, "But someone may well say," introduces an imaginary opponent, then the longer quotation does not make sense, because now the opponent is saying, "I will show you my faith by my works," which is actually James's point, not his opponent's.

Even with the shorter quotation, there remains a second issue to clarify—the identity of the speakers. The shorter quotation could be literally translated, "You are having faith, and I am having works." The question is: Who is the "you" and who is the "I"? The most likely solution is that the pronouns are not intended to identify James and his opponent specifically, but rather they are marking out two different positions in the argument generally. That is, the "you" and the "I" refer, on the one hand, to a person who has faith (the "you") and on the other hand, to one who has works (the "I"). Thus, the objection of the imaginary opponent is that faith and works can or must be separated—one person can have faith and another person can have works. But this is what James is arguing against; rather than being separated, James argues that faith and works must go together. Therefore, he argues: "Show me your faith without works, and I will show you faith by my works" (Jas 2:18). Then, to drive the point home, James offers an example: "You believe that God is one. Good! Even the demons believe—and they shudder" (Jas 2:19). This is a reference to the *Shema*, Israel's statement of faith in the one God (Deut 6:4). Though James's audience believes the right thing—God is one—they do not respond, in contrast to the demons, who actually respond to this theological truth by trembling.

James, then, offers two positive examples of faith in contrast to the false notion that works can be detached from true faith. First, he offers the example of father Abraham (Jas 2:21, 23) and then, somewhat ironically, Rahab (Jas 2:25). Both individuals are offered as examples that demonstrate faith is made complete by works (Jas 2:22) and that a person "is justified by works and not by faith alone" (Jas 2:24).

First, in James 2:21, James refers to Abraham's obedience in offering his son Isaac: "Wasn't Abraham our father justified by works in offering Isaac his son on the altar?" (Jas 2:21). From this lived example, James draws the general conclusion, "You see that faith was active together [*synergeō*] with his works, and by works, faith was made complete, and the Scripture was fulfilled that says, Abraham believed God, and it was credited to him as righteousness, and he was called God's friend" (Jas 2:22-23). It is in Genesis 15:6 that Abraham believes what God says, and he is counted righteous, yet it is later, in Genesis 22, that Abraham demonstrates his faith through his willingness to sacrifice Isaac. This act is the supreme instance of Abraham's faith working along with his works (Jas 2:22). In Genesis 15:6, God declares Abraham righteous on account of his faith (Gen 15:6), yet this declaration is confirmed by Abraham's test of faith in sacrificing Isaac (Gen 22). This test demonstrated the genuineness of Abraham's faith (note the link back to Jas 1:2-4). Therefore, James concludes that a person is justified by works and not by faith alone (see "Going Deeper: Paul and James on Justification" following).

Like the events in Abraham's life, James also calls on the story of Rahab the prostitute (Josh 2:4, 15; 6:17) in James 2:25. Rahab acts in faith when she hides the Israelite spies while confessing, "the LORD your God is God in heaven above and on earth below" (Josh 2:11). So, just like Abraham, Rahab acted in confirmation of her faith, which resulted in her being listed as one of the examples of faith in the catalogue in Hebrews 11:31. Doug Moo observes:

> ## Faith and Works
>
> The necessary unity of confession and ethics—or faith and works—is a central concern for James, and it is examined in detail here in James 2. The connection between faith and works is implicit throughout 1 Peter (where the good works of Christians are on display for nonbelievers), and it surfaces again in 1 John 3:16-18.

> Critical to understanding the argument of the section and integrating it successfully into a broader biblical perspective is the recognition that James is not arguing that works must be added to faith. His point . . . is that genuine biblical faith will inevitably be characterized by works. Trying to add works to a bogus faith is an exercise in futility. . . . James, in a sense, proposes for us in these verses a "test" by which we determine the genuineness of faith: deeds of obedience to the will of God.[23]

This series of examples regarding faith, like the previous section (Jas 2:1-13), is brought to a conclusion with a proverb that contrasts living (with works) and dead (without works) faith: "For just as the body without the spirit is dead, so also faith without works is dead" (Jas 2:26).

---

[23]Moo, *Letter of James*, 120.

GOING DEEPER: PAUL AND JAMES ON JUSTIFICATION

The interpretation of James has been greatly influenced by the question of how the letter is related to Paul. Simply put, the central question is whether James's language in James 2 is a deliberate response to and rebuttal of either Paul himself or a misunderstanding of Paul's teaching. This tension arises from what has been seen as a flat contradiction between their teaching on justification. For Paul, justification comes through faith alone and not by works (Rom 3:28; Gal 2:16); for James, justification is bound up with works because a person "is justified by works and not by faith alone" (Jas 2:24).

In the face of this apparent contradiction, there have been several attempts to make sense of the tension: (1) James is understood to be written very early (pre-AD 48), and thus prior to and independent of both Paul's letters and the subsequent reception of his teaching; (2) James composed his letter later (late 50s or early 60s) and constitutes a direct response to and rebuttal of Paul himself or his theology; (3) James was much later (AD 80–120) and is a self-conscious correction of a distorted form of Paul's law-free gospel; and (4) James, regardless of being early or late, is not comparable with Paul.[24] Positions (1) and (4) both find ways to avoid conflict, while (2) and (3) posit some kind of direct or indirect tension between Paul and James.

Three central issues must be considered in the debate. First, James never addresses the key issues of circumcision or food laws, both of which are at the heart of the conflict. Second, Paul and James refer to works in different ways. Whereas Paul speaks against works of the law (Gal 2:16; 3:2, 10), James never speaks of works of the law but rather uses *works* as a neutral term for good deeds and charitable action. Third, Paul and James must be set within their own contexts. Where Paul is combating those who would have Gentiles practice Jewish circumcision in order to be included in the people of God, James speaks to Christian Jews who, by virtue of their perceived special status, think that a verbal profession of faith (Jas 2:19) is adequate for justification and

---

[24] Andrew Chester and Ralph P. Martin, *The Theology of the Letters of James, Peter, and Jude*, NTT (Cambridge: Cambridge University Press, 1994), 47.

thus are ignoring social responsibilities (Jas 2:2-6, 14-17). Finally, one must consider how James and Paul use the key verb "justify" (*dikaioō*). The word is used three times in James (Jas 2:21, 24-25), but Paul uses it twenty-three times in Romans and Galatians. The verb can either be translated "to pronounce righteous" or "to demonstrate something or someone right" (examples of this usage are found in Mt 11:19; 12:37). Matthew follows typical use of the term where referring to the demonstration of something as righteous or just. James uses the word in this latter, demonstrative sense. That is, James speaks of Abraham's works as evidence or demonstration that God had previously declared him righteous. So, whereas Paul uses the term in the sense of "pronounced or conferred righteous," James uses the term simply as "shown to be righteous." As with so many issues in interpretation, one's conclusions regarding the relationship between the teaching on faith and works in James and Paul rest on the conclusions one reaches in the areas of authorship, audience, and genre. Here it is at least plausible that both James and Paul articulate the importance of justification within their own unique contexts independent of each other.[25]

The tongue (James 3:1-12). In the next section James warns his readers of the disproportionate influence of the tongue by contrasting the ability to control speech with stumbling in one's use of the tongue. As James turns his attention to speech ethics, the right use of the tongue could be understood as an example of faith and works going together—one who controls the tongue has both faith and works. James argues that the one who "does not stumble in what he says, he is mature, able also to control [*chalinagōgēsai*] the whole body" (Jas 3:2), as opposed to the one who stumbles in the use of the tongue (Jas 3:6). This forms a direct link back to James 1, where the concern for speech ethics was first noted. There the one who "thinks he is religious without controlling [*chalinagōgōn*] his tongue" is deceived, and his piety before God is useless (Jas 1:26)— the rare word "to bridle" or "control" [*chalinagōgeō*] only appears in

---

[25]Bauckham, *James*, 127-40.

James 1:26; 3:2 in all the New Testament, thus even more drawing the two passages together.

This section opens with a warning that not many should become teachers due to the greater judgment they will face. It is unlikely that this means teachers will be judged by a higher standard or that they will be judged more severely, but rather, teachers will be scrutinized more closely because of their very public and influential position. This is similar to Jesus' declaration that the scribes will receive a harsher sentence because of their influential position (Mk 12:38-40; Mt 23:13-15).

The power of the tongue is illustrated in James 3:3-5 through a series of examples of small or weak things exerting disproportionate influence over large things (e.g., a bit in a horse's mouth, a ship's rudder, and a spark igniting a large forest). These illustrations are drawn to a conclusion in James 3:6, where the tongue, though small, is a world of evil able to defile "the whole body." The repetition of the phrase "the whole body" in James 3:6 connects back to James 3:2, reinforcing the influence of the tongue especially over the entire body. The imagery of the tongue and the whole body can be taken in two different, yet related, ways: first, the tongue could simply refer to the physical muscle that controls speech and thus disproportionally influences one's entire body. A small organ can negatively affect the entire person. However, second, the image of the tongue could represent the influence of a teacher who exercises a degree of control over the entire community (the whole body). Either way the disproportional influence of the tongue is highlighted.

The passage then moves on to further contrasts: tamable animals versus the untamed tongue (Jas 3:7-8), and the blessing (correct) versus cursing (incorrect) tongue (Jas 3:9-10). The general contrast between the right and wrong use of the tongue is illustrated by several images from nature in James 3:11-12. In James 3:7-8, James draws a contrast between taming animals and the untamable tongue. The list of animals resembles the categories of animals found in Genesis 9:2 and must include all animal life, which is under the domain of humans. It is, then, ironic that humans can bring the largest animals under their control but cannot tame the small muscle in their mouths.

The specific way in which humans are unable to tame the tongue is illustrated next, the inconsistency of the tongue: "With the tongue we bless our Lord and Father, and with it we curse people who are made in God's likeness. Blessing and cursing come out of the same mouth" (Jas 3:9-10). Highlighted by the clear reference to creation in the reference to humans made in the image of God (Gen 1:26), the utter duplicity of humanity is demonstrated most clearly in speech ethics. The same instrument of God's praise is used, in turn, to defame creatures made in his image.

The illustrations in James 3:11-12 show, ironically, that nature cannot do what humans can—nature cannot be double-minded or duplicitous in speech. These powerful metaphors indicate that plants (and water from a spring) produce according to their kind, and failure to produce according to kind goes against nature. The paradigmatic act of ordering living things after their kind is present in Genesis 1 (plants, Gen 1:11-13; animals, Gen 1:24-25), while Leviticus 19:19 reinforces this order. James drives home the point that while nature itself cannot transgress God's order, humans unfortunately can. Thus, this section is more lament over human sinfulness than moral instruction—James concludes: "My brothers and sisters, these things should not be this way" (Jas 3:10).

True and false wisdom (James 3:13-18). This passage describes two types of wisdom and contrasts them with respect to their origin ("from above" versus "earthly, unspiritual, demonic") and also with respect to what they produce in the life of the community. As in James 2:14-26, this section starts with a rhetorical question: "Who among you is wise and understanding?" The question is followed by the indication that wisdom is demonstrated by "good conduct" and the "gentleness that comes from wisdom" (Jas 3:13). The implication is that true wisdom is not reducible to content or knowledge—knowing the right truths or doctrines is not enough to be wise. Rather, wisdom is demonstrated through good works and the general disposition of gentleness, which is wisdom's product. This seems deeply challenging to the notion that knowledge is power or that the wise exert control over others; rather, for James, true wisdom produces meekness.

James begins first with the so-called wisdom that stands in opposition to God's wisdom. The origin of this wisdom reveals something about its character. This so-called wisdom "does not come down from above but is earthly, unspiritual, demonic" (Jas 3:15)—it is wisdom from below. Each adjective—*earthly* rather than heavenly; *unspiritual* or *natural*, describing life apart from God; and *demonic*—indicates intensifying degrees of distance from and opposition to God. Related to its origin, this wisdom from below produces the destructive characteristics of "bitter envy and selfish ambition" (Jas 3:14), both of which destroy compassion and community.

On the other hand, James describes true wisdom as "wisdom from above" (Jas 3:17). Because this wisdom is from above, it, of course, originates with God himself. James 1 claims: "Every good and perfect gift is from above, coming down from the Father of lights" (Jas 1:17), and that if one lacks wisdom one should ask God, and he will give it (Jas 1:5). These connections help clarify James's understanding that wisdom is not just acquired by human effort or learning, but wisdom is a divine gift, given by God. Because wisdom comes from God as a gracious gift, it cannot be manipulated or faked. Rather, as a gift, it must be received with humility and treated as an unmerited grant. The remainder of James 3:17 lists the qualities produced by wisdom from above: it is first pure (*hagnē*; compare Jas 1:27, where religion is "pure"); peaceable (*eirēnikos*); "gentle" (CSB) or "willing to yield" (NRSV); "compliant" (CSB) or "open to reason" (ESV); "full of mercy and good fruits"; "unwavering" (CSB; *adiakritos*, most other translations have "impartial"); "without pretense" (*anypokritos*). This list of character qualities has been compared to the fruit of the Spirit in Galatians 5. Finally, the section contrasting earthly wisdom and wisdom from above is rounded off by a proverb: "And the fruit of righteousness is sown in peace [*eirēnē*] by those who cultivate peace [*eirēnēn*]" (Jas 3:18). There is a key thematic connection made between the list and the closing proverb. Wisdom from above is peaceable, and righteousness is sown in peace by those making peace. This connection highlights the primary orientation and effect of wisdom from above—it is characterized by and thus produces peace, especially peace within the community. Such peace (and its harvest) is the product of wisdom from above, in contrast to the "bitter envy and selfish ambition" and consequent "disorder and every evil practice" of wisdom from below.

A call to the double-minded to repent (James 4:1-10). The central contrast in James 4:1-10 is between the one who humbly draws near to God and the one who stands in proud friendship with the world. The contrast in this passage echoes the contrast between the two kinds of wisdom in the previous section—wisdom from below animates "wars and fights" in the community (Jas 4:1), whereas wisdom from above leads to humble repentance (Jas 4:7-11). The passage opens with an indictment (Jas 4:1-6) and then moves to a call for repentance—to return to humble loyalty to God (Jas 4:7-10).

The central focus of the passage comes to the surface in James's opening question: "What is the source of wars and fights among you? Don't they come from your passions that wage war within you?" (Jas 4:1). Notice that the question sets up a focus on the cause rather than the result of the conflict. The cause of the conflict is misguided human "passion" or "desire" (note the connection between "your passions" [*hēdonōn*] in Jas 4:1 and one's "own evil desire" [*epithymias*] in Jas 1:14). Shifting from a rhetorical question to an accusation, James continues: "You desire [*epithymeite*] and do not have. You murder and covet and cannot obtain" (Jas 4:2). James's relentless rhetoric points to the underlying problem: misalignment with God as a result of human desire. James's audience does not have what they need because they either fail to ask or ask with wrong motives—certainly they are not asking God for wisdom (Jas 1:5), as previously instructed. James says "you ask with wrong motives," or literally "you ask evilly," which does not indicate a failure to use the correct formula in prayer but rather an evil purpose (a desire to manipulate) when approaching God (Jas 4:3).

The accusation against his audience comes to a climax in James 4:4: "Adulteresses! Don't you know that friendship with the world is hostility toward God? So whoever wants to be the world's friend becomes God's enemy" (HCSB). Frustrated desires are due to wrong asking, and wrong asking is an indication of a rebellious disposition toward God. The label "adulteresses" (*moichalides*, a feminine plural noun) connects back to the Old Testament, where Israel (the bride) is in covenant relationship with God (the groom). This covenant relationship is found in the Torah and the Prophets, where it is couched in terms of marriage (Is 54:4-8). There God is rejected by unfaithful Israel, and thus the unfaithfulness of Israel is metaphorically depicted as adultery (Ps 73:27; Jer 3:6-10; 13:27; Is 57:3; Hos 3:1; 9:1; Ezek 16:38; 23:45). Alongside the covenant-marriage image, the language of friendship here does not refer merely to enjoyable company but rather to loyalty and allegiance—the two images (marriage and friendship) reinforce the conflict between competing loyalties to God or to the world.

God and the World as Incompatible Allegiances

James is clear that one cannot be loyal to both God and the world. This contrast is also clear in James 1:27; 3:14-17. The sharp contrast between God and the world is also clearly articulated in 1 John 2:15-17 and is implicit in 1 Peter, 2 Peter, and Jude.

Because of their equivocation in loyalty to God, James calls his audience to repentance by quoting the Old Testament: "God resists [*antitassetai*] the proud, but gives grace to the humble [*tapeinois*]" (Jas 4:6, quoting Prov 3:34). The rest of the passage uses a series of commands urging his readers to repent from friendship with the world. It is especially the first and last commands that bookend the section: "Therefore, submit to God" (Jas 4:7) and "Humble [*tapeinōthēte*] yourselves before the Lord and he will exalt you" (Jas 4:10). Repentance is accomplished in part through submission to God and thereby resisting the devil. Repentance is never just a turning away from evil, but also entails turning to God in complete loyalty. Repentance is further described by cleansing the hands and purifying the heart, both ideas richly attested in the Old Testament.[26] In James 4:8, hands and heart refer to both external behavior and internal attitude, or, in other words,

---

[26]The command is to "cleanse your hands" and "purify your hearts" is reminiscent of Ps 24:4.

the whole person. Finally, James commands the repentant to mourn and weep, and let laughter be turned into mourning and joy to gloom. These are common expressions of sorrow over judgment in Israel's prophetic literature, especially in the context of covenant unfaithfulness.[27]

The section calling for repentance (Jas 4:7-10) concludes with a reiteration toward humility: "Humble [*tapeinōthēte*] yourselves before the Lord, and he will exalt you" (Jas 4:10). The verb "to humble" (*tapeinoō*) is related to the noun "humble" (*tapeinos*) in James 4:6 from the quotation of Proverbs 3:34 and connects back to the "lowly" (*tapeinos*) person in James 1:9. The call to repentance and humility is a means to restore wholeness. Throughout the letter we have seen James's primary concern is that his readers be whole before God in action and devotion. From the beginning of James 2, the author notes several ways to fail in being whole: ignoring God's standard of measure by showing favoritism (Jas 2:1-13), wrongly living as if faith and works can be separated (Jas 2:14-26), allowing what one says to stain the whole body (Jas 3:1-12), and allowing oneself to be animated by the wrong kind of wisdom (Jas 3:13-18). In light of these ways of failing to live in God's wholeness, James calls his readers to repentance and humble submission to God in James 4:1-10.

Against judging one another (James 4:11-12). The flow of thought from this point on in the letter is not easy to identify—it is even more difficult than previous sections. There are at least six, perhaps seven individual sections in the final portion of James: James 4:11-12, 13-17; 5:1-6, 7-11, 12, 13-18, 19-20. Even though these sections are grammatically (and topically) disconnected from one another, the underlying issue running through this part of the letter is a clash of worldviews. In James 4:11-12, James speaks of slanderous speech that runs the risk of denying love of neighbor, followed by examples of arrogant self-reliance seen in merchants (Jas 4:13-17) and the greedy indulgence of the rich (Jas 5:1-6), then by lack of prayer (Jas 5:13-18) and wandering away from the path of life

---

[27]Lam 5:15: "The joy of our hearts has ceased; Our dancing has been turned into mourning." See also Joel 1:5, 12, 16; Jer 16:9; 25:10.

(Jas 5:19-20). A common thread running through these passages in particular is a denial of God as the ultimate judge. By contrast, those who remain patient and wait for God must respond with a resolute reaffirmation of God's will, marked by his ordering of events (Jas 4:15) and the reality that he is returning to reward the faithful and judge the sinful (Jas 5:1, 3, 5, 7)—it is to this path or way that the erring brother or sister must return (Jas 5:19-20).

The major thrust of James 4:11-12 is the warning against slanderous speech used against fellow believers. The contrast, implicitly, is between two behaviors: either slandering a brother and thus judging the law, or refusing to slander because the fellow believer is a neighbor to be loved, not judged. James warns, "The one who slanders or judges a brother or sister, slanders and judges the law" (Jas 4:11, my translation).

> ## The Love Command
>
> The command to love one's neighbor already surfaced in James 2:8, and it appears here too. This theme runs through each of the Catholic Epistles (e.g., 1 Pet 1:22; 2:17; 3:8; 1 Jn 2:7-11; 3:10-11; 4:20-21; 5:1-2).

It is important to notice that James equates slander and judgment. This is because when one slanders another person, a judgment is rendered against that person. The association of slander and judgment likely comes from Leviticus 19:15-16: "Do not act unjustly when deciding a case. Do not be partial to the poor or give preference to the rich; judge your neighbor fairly. Do not go about spreading slander among your people." Thus, slander is a kind of unjust judging that is not loving toward the neighbor. In turn, judging a brother is equivalent to judging the law of God, specifically because while judging the brother or neighbor one is failing to love. If one is judging the law, one is certainly not doing it—James has already stressed being a doer of the law in James 1:22-25 and expanded on it in James 2:14-26. In the end, to judge one's brother, and thus God's law, is to forsake God's instruction, the Torah. In the act of slander, one sets oneself above God's law as a critic, and a critic does not obey the commands of the Torah—most importantly to "love your neighbor as yourself" (Lev 19:18)—but rather stands as judge over such commands.

There is no greater way to fail in complete and single devotion to God than to act as God's rival in deciding which of his instructions to follow.

Denunciation of merchants (James 4:13-17). In the next two sections James illustrates the danger of judging God's law by deciding which instructions to follow—both are examples of double-mindedness. The two passages (Jas 4:13-17; 5:1-6) are stylistically similar, and both read like a prophetic denunciation. They share the distinct opening phrase, "come now" (*age nyn*), which is a frozen imperative or a phrase that once was a command but now has become a stock expression used to gain the attention of the one singled out for judgment. It is a phrase used especially in Israel's prophetic literature.

First, James warns merchants: "Come now, you who say, 'Today or tomorrow we will travel to such and such a city and spend a year there and do business and make a profit'" (Jas 4:13). Yet, we might ask, why does James find fault with them? He calls special attention to the comprehensive way in which these merchants fail to acknowledge God in their plans. The merchants neglect God's providence temporally ("today or tomorrow"), geographically ("we will travel to such and such a city"), in duration ("spend a year there"), nature of activity ("do business"), and outcome (will "make a profit"). It is not business per se but the arrogant attitude of assuming human control over all these aspects of life that James condemns. This is living out a kind of practical atheism—one might confess trust in God but functionally live as though God does not exist. James goes on to warn, "You do not know what tomorrow will bring. . . . You are like a vapor that appears . . . then vanishes" (Jas 4:14-15). Rather than acknowledging God's will in life, planning and acting without reference to God's providence is the height of arrogant pride. The contrast between arrogant boasting and humble submission ("If the Lord wills") is underlined with the implicit juxtaposition between the one knowing the good and doing it and the one knowing to do good and not doing it (Jas 4:17).

Denunciation of landowners (James 5:1-6). James 5:1-6, 7-11 may be considered separately, with James 5:1-6 serving as the second of two examples of double-mindedness along with James 4:13-17. However, it is also possible to understand the section denouncing the rich (Jas 5:1-6) as directly connected to what follows, serving as the negative contrast to James 5:7-11, where brothers and sisters are encouraged to wait patiently for the coming of the Judge. There are good reasons for understanding either connection, but the present discussion will consider James 5:1-6 in conjunction with James 5:7-11 because of James's preference for presenting two possible ways in contrast.

James 5:1-6 is composed of two subsections, an announcement of judgment (Jas 5:1-3) and an accusation (Jas 5:4-6), and both are reminiscent of Israel's prophets (Is 13:6; 14:31; 23:1, 6, 14; 32:9-14; Jer 49:3). "The rich" refers to the landed aristocracy, who employed the very poor to work their land for the sake of enriching themselves. James announces future judgment on the oppressive actions of the rich as if they are actually happening to them now (prolepsis). James commands the rich to "weep and wail" because "your wealth has rotted. . . . Your gold and silver are corroded, and their corrosion will be a witness against you. . . . You have stored up treasure in the last days" (Jas 5:2-3). The combination of the two commands, "weep [*klausate*] and wail [*ololyzontes*]," was not common in the Greek of the day and likely came directly from Israel's prophets, where the message was directed at those confronting divine judgment.[28] That the rich have stored up treasure "in the last days" not only is an indication that their judgment is about to begin but further illustrates the object of their confidence and trust in the time of judgment.

After the proleptic announcement of judgment (Jas 5:1-3), James offers a list of accusations against the rich: they defraud day laborers (Jas 5:4), live self-indulgent lifestyles (Jas 5:5), and condemn and murder the innocent (Jas 5:6).

In first-century Palestine, day laborers depended on their wages each day to feed and clothe their families, and thus going the night without payment often could lead to economic ruin or threaten starvation. The

---

[28]See especially Is 10:10; 13:6; 14:31; 15:2-3; 16:7; 23:1, 6, 14. Is 15:2, 3, 5, 8 combine both terms in the same passage.

concern for justice specifically with regard to the payment of day laborers is reflected in the Torah and the Prophets:

> Do not oppress your neighbor or rob him. The wages due a hired worker must not remain with you until morning. (Lev 19:13)

> "I will come to you in judgment; . . . against those who oppress the hired worker, the widow, and the fatherless; and against those who deny justice the alien. They do not fear me," says the LORD of Armies. (Mal 3:5)

It is interesting that James describes the wages owed to the day laborers as crying out to the Lord of Hosts (or the Lord of Armies). First, this is reminiscent of the blood of Abel crying out to God (Gen 4:10). Both the blood and the wages are personified as the weak and vulnerable crying out to God for justice. Second, it is significant that James says the cries of the wages reach the ears of the Lord of Hosts because this phrase emphasizes God's power and ability to bring judgment. Withholding the laborers' wages, for James, is tantamount to judicial murder ("you have condemned, you have murdered," Jas 5:6), which is especially wicked in light of the fact that the rich have lived in self-indulgence and luxury (Jas 5:5). Both the merchants and the rich are examples of ignoring God's law (they are double-minded), and both represent ways of judging by the world's standard of judgment—there is a clear connection back to James's examples in James 1:9-11; 2:1-13.

Holding out until the coming of Christ (James 5:7-11). Because the next section starts with the connective "therefore" (*oun*), some argue that James 5:7-11 is to be read in close connection with James 5:1-6. On the other hand, because James shifts from "come now," you rich, in James 5:1 to "brothers and sisters" in James 5:7, and because the tone turns from judgment to encouragement, some consider James 5:7-11 as a new and separate section. As we have seen before, many of the sections in James are loosely related yet can stand independent from one another.

Here James encourages his audience to be patient (Jas 5:7-8, 10) and to strengthen their hearts (Jas 5:8) in light of the coming of the Lord.

Though a different term, the command to "be patient" (*makrothymēsate*) in James 5:7 thematically relates back to the endurance (*hypomonē*) amid trials at the beginning of the letter in James 1:2-4. James offers the example of the farmer who waits patiently for his crops to grow. This image of crops receiving the early and late rains recalls the conditions common in Palestine, where the fall rains, beginning in October, are followed by more rainfall in mid-November. Again, James's language echoes phrases that occur in the Torah (Deut 11:14) and the Prophets (Jer 5:24; Hos 6:3; Joel 2:23; Zech 10:1). In addition to being patient (Jas 5:7, 8), James commands his readers to "strengthen" (*stērixate*) or "set firmly" or "establish" their hearts. In this context, readers are to be patient and strengthen their hearts because of the Lord's coming (Jas 5:7-8).

The Lord's coming could refer to either the return of Christ or the impending judgment of God—perhaps specifically the destruction of Jerusalem. Those who argue that "Lord" refers to God's judgment understand the references to "judge" (Jas 4:12; 5:9), along with "lawgiver" (Jas 4:12), as pointing to God, who himself gave the law at Sinai. However, because James describes the judge as standing at the door (Jas 5:9), and because James 5:7 uses the term *coming* (*parousia*), which in the New Testament is a technical term for Christ's return, it is more likely that the Lord who is coming is Jesus Christ. This means that in James 4:12 James could understand the judge and lawgiver as referring to Christ, which would significantly strengthen the letter's Christology. It is significant to note that whereas the most common translation for the Hebrew name for God (Yahweh) is "Lord" (*kyrios*) in the Greek Old Testament, the New Testament consistently uses the term *kyrios* to identify Jesus Christ. Thus, though James is often disparaged for its lack of christological language, it is quite possible that this passage is more christological than usually acknowledged. So here, patience in waiting (Jas 5:7-8), refusal to grumble (Jas 5:9), and even willingness to suffer (Jas 5:11) are all within the context of expectation of Christ's return.

Speaking the whole truth (James 5:12). The next passage is both one of the shortest of the main body of the letter and perhaps the most detached from its surrounding context. The use of "my brothers and sisters," along with the phrase "above all" (*pro pantōn*), indicates a new section. This short, almost proverbial statement warns against oath taking and strikes the contrast of using one's words with simple honesty versus "swearing" or taking an oath in order to bolster the credibility of one's words. James commands, do not swear, but "let your 'yes' mean 'yes,' and your 'no' mean 'no.'" Of all the passages in James, this command most closely echoes Jesus' teaching, found in Matthew 5:34-37. The prohibition against swearing does not have in view cussing or vulgarity per se but rather the inappropriate use of God's name for the purpose of convincing others regarding the trustworthiness of one's speech. Thus, it is not that the oath is in itself wrong; oaths are not forbidden in the Bible. Rather it is dividing speech into two levels—that is, normal speech that could be true or false, and sworn speech, guaranteed by taking an oath.[29] Not only does the need to swear in order for one's speech to be trustworthy call into question one's normal speech, but swearing to God to bolster one's credibility is a form of manipulating God's name—or taking God's name in vain. The point of the passage is that all speech should be simple and truthful; if you mean "yes," then say "yes."

Prayer (James 5:13-18). The next-to-last section of James focuses on prayer and implicitly contrasts effective and ineffective prayer. Structurally, the section is marked by rhetorical questions in James 5:13-14, each of which addresses a different situation in a public worship context: "Is anyone among you suffering?" "Is anyone cheerful?" "Is anyone among you sick?" After each question there is a call to action: "pray" (*proseuchesthō*), "sing praises" (*psalletō*), and "call for the elders . . . and pray." The focus of these commands indicates that the passage is concerned with the proper context of prayer, namely, the context of public worship (Jas 5:13-14a). The next two sections focus on the correct procedure (Jas 5:14b) and effectiveness of "the prayer of faith" (Jas 5:15-16).

---

[29]On this see Moo, *Letter of James*, 232.

What is a bit confusing is the proper procedure for prayer (Jas 5:14). What does it mean to have the elders "pray over him, anointing him with oil in the name of the Lord"? First, it is important to note that the anointing *accompanies* the main act of praying—prayer appears to be the focal act, and anointing with oil accompanies that act. Second, the word "sick" (*astheneō*, "to be weak") is applied to all kinds of situations in the New Testament: one's appearance mentally, one's spiritual condition, or one's general physical appearance. Therefore, the one receiving special prayer and anointing could be suffering any number of troubles. Third, what is the meaning or significance of the oil? Some understand the oil as having a practical purpose, for example, a medicinal use. Using oil for medical purposes was a common practice in the ancient world and is reflected in other New Testament contexts. In the parable of the Samaritan, oil and wine are used to soothe wounds (Lk 10:34). Others think the oil has a religious function. A sacramental view understands that the oil itself possesses a mediating divine power. It is more likely that the oil has a representative function in setting aside particular individuals for special prayer (especially those experiencing unusual or severe sickness or distress).

This climax of the unit (Jas 5:15-16) addresses the effectiveness of the prayer of faith, which in the context of James as a whole suggests an implicit contrast between asking God for wisdom in faith without doubt, referring back to James 1:6 and asking "with wrong motives" (Jas 4:3). James asserts that the "prayer of faith will save the sick person, and the Lord will raise him up; if he has committed sins, he will be forgiven" (Jas 5:15). The phrase "will save the sick" most likely is not eschatological but rather refers to delivering someone from a physical illness. The verb "save" (*sōzō*) can indicate a temporary (i.e., non-eschatological) salvation (the imagery of salvation to express healing is frequent in the Gospels; Mt 9:21-22; Mk 5:23, 28, 34; 6:56; 10:52). So, this section clarifies the context, procedure, and effectiveness of prayer.

Reclaiming those who err (James 5:19-20). The last two verses of James are an appropriate conclusion to the entire letter. The central focus of this concluding passage in James is recovering the erring brother or sister and contains an understood contrast drawn between the way that leads to death and the way of truth that leads to life (similar to the contrast between the desire–sin–death sequence and the God's choice–by the word–life sequence seen in Jas 1:14-15, 18).

This concluding passage is a command to recover any person who might wander from the truth, and a promise that whoever brings back a sinner "from the error of his way" (*ek planēs hodou autou*) will "save" (*sōsei*) that person's soul "from death." In these final verses, we again encounter the two ways. In the textual tradition of James 5:19, some manuscripts read "from the way of truth" (*apo tēs hodou alētheias*). The addition of the word *way* suggests that some early transcribers of this passage understood the truth as a way one follows. There is a way of error that leads to death and a way of truth that implicitly leads to life. The one recovering their brother from the way of error covers a multitude of sin. The descriptions of wandering, bringing back, and error of his way communicate a concern for restoration rather than conversion. As the call for repentance in James 4:1-10 was addressed to believers, so too here James concludes his letter with the call for the community to reclaim wayward brothers and sisters. In general, returning wandering brothers and sisters from the path of error is to return them on the way to wholeness or perfection. This seems to be the overarching goal of the letter—living before God in wholeness by means of his gracious word, law, and wisdom.

FURTHER READING | JAMES COMMENTARIES AND MONOGRAPHS

T: technical; ★: recommended; ★★: highly recommended

T★★ Allison, Dale C. *James*. ICC. London: Bloomsbury, 2013.

★Bauckham, Richard J. *James: Wisdom of James, Disciple of Jesus the Sage*. New York: Routledge, 1999.

Cheung, Luke L. *The Genre, Composition, and Hermeneutics of the Epistle of James*. Paternoster Biblical Monographs. Eugene, OR: Wipf & Stock, 2007.

т Davids, Peter H. *The Epistle of James: A Commentary on the Greek Text.* New International Greek Testament Commentary. Grand Rapids, MI: Eerdmans, 1982.

т Dibelius, Martin. *James: A Commentary on the Epistle of James.* Hermeneia. Philadelphia: Fortress, 1976.

Johnson, Luke T. *Brother of Jesus, Friend of God: Studies in the Letter of James.* Grand Rapids, MI: Eerdmans, 2004.

———. *The Letter of James: A New Translation with Introduction and Commentary.* AB. New York: Doubleday, 1995.

Laws, Sophie. *A Commentary on the Epistle of James.* Black's New Testament Commentary. San Francisco: Harper & Row, 1980.

т Martin, Ralph P. *James.* WBC. Nashville: Thomas Nelson, 1988.

McCartney, Daniel G. *James.* BECNT. Grand Rapids, MI: Baker, 2009.

★ McKnight, Scot. *The Letter of James.* NICNT. Grand Rapids, MI: Eerdmans, 2011.

★★ Moo, Douglas J. *The Letter of James.* PNTC. Grand Rapids, MI: Eerdmans, 2000.

CHAPTER TWO

The Letter of I Peter

WHEREAS THE LETTER OF JAMES addresses readers of a Jewish heritage who live in the diaspora (outside the land of Israel), 1 Peter addresses those of non-Jewish heritage who are "chosen, living as exiles dispersed abroad" (1 Pet 1:1). The previous chapter argued that reference to the twelve tribes in James is a reference to the reconstituted people of God, which now includes Gentiles. Richard Bauckham notes:

> If we read the catholic epistles in the order which at an early date came to be the accepted canonical order, with James in first place and 1 Peter immediately following, then we read first a letter addressed only to Jewish Christians as the twelve tribes in the Diaspora and then a letter apparently addressed only to Gentile Christians as "exiles of the diaspora," to whom defining descriptions of Israel as God's people are applied. One effect is to portray the inclusion of Gentiles in the eschatological people of God, which retains through its Jewish Christian members its continuity with Israel and yet is also open to the inclusion of those who had not hitherto been God's people (1 Pet 2:10).[1]

Something that would be striking, even to the earliest readers, who would have read James and 1 Peter as the first two letters of a collection,

---

[1]Richard Bauckham, *James: Wisdom of James, Disciple of Jesus the Sage* (London: Routledge, 1999), 156-57.

is the significant number of parallels between the two texts. There are thirteen similarities in theme and vocabulary that are significant.

1. addressed to diaspora audiences: James 1:1; 1 Peter 1:1

2. command rejoicing in suffering: James 1:2; 1 Peter 1:6-9

3. the proving of faith and perfection: James 1:3-4; 1 Peter 1:7-9

4. allude to Isaiah 40:6-8: James 1:10-11; 1 Peter 1:24

5. use imagery of birth by the divine word: James 1:18; 1 Peter 1:23

6. command the ridding of the self of evil: James 1:21; 1 Peter 2:1

7. quote from and give an interpretation of Leviticus 19: James 2:8; 1 Peter 1:16

8. make the call to good conduct: James 3:13; 1 Peter 2:12

9. warn about desires at war with the self: James 4:1-2; 1 Peter 2:11

10. quote LXX Proverbs 3:34: James 4:6; 1 Peter 5:5

11. give the command to resist the devil right after the citation of the proverb: James 4:7; 1 Peter 5:8-9

12. promise that God will exalt those who humble themselves: James 4:10; 1 Peter 5:6

13. and finally, quote the same portion of Proverbs 10:12: James 5:20; 1 Peter 4:8

What is remarkable about this list is not only the similarity in vocabulary and theme, but even more the agreement in sequence. When comparing the ordering of these thirteen parallels, there are only three instances where the material in James is out of sequence from that of 1 Peter.[2] These are striking examples of how James and 1 Peter are related to each other and thus would have been similarities early readers would have observed when compiling the Catholic Epistles.[3]

---

[2] "If the relevant verses from James are numbered 1-12, the order in 1 Peter is this: 1, 2, 3, 5, 4, 6, 7, 8, 9, 11, 10, 12." See Dale C. Allison, *James*, ICC (London: Bloomsbury, 2013), 68.
[3] For fuller discussion of the relationship between James and 1 Peter see Darian R. Lockett, "The Use of Leviticus 19 in James and 1 Peter: A Neglected Parallel," *CBQ* 82 (2020): 456-72.

Though Peter's audience is also in the diaspora ("dispersed abroad"), this description functions more as a metaphor for Christians living in hostile territory. Rather than living in a place of safety and belonging, Peter's audience lives in the midst of a hostile and watching world. Because of their Christian commitments, they live as aliens and strangers in a setting where the community does not accept the values and worldview of God's kingdom. It is in this context that Peter writes to remind his readers of their new identity in Christ as they witness to a watching world—usually in the form of enduring hardship and persecution for the sake of witness to the truth of Christ.

OCCASION AND SETTING

Authorship. Like the authorship of James, there is little doubt regarding which Peter is intended in the opening verse of the letter: "Peter, an apostle of Jesus Christ." The individual in view can be none other than Peter the disciple of Jesus. Peter's given name was Simeon (or the Greek spelling of the name Simon, *Simōn*), after the patriarch of Israel, yet Jesus renamed him Peter, or "rock" (Aramaic: *Kêpā'*; Greek: *Petros*; see Mt 16:18; Jn 1:42). Paul himself uses both forms of Peter's nickname: he refers to Peter as *Petros* (Gal 2:7-8) and as *Kēphas* (the Greek transliteration of the Aramaic, found in 1 Cor 1:12; 3:22; 9:5; 15:5; Gal 1:18; 2:9, 11, 14), and it is interesting that even among Greek-speaking Christians, Peter was called Cephas (*Kēphas*). Peter apparently preferred to use the Greek Peter (*Petros*) for himself, as does the rest of the New Testament, and thus we find this form of his name in 1 Peter 1:1 and 2 Peter 1:1.

Few doubt that the Peter in view here is the apostle of Jesus; however, there is disagreement over who actually wrote the letter. The traditional view, held throughout antiquity to the modern period, understood that 1 Peter was written by Peter himself (see Eusebius, *Hist. eccl.* 4.14.9). This view hangs on several factors. First, this view reads the self-identification of the author in 1 Peter 1:1 as an authentic reference to the real author of the letter. Second, the author's claim to have been a "witness to the

sufferings of Christ" (1 Pet 5:1) reinforces the view that Peter himself was
the author. Though all of the disciples, except John, fled at Jesus' arrest
(Mk 14:50; Mt 26:56), in Luke's Gospel Peter also remained, following
Jesus at a distance, and then witnessed the crucifixion (Lk 22:54, 61).
Third, the similarities in vocabulary and themes between 1 Peter and
Peter's speeches in the book of Acts also strengthen the authenticity
of authorship.

Some argue that 1 Peter was composed by Silvanus, written either
during Peter's lifetime or soon after his death. The letter's use of the
idiom "Through Silvanus . . . I have written" (*dia Silouanou . . . egrapsa*,
1 Pet 5:12) may imply that Silvanus (Silas) wrote the letter as Peter's secretary or amanuensis. A similar use of this particular phrase is found in
Dionysius of Corinth, who refers to the Clement's letter to the Corinthians (*1 Clement*) as "written to you through Clement" (*hymin dia
Klēmentos grapheisan, Hist. eccl.* 4.23.11), which could support the idea
that Silas wrote on Peter's behalf. This would explain the letter's excellent
quality of Greek prose and the abundant use of the Greek translation of
the Old Testament. However, others have pointed out that the phrase "to
write through" was a common idiom referring to the letter carrier, not
the secretary.[4]

Whether Peter is the historical author of 1 Peter or not, there is a clear
indication of where the letter was written in 1 Peter 5:13: "She who is in
Babylon . . . sends you greetings." It is unlikely that Peter would have used
the term *Babylon* with reference to the city in Mesopotamia, because
there is no evidence that Peter was ever in Babylon. Rather, most understand Babylon to be a reference to another city altogether—namely,
Rome (Rev 14:8; 16:19; 17:5; 18:2, 10, 21).[5] This is strengthened by the fact
that postbiblical tradition places Peter in Rome at the end of his life and
that Rome and Babylon shared a similar role in early Christian writings

---

[4]See Acts 15:23; possibly also Ign. *Rom.* 10.1; *Smyrn.* 12.1; *Phld.* 11.2; Paul J. Achtemeier, *1 Peter* (Minneapolis: Fortress, 1996), 349-52; John H. Elliott, *1 Peter*, AB (New York: Doubleday, 2000), 872-76.

[5]Other texts roughly contemporary with 1 Peter also use the term *Babylon* symbolically: 2 Baruch 10.1-2; 11.1; 67.7; 4 Ezra 3.1-2, 28, 31; Sibylline Oracles 5.143, 158-159.

because, whereas Rome was interpreted as the symbolic (and at times literal) origin of opposition to God on earth, so too was Babylon in the Old Testament. So, it would seem natural for Peter to use the symbolic name "Babylon" as a label for Rome. This conclusion is supported in the early church. Clement of Alexandria, as recorded in Eusebius, understood the reference to Babylon as a metaphor for Rome: "Peter mentions Mark in his first letter and that he composed this in Rome itself, referring to the city metaphorically as Babylon in the words 'The elect one in Babylon greets you, and Mark, my son'" (*Hist. eccl.* 2.15).

Audience. Though the ethnic and religious identity of the audience has been contested, its geographic location is much clearer. In the words of the letter's opening, the recipients lived in "Pontus, Galatia, Cappadocia, Asia, and Bithynia" (1 Pet 1:1). These are Roman provinces located in central Asia Minor. This list of regions is a significantly large geographical area, such that John Elliott notes, "1 Peter is addressed to a larger area than any other letter of the NT, with James . . . constituting the only possible exception."[6]

First Peter 1:1 also indicates something about the identity of the audience. The letter is addressed "to those chosen, living as exiles dispersed abroad." Each of these terms, "chosen" (or "elect," *eklektois*), "living as exiles," and "dispersed abroad" (*diaspora*, which is the same word found in Jas 1:1), are terms carefully selected from the Old Testament's description of Israel. Throughout the Old Testament, Israel stood as God's chosen people (Ex 19:3-8; Deut 7:6), who were called to a holy way of life (Lev 19:2, quoted in 1 Pet 1:16), and as such, God's elect people were set apart from the nations. Yet, as the narrative of the Old Testament unfolds, God's elect people were scattered from their land. Dispersion was God's punishment as a direct result of Israel's failure to keep the demands of Yahweh's covenant. As a result of this covenant breaking, God's chosen people were scattered among the nations and thus lived as exiles among these foreign nations.

---

[6]Elliott, *1 Peter*, 84.

Though these references have been traditionally understood as references to Jewish converts (Eusebius, *Hist. eccl.* 3.1.2; 3.4.2; Jerome, *On the Lives of Illustrious Men* 1), most modern commentaries argue for a predominantly Gentile audience in 1 Peter. Several statements in the letter indicate that the author had Gentile converts in mind. In 1 Peter 1:14 the author warns the readers not to conform to their "desires of your former ignorance," which is suggestive because no Jewish author would describe Jewish law or practice as ignorance. This was a common way of specifically referring to Gentiles from a Jewish perspective. Likewise, in 1 Peter 1:18 we learn that the readers have been redeemed from "your empty way of life inherited from your ancestors." Again, "empty way of life" would refer to the previous way of life for a Gentile, not a Jew. Finally, the author clearly reasons with the audience, saying, "You have already spent enough time in doing what the Gentiles like to do, living in licentiousness, passions, drunkenness" (1 Pet 4:3-4 NRSV). However, even this evidence is disputed. With this last passage specifically in view, Karen Jobes argues that it is possible that the author is describing Jewish converts.[7] In the end, it is difficult to know with confidence whether a Gentile, Jewish, or mixed audience was in view, though a predominantly Gentile audience is most plausible.

Genre. First Peter is clearly constructed as a letter. The opening conforms to the traditional Greek letter: "Peter, apostle of Jesus Christ: To those chosen, living as exiles dispersed abroad. . . . May grace and peace be multiplied to you" (1 Pet 1:1-2). In addition to this formal letter introduction (composed typically of a named sender, audience, and terms of greeting), 1 Peter also contains a clear letter body (1 Pet 1:3–5:11) and a personalized letter conclusion (1 Pet 5:12-14). Many have understood the text as a specific type of "diaspora letter." Most recently Lutz Doering has argued that 1 Peter contains several elements of form and intention that parallel Jewish and Christian examples of this genre of diaspora letter.[8]

---

[7]Karen Jobes, *1 Peter*, BECNT (Grand Rapids, MI: Baker Academic, 2005), 268-69; see also 23-24.
[8]Lutz Doering, *Ancient Jewish Letters and the Beginnings of Christian Epistolography*, WUNT 298

First, as with typical diaspora letters, the explicit theme of exile appears in 1 Peter: the letter is bookended by the opening address to those in the diaspora (1 Pet 1:1) and in Babylon (1 Pet 5:13), both of which frame the text in an exilic context. Second, both 1 Peter and such diaspora letters are addressed to a wide range of audiences and, whereas many of these letters were specifically written from a central location (namely, Jerusalem, as for Jer 29 and, perhaps, the letter of James), some were written from areas outside Israel addressed to those in Jerusalem (for example, Baruch, sent from Babylon to Jerusalem). In this case it is all the more interesting that 1 Peter is addressed from Babylon in 1 Peter 5:13, which may intentionally conform to this kind of letter type. Finally, both 1 Peter and diaspora letters focus on instructing readers in their conduct amid a hostile culture.

A final issue to take up in considering the genre of 1 Peter is the text's use of various traditions. Allusions throughout the text primarily originate from Jewish and Christian traditions. Along with Romans and Hebrews, 1 Peter is the most dependent on the Old Testament. William Schutter, whose work is especially helpful in this area, notes 1 Peter's "extraordinary dependence on the OT," finding a total of forty-six quotations and allusions to the Old Testament.[9] Most of these come from the Greek version of the Old Testament (LXX) and originate primarily from Isaiah (21×), Psalms (11×), and Proverbs (6×). These indications of such prolific use of the Old Testament in 1 Peter, along with the carefully selected terms from Israel's story used to identify the readers, signals one of the major conceptual worlds that helps to shape the letter's theological worldview.

STRUCTURE

The natural structure coming from the flow of thought in the letter suggests the two main sections focus on the new identity of the audience (1 Pet 1:3-2:10) and the corresponding conduct flowing from that identity (1 Pet 2:13–5:11), with a transition in between (1 Pet 2:11-12).

(Tübingen: Mohr Siebeck, 2012), 431.
[9]William Schutter, *Hermeneutic and Composition in 1 Peter*, WUNT (Tübingen: Mohr Siebeck, 1989), 3.

GOING DEEPER: SUFFERING IN 1 PETER

First Peter was written with two aims in mind: first, to comfort and encourage Christians suffering for their faith, and second, to instruct them to stay unified as a community in their current context. Throughout the letter, Peter urges his readers to understand suffering in three ways. First, he explains that because they are followers of Christ—who himself suffered innocently—his audience should understand that suffering for their faith is natural and to be expected (1 Pet 4:12-13). Second, Peter clarifies that the suffering they should expect is very specific—they are to suffer for doing what is right, or they should expect to experience innocent suffering (1 Pet 3:14-17; 4:14-15). Finally, Peter highlights the outcome of this particular kind of suffering, namely, it should serve as a testimony to the goodness of God. That is, Peter urges his readers to live holy lives in the midst of a watching world so that when outsiders observe their conduct and endurance of suffering they too might repent (1 Pet 2:11; 3:13-15).

Though the audience is clearly suffering, it is not clear exactly what kind of suffering is in view and what is causing the suffering. There is clear historical evidence of Christians suffering persecution in the Roman region of Bithynia during the time of Trajan. Using the correspondence between Trajan and Pliny (Pliny, *Letters* 10.96-97), some have concluded 1 Peter was written between AD 109 and 111. Others have argued the letter was written shortly before the outbreak of persecution during Nero's reign. On July 19, AD 64, a fire broke out in Rome that destroyed most of the city. Tradition has it that initially Nero himself was under suspicion for the catastrophe, so he in turn blamed the Christians in Rome for the fire, and this marked a time of intense persecution of the church (*1 Clement* 6). During this time there is clear evidence that Christians in general were both suspect and mistrusted in Roman culture. For example, Suetonius calls Christianity "a new and mischievous [evil] superstition" (*superstitionis novae ac maleficae*) (*Nero* 16.2), and Tacitus says that it is "pernicious superstition" (*exitiabilis superstitio*), an unpopular religious sect, infamous for its antisocial attitude (*Ann.* 15.44).[a] Finally, a third option is the time of persecution under Domition

(AD 81–96). Each of these periods is consistent with the information in 1 Peter regarding the suffering and persecution of the audience, yet the time of Nero's persecution seems most likely.

The nature of the persecution in many passages of 1 Peter was limited to verbal slander and false accusation (1 Pet 2:12, 15; 3:9, 16). It is hard to know whether 1 Peter 4:12 refers to physical persecution. If persecution went beyond verbal criticism to include physical suffering and death the further related question is whether the Roman government gave official sanction to such action—in other words, was such persecution a part of official Roman policy, and thus, empire-wide? Even though 1 Peter 5:9 speaks of worldwide suffering, many argue this cannot refer to an official persecution of Christians by Rome because the first recorded official persecution of Christians undertaken by Rome occur during Decius's reign (249–251 CE). Therefore, an empire-wide persecution in the time of 1 Peter is unlikely. Thus, the suffering and persecution in 1 Peter seems to be sporadic, personal (rather than empire-wide), and varied in intensity.

---

[a]Suetonius, *Lives of the Caesars*, trans. J. C. Rolfe, LCL 38 (Cambridge, MA: Harvard University Press, 1914), 2:106-7; Tacitus, *Annals, Books 11-16*, trans. John Jackson, LCL 322 (Cambridge, MA: Harvard University Press, 1937), 282-83.

OUTLINE

I. Salutation of the letter (1 Pet 1:1-2)

II. Main body of the letter (1 Pet 1:3–5:11)

    A. Theological identity (1 Pet 1:3–2:10)

        1. The elect's new identity through the work of the Father, Jesus Christ, and the Spirit (1 Pet 1:3-12)

        2. Call to be holy (1 Pet 1:13–2:10)

    B. Conduct or responsibility of those with a new theological identity (1 Pet 2:11–5:11)

        1. Transition from theological identity to conduct (1 Pet 2:11-12)

    2. New life in society (1 Pet 2:13–4:6)

       a. Submission in society (as witness)

         (1 Pet 2:13–3:12)

       b. Doing what is right in the midst of opposition

         (1 Pet 3:13-17)

       c. The suffering and triumph of Christ

         (1 Pet 3:18-22)

       d. Doing what is right in the midst of outsiders

         (1 Pet 4:1-6)

    3. Love one another: Maintaining unity to God's church

      (1 Pet 4:7-11)

    4. Christian endurance in a persecuted church

      (1 Pet 4:12–5:11)

       a. Suffering as fellowship with Christ (1 Pet 4:12-19)

       b. Unity in community: Leadership in service to the

         community (1 Pet 5:1-5a)

       c. Final exhortation: Mutual humility—resisting the

         devil and trusting God (1 Pet 5:5b-11)

  III. Conclusion of the letter (1 Pet 5:12-14)[10]

COMMENTARY | SALUTATION OF THE LETTER | 1 PETER 1:1-2

The letter opening clearly names the author and the geographic areas where the audience(s) lives. At the same time, even here in the letter opening, Peter articulates something about the identity of the audience: "chosen according to the foreknowledge of God the Father, through the sanctifying work of the Spirit, to be obedient and to be sprinkled with the blood of Jesus Christ. May grace and peace be multiplied to you" (1 Pet 1:1-2). The striking phrase "chosen, living as exiles dispersed abroad" was briefly set in the context of the Old Testament story line above and will receive further comment below, but here it is important to note three phrases in 1 Peter 1:2 that highlight the work of the triune God in the

---

[10]This outline roughly follows Elliott, *1 Peter*, 82-83.

election of God's people. These three prepositional phrases describe the origin, means, and purpose of the audience's elect status.

First, Peter's readers are "elect . . . according to the foreknowledge [*prognōsin*] of God the Father." The phrase "according to" marks the norm or authority that governs the audience's elect status, namely, God's foreknowledge. Though the term *foreknowledge* only occurs here and in Acts 2:23 in the New Testament, 1 Peter 1:20 also refers to the concept of God's foreknowledge—Christ "foreknown [*proegnōsmenou*] before the foundation of the world." The word denotes not just God's passive knowing of an event beforehand but God's predetermining knowledge. Divine election and foreknowledge are linked in 1 Peter 1:2 (as they are in Paul: Rom 8:28-30; Eph 1:4-5; 3:13; 2 Thess 2:13) and are furthermore consistently related to Christology throughout the letter (1 Pet 1:2, 20; 2:4-10). God's predetermining election of Peter's audience is accomplished through the divine work of Jesus.

Second, the audience is "elect . . . through the sanctifying work of the Spirit." Election is worked out in the lives of believers by means of the sanctifying action of the Holy Spirit. This means the instrument by which Peter's audience is made holy is the Spirit. The chosen status of the audience (election) is not just a "favored people" designation void of real-life change. Those whom God predetermined as chosen are also transformed by the work of God's Spirit. The second half of the letter has much to say about the quality of this transformation.

Third, they are "elect . . . to be obedient and to be sprinkled with the blood of Jesus Christ." This last prepositional phrase indicates the purpose of election in Jesus Christ, which is obedience made possible by Jesus' own suffering and death. The purpose of the Father's foreknowledge and the Spirit's sanctifying work is the obedience of those who have been chosen, but this obedience is made possible by the sprinkling of Jesus' blood, or his redeeming work on behalf of the elect. Both obedience and sprinkling of the blood of Christ refer back to the Old Testament account of establishing a covenant between God and Israel (especially Ex 24:3-8, where both obedience and sprinkling of blood are noted).

Though some have argued for an allusion to Christian baptism here, Paul Achtemeier is convinced that there is a more convincing parallel with the covenant renewal ceremony in Exodus 24. With regard to Exodus 24 he notes, "In that ceremony, the people pledge their obedience (24:3), after which a sacrifice is made and blood is sprinkled on the altar (24:4-6). After a second pledge to obey God (24:7), the remaining blood is sprinkled on the people (24:8), and the covenant is declared to be in force." Therefore, he concludes, "the two elements in the ceremony, obedience and sprinkling of blood, reflect the order and content of 1 Peter 1:2, and present a closer parallel."[11]

Furthermore, the final prepositional, phrase noting obedience and Christ's sprinkling of blood, in effect introduces two major themes developed throughout the letter. First, the innocent suffering of Christ included the shedding of his blood (1 Pet 1:11, 19; 2:21, 23, 24; 3:18; 4:1, 13; 5:1). Second, election (1 Pet 2:4-10), holiness (1 Pet 1:14-16), and obedience to God in the face of innocent suffering are rooted in the election, holiness, and obedience of Christ, who serves as both the enabler and example of the believing community (1 Pet 1:6; 2:19-20; 3:14-17; 4:1, 13, 15, 19; 5:9, 10). This is how foreknowledge and election are grounded christologically in the letter.

COMMENTARY | MAIN BODY | 1 PETER 1:3-5:11

Theological identity (1 Peter 1:3–2:10).

The elect's new identity through the work of the Father, Jesus Christ, and the Spirit (1 Peter 1:3-12). In the first part of the letter Peter outlines the theological identity of his readers (1 Pet 1:3–2:10). The first section of theological identity (1 Pet 1:3-12) expresses praise for God's mercy and saving benefits. This is one long sentence in the Greek broken up by three relative clauses, which mark the distinct thoughts in the paragraphs. The threefold structure of 1 Peter 1:3-12 focuses on the Father (1 Pet 1:3-5), Jesus Christ (1 Pet 1:6-9), and the Spirit (1 Pet 1:10-12). Each of these

---

[11]Achtemeier, *1 Peter*, 88.

phrases reinforces the new identity Peter's readers have received by incorporation into Christ, and they echo—though in a different sequence—the trinitarian structure of 1 Peter 1:2.

The first of three subunits of this section (1 Pet 1:3-5) announces praise to God for three specific transforming benefits that believers have received: a living hope (1 Pet 1:3), an imperishable inheritance (1 Pet 1:4), and a salvation about to be revealed (1 Pet 1:5).

First, in 1 Peter 1:3, God the Father himself causes believers to be born into a living hope, and this hope is "through [*dia*] the resurrection of Jesus Christ from the dead." God is the agent of new birth, and the means or instrument of new birth is the resurrection of Jesus Christ. Peter encourages his readers that their present new identity as children of God is established by the reality of Christ's resurrection as a past and complete event. They have a "born-into-living-hope-by-the-resurrection" identity by God's gracious action. Second, new birth has brought Peter's readers into a new family, and, by extension, they have been given an inheritance that cannot be destroyed by time or circumstance. New birth is for (*eis*) an inheritance (1 Pet 1:4). Three adjectives describe this inheritance—*imperishable, undefiled,* and *unfading*—all of which stress the permanence of the inheritance over against transitoriness. Peter's readers are born into a new family where they are now full heirs of an inheritance that cannot be lost. Third, not only can the inheritance not be lost, but the heirs themselves are kept by God's power through faith. Peter says his readers are being "guarded by God's power through faith for [*eis*] a salvation that is ready to be revealed" (1 Pet 1:5). As we will see moving forward in the letter, paradoxically, it is their faith in Christ that has put them in jeopardy in the first place, but because faith in Christ marks them out as legitimate heirs, it is God who will powerfully protect them in the midst of danger and suffering. God, the Father, has caused Peter's readers to be born into this living hope, which enables them to suffer in Christ's strength—this new birth is their new identity.

Again, the threefold structure of 1 Peter 1:3-12 focuses on God the Father (1 Pet 1:3-5), Jesus Christ (1 Pet 1:6-9), and the Spirit (1 Pet 1:10-12).

First Peter 1:6-9 constitutes the second subunit of this section, with attention now shifting from the praise of God to the consolation and joy of believers in Jesus Christ. Peter makes the challenging claim that the suffering Peter's audience presently experiences is a test of faith that will end in praise, glory, and honor when Jesus Christ is revealed. The repeated command "you rejoice" in 1 Peter 1:6, 8 forms bookends to a series of concessions:

> You rejoice in this,
>> *even though* now . . . you suffer grief in various trials . . .
>> *Though* you have not seen him, you love him;
>> *though* not seeing him now, you believe in him, and
> you rejoice. (1 Pet 1:6-8)

Enduring Trial

Rejoicing in the midst of trials is a common theme in the Catholic Epistles. James 1:2-4, 12 echo the same words and concerns as 1 Peter 1:6-9. Second Peter 1:5 encourages endurance, and 1 John revolves around testing and true orthodoxy.

The new identity in Christ allows believers to rejoice in the face of present suffering, knowing such suffering demonstrates the genuineness of their faith in Christ (which is the same theme in Jas 1:2-4). In light of such rejoicing, readers obtain "the goal of your faith, the salvation of your souls" (1 Pet 1:9). The word *salvation* acts as a link word joining 1 Peter 1:6-9 to 1 Peter 1:10-12. Because salvation is theirs, Peter's readers rejoice in their present suffering, not because suffering is itself enjoyable but because joy is the characteristic of their new identity in Christ.

The final subunit (1 Pet 1:10-12) focuses on the Spirit, who makes known the work of Christ. After announcing that the goal of rejoicing in suffering is salvation, Peter then turns to address the announcement of this salvation: "Concerning this salvation, the prophets . . . searched and carefully investigated" (1 Pet 1:10). The prophets sought out and carefully inquired about this salvation that had come to the Christians of Peter's day. Here Peter draws a line of connection between what had been "witnessed to beforehand" in the Old Testament and what has been realized in the life of Jesus and preached in the gospel. In other words, Peter is stressing that the prophets and the Christian evangelists share the same message about the suffering and glory of Jesus Christ (the continuity between Old Testament prophets and New Testament apostles also appears in 2 Pet 1:16-20; 3:2).

Peter goes on to argue, "It was revealed to them [the prophets] that they were not serving themselves but you [Peter's audience]" (1 Pet 1:12). Peter then claims his readers' knowledge of God's redemptive work as superior to both the prophets and the angels. Though the Spirit of Christ revealed knowledge to the prophets, they did not enjoy complete understanding of what God's redemptive plan was. Because Peter's readers have received and accepted the gospel, they are both historically privileged, giving them superior vantage to the prophets, and cosmically privileged, rendering their access to the saving act of Christ greater even than the angels'. Throughout this brief but important section, Peter is arguing that the purpose of the Jewish prophets was to point to Christ. David Horrell concludes: "So the author claims that the goal, the fulfilment, to which Jewish prophecy pointed was the Christ-event, and that the recipients of grace and salvation are his Gentile readers. Clearly this constitutes a christological claim over the Jewish scriptures, the Christian 'Old Testament.'"[12]

Call to be holy (1 Peter 1:13–2:10). In the next section of 1 Peter 1, the author shifts from the indicative mood ("is") to the imperative ("ought") but continues to outline his readers' new identity. The subtle shift in the focus here is that, if his readers are now ones born into a living hope unable to be lost or corrupted, if they rejoice in Christ as he strengthens their faith through trial, if they receive from the Holy Spirit the truth about the suffering and glory of Christ, then they should be holy. New identity flows into a new way of living.

1 Peter 1:13-21. God causes birth into a living hope that results in a new identity (1 Pet 1:3-12), which is characterized by a new way of living.

---

[12]David Horrell, *The Epistles of Peter and Jude* (Peterborough, UK: Epworth, 1998), 29.

The emphasis on hope in 1 Peter 1:13 and the end of 1 Peter 1:21 forms bookends drawing the next section (1 Pet 1:13-21) together and links it back to the prime characteristic of new identity in Christ in 1 Peter 1:3, born "into a living hope."

The section roughly falls into three units. First, Peter instructs his audience to "set your hope completely on the grace to be brought to you at the revelation of Jesus Christ" (1 Pet 1:13). As "obedient children" (recall the theme of obedience, announced in 1 Pet 1:2), second, Peter's readers should "not be conformed to the desires of your former ignorance" (1 Pet 1:14-16). And finally, because of their new identity as those freed by the death of Christ, Peter urges them "to conduct yourselves in reverence" so that "your faith and hope are in God" (1 Pet 1:17, 21).

In 1 Peter 1:13, Peter draws an implication from his readers' new identity: "Therefore, with your minds ready for action . . . set your hope completely on the grace to be brought to you at the revelation of Jesus Christ." The phrase "with your minds ready for action" is a translation of a literal phrase "bind up the loins of your mind." This phrase would be common in the ancient context for a person preparing for physical activity—he must first tuck his loose robe into his belt so that he could move without restriction. A similar idiom today might perhaps be, "Roll up your sleeves and get to work." Peter instructs his readers to set their hope on the grace that will be theirs when Jesus returns. That is, to set their minds on the living hope that they have been born into and which will be brought to them "at the revelation of Jesus Christ." Peter makes several time references in 1 Peter 1, of which this last phrase of 1 Peter 1:13 is a part. Jesus was "foreknown before the foundation of the world," referring to primordial time; the readers lived in a time of "former ignorance" (1 Pet 1:14), the "empty way of life inherited from your fathers" (1 Pet 1:18). This refers to the audience's past life before hearing the gospel. Peter speaks of Jesus being "revealed in these last times" (1 Pet 1:20), which is a reference to the revelation of Jesus as the Christ especially in his suffering and resurrection. Now that Peter's readers have been born anew, they live in the present time as strangers and exiles

(1 Pet 1:17) and await the final eschatological revelation of Jesus at his second coming (1 Pet 1:13).

The next subsection (1 Pet 1:14-16) stresses obedience and warns against conforming to a former way of life. Because Peter describes their previous way of living as being in ignorance, many have argued that this strongly suggests they were Gentiles (or at least predominantly Gentile). It was common for Jews to describe Gentiles as ignorant, not because they lacked information or were not intelligent in general but because of their profound failure to grasp the character and purpose of God especially revealed in the Torah.

In contrast to their previous way of life (in ignorance), Peter calls his audience to a new, holy way of life in 1 Peter 1:15: "But as the one who called you is holy, you also are to be holy in all your conduct." Not only does Peter ground Christian morality in the very character of God, but 1 Peter 1:15 serves as a kind of introductory paraphrase of Leviticus 19:2, which is quoted in the next verse. Rather than conforming to the previous way of life characteristic of his audience, Peter challenges them to be conformed to God's holiness, articulated in Israel's law. It is important to note that Peter quotes directly from Leviticus 19:2 (in 1 Pet 1:16), assuming that such a command first articulated to Israel now quite reasonably applies to a predominantly Gentile audience.

The third and final subunit of this larger section, 1 Peter 1:17-21, explains the call to a new life of holiness. Peter calls those born to a living hope to "conduct yourselves in reverence during your time living as strangers" (1 Pet 1:17). The audience's faith in Christ results in their new citizenship in God's kingdom, and as a result they are now exiles, living as strangers in their current surroundings. While living in exile, they need to live in reverent fear because the Father is an impartial judge (1 Pet 1:17; *impartiality* is picked up from Lev 19:15). Yet God's impartial judgment is not a threat because they have been redeemed by the death of Jesus from their former way of life (1 Pet 1:18-19) and, as a result, their "faith and hope" (1 Pet 1:21) are in God. It is interesting to note how this section of 1 Peter is indebted to Leviticus 19. Peter paraphrases and then quotes Leviticus 19:2 in 1 Peter 1:15-16, then refers to impartiality with a rare word that calls to mind similar terms from Leviticus 19:15. Finally, in 1 Peter 1:22 Peter refers to loving others as the climax of holiness, which resonates with the call to love one's neighbor in Leviticus 19:18. This dependence on Leviticus 19 is very similar to the same dependence seen in James (note textbox in chapter two).

Two final comments about 1 Peter 1:20-21. As mentioned in 1 Peter 1:2, foreknowledge and election of the believers are christologically grounded. The sacrificial death of Jesus is anchored in the timeless plan of God, which provides the foundation for the election of believers. Furthermore, because God has worked in Christ by raising him from the dead and giving him glory, the believer's hope is in God. This again echoes back to 1 Peter 1:13, "set your hope," and 1 Peter 1:3, "new birth into a living hope."

1 PETER 1:22–2:3. The end of 1 Peter 1 and the beginning of 1 Peter 2 continue the construction of the theological identity of Peter's readers. In 1 Peter 1:22-25 Peter calls his readers to love one another because of their birth through the imperishable word of God, and in 1 Peter 2:1-3 to therefore desire the word as a newborn baby desires milk.

Here Peter offers a final command to love one another (1 Pet 1:22-25), which, due to the other references to Leviticus 19, might be an allusion to the love command in Leviticus 19:18. Following the exhortations to be holy (1 Pet 1:15-16) and to fear God (1 Pet 1:17), Peter's readers are also to "love one another earnestly" (1 Pet 1:22 ESV). Peter then gives the grounds for such love: "because you have been born again—not of perishable seed but of imperishable—through the living and enduring word of God" (1 Pet 1:23). The grounds for the command to love is that "you have been born again"—the general idea introduced in 1 Peter 1:3 is reiterated here. Peter, then, stresses the instrument of such rebirth: the word of God preached as good news concerning Jesus Christ (1 Pet 1:23-25). Note that this gospel about Jesus is the prophetic word announced by Isaiah. Isaiah 40:6-8 speaks of the enduring word of God, by which Peter's readers have been reborn. The broader context of the passage in Isaiah indicates its particular relevance for all of 1 Peter: "A voice of one crying out: Prepare the way of the Lord in the wilderness; make a straight highway for our God. . . . And the glory of the Lord will appear, and all humanity together will see it. . . . The grass withers, the flowers fade, but the word of our God remains forever" (Is 40:3, 5, 8).

These verses in Isaiah introduce the promises God makes to redeem his people exiled in Babylon "without silver and without price." Karen Jobes argues, "Peter identifies the word of God as understood by Isaiah with the word that has been preached to Peter's readers, the gospel of the Lord Jesus Christ. . . . Remarkably, Peter does not hesitate to redirect covenant language first addressed to Israel in exile to his first-century Christian readers in Asia Minor."[13] Thus the very same "enduring word of the Lord spoken through Isaiah to ancient Israel is respoken by Peter to first-century Christians in a letter that is framed by allusion to the Babylonian exile." Jobes continues, "Peter fully recognizes that God's message to 6th century Israel stands as Christ's word to 1st century Christians because he recognizes that it is the Spirit of Christ who revealed God's promises to Isaiah."[14]

Furthermore, the exact quotation of Isaiah 40:6-8 comes from the Greek Old Testament, yet with one key alteration, changing the subject of the phrase from "God" (*theos*) to "Lord" (*kyrios*). Because *kyrios* was the most common way for New Testament authors to refer to Jesus Christ, it seems that Peter applied the phrase to Christ, and thus it would mean "the word spoken by Christ the Lord" or perhaps "the word which is about Christ the Lord." Peter's conclusion to the Isaiah quotation is that this very word, the word of Isaiah, is the gospel message about Jesus preached to Peter's audience. Thus, God's promises announced in Israel's prophet Isaiah, which have been kept in Christ, are now announced and applied to Peter's readers. This echoes the conclusion of 1 Peter 1:10-12, where the spirit of Christ witnessed beforehand to the suffering and glory of Christ "for you," Peter's audience.

[13]Jobes, *1 Peter*, 126-27.
[14]Jobes, *1 Peter*, 127.

After Peter explains that his readers' new life is generated by God's eternal word (1 Pet 1:22-25), he argues for the necessity of sustaining this new life by that same word. This new life requires changed behaviors—"putting off" or literally "taking off" an old way of living, malice, deceit, hypocrisy, evil, and slander. But it is not enough to take old vices off. Peter also commands his audience to do something positive: to desire the "milk of the word" (1 Pet 2:2). English translations render the Greek phrase *logikon adolon gala* either as "pure spiritual milk" (ESV, NRSV, NIV) or "pure milk of the word" (CSB, NASB, KJV). Though there is question regarding the clearest translation of this phrase, the one command in the passage is without doubt; while putting off moral vices, the audience is commanded to long for or desire milk like a newborn.

The question in the translation is whether they are to desire "spiritual milk" or the "milk of the word." The key word *logikon* can be translated "spiritual" (as opposed to literal "milk"), or, as one might recognize in the root of the adjective, it could be translated simply as "word." The second translation clearly connects back to the preceding context of 1 Peter 1:23-25, where the *logos* or word was described metaphorically as a seed (1 Pet 1:23) and where the quotation from Isaiah 40:6-8 speaks of God's enduring word. Taking both the image of the word as seed in 1 Peter 1:23 and the image of the word as milk in 1 Peter 2:2-3 together indicates that God's word gives new life and sustains it. Furthermore, the metaphor connects back to the idea of new birth in 1 Peter 1:3. Finally, the image of longing for milk is supported by the allusion to Psalm 34:8: "if you have tasted that the Lord is good." The context, in light of Psalm 34, is of God himself as sustainer of our spiritual new birth. It is noteworthy that Peter changes the two imperative verbs "Taste and see!" in the Greek Old Testament to the single indicative statement "you have tasted" in 1 Peter 2:3. This suggests that Peter's readers have already tasted of the Lord's goodness; they have already been made alive to a living hope. Thus, 1 Peter 2:2-3 is encouraging those who have already been made alive to stay alive by longing for God's word.

1 PETER 2:4-10. This is the final section where Peter is constructing the theological identity of his readers. Here the line of thought begun in 1 Peter 1:3 is brought to its climax. Changing the metaphor from milk to living stones, in 1 Peter 2:4-10 Peter completes his instruction about his readers' new identity.

This passage is intricately structured and plays an important function in the letter as a whole. The entire section seems to function like a midrash, or a Jewish exegesis or interpretation of Old Testament text where key words draw the various texts together. First Peter 2:4 introduces the theme expounded in 1 Peter 2:6-8, where the keyword "stone" (*lithos*) forms a link, and 1 Peter 2:5 introduces the theme expounded in 1 Peter 2:9-10, where the word "people" (*laos*) draws the connection. Jesus Christ, the living Stone in 1 Peter 2:4, is rejected by humans, yet chosen by God. Likewise, the living stones, or believers in 1 Peter 2:5, are built up as a spiritual house, a holy priesthood to offer spiritual sacrifice.

The phrase "As you come to him" flows without break from 1 Peter 2:3-4 and refers to Jesus as "a living stone—rejected by people but chosen and honored by God." The contrast between human and divine evaluation of Jesus is further developed in 1 Peter 2:6-8. Peter makes it clear that Jesus is the stone set in Zion by God (Is 28:16), who is chosen and honored. Peter already noted how the Old Testament prophets inquired into the fulfillment of God's promised salvation in 1 Peter 1:10-12, and here Peter understands that God revealed to Isaiah both the sufferings and the glory of the Christ. Because Jesus is chosen and honored, it will be the same for those who believe in him. Likewise, those who do not believe in Jesus, to them the rejected building material is something to stumble over. Yet, though the unbelieving stumble over Jesus, he in fact is the cornerstone, the most important piece of the entire building.

Peter's reference to Isaiah 28:16 and Psalm 118:22 in 1 Peter 2:6-7 gives his readers the assurance that though people reject Jesus, the stone, this was already announced in Israel's prophets and thus should be no surprise. A second outcome of Peter's references to this passage is to clearly "present Jesus Christ as the only means of salvation by which all will be judged."[15]

---

[15]Jobes, *1 Peter*, 154.

Because Peter's readers come to Jesus, a living stone, they too are "living stones, a spiritual house . . . to be a holy priesthood" (1 Pet 1:5)—an identity further developed in 1 Peter 2:9-10. The series of labels here constitute an amazing and powerful description of the elect, newborn identity of Peter's readers. "But," Peter says, contrasting his audience with those who disobey the word and stumble,

> you are a chosen race [Is 43:20], a royal priesthood, a holy nation [Ex 19:5-6], a people for his possession [Is 43:21], so that you may proclaim the praises of the one who called you out of darkness into his marvelous light [Is 9:2]. Once you were not a people, but now you are God's people; once you had not received mercy, but now you have received mercy [Hos 1:6, 9; 2:23]. (1 Pet 2:9-10)

Just as Peter interpreted the Old Testament as referring to Jesus using the keyword *stone* (in 1 Pet 2:6-8), here he understands the Old Testament descriptions of God's people, Israel, as referring to his Christian audience. They are a chosen race, which echoes Isaiah 43:20-21, where Yahweh declares himself Israel's only deliverer from their exile in Babylon. Yahweh declares that he will provide water in the desert for his chosen people. Jobes comments, "Israel's deliverance from exile in Babylon is the typological forerunner of the greater deliverance achieved by Jesus Christ."[16] A royal priesthood, a holy nation, a people for God's special possession: all are phrases taken from the Greek version of Exodus 19:5-6. It is important to note that all of these descriptions of God's people are corporate, meaning that the new identity of Peter's readers is essentially that of a community.

The opening section of 1 Peter focusing on his readers' new identity in Christ (1 Pet 1:3–2:10) comes to a climax here in 1 Peter 2:4-10 with a thick series of quotations and allusions to the Old Testament. Peter uses labels from the Old Testament story line to inscribe his mixed audience firmly within the narrative of God's story. Peter's readers are the regathered people of God, and because they have been reborn as the children of God,

---

[16]Jobes, *1 Peter*, 159.

they have been given a new name ("chosen race, royal priesthood") and a new identity.

Conduct or responsibility of those with a new theological identity (1 Peter 2:11–5:11).

Transition from theological identity to conduct (1 Peter 2:11-12). These two verses constitute the hinge around which the letter of 1 Peter turns. In 1 Peter 1:3–2:10 Peter describes his readers' new identity in Christ as reborn ones, living stones like their savior. He then moves on to the ethical instructions of 1 Peter 2:13–5:11, where he instructs his readers how to live out their new identity in the particular situation of a hostile culture. Peter once again addresses his readers as "aliens and strangers" (in keeping with their status as exiles, 1 Pet 1:1) and then challenges them to keep their internal passions in check so that they may live conspicuously holy lives before nonbelievers. In these ways the passage looks back summarizing the message so far. At the same time, 1 Peter 2:12 anticipates what comes next. Living before a watching world means, in this context, setting aside one's rights and submitting to ridicule, misunderstanding, and even innocent suffering all for the purpose of witnessing to the hope that now lives within them. The major theme of 1 Peter 2:13–3:12 is submission, and this submission is an illustration of the larger theme that dominates 1 Peter, namely, the necessity of doing what is right, even if it results in innocent suffering, so that the watching world might see the glory of God.

New life in society (1 Peter 2:13–4:6).

SUBMISSION IN SOCIETY AS WITNESS (1 PETER 2:13–3:12). This next major section revolves around the theme of submission and addresses specific groups within the community: 1 Peter 2:13-17 addresses the entire community; 1 Peter 2:18-20 instructs household slaves; 1 Peter 2:21-25, the climax of the section, offers the supreme example of innocent suffering, Jesus himself; 1 Peter 3:1-7 discuss the submission of wives; and in 1 Peter 3:8-12 the section concludes by addressing the entire community again. This section of instruction contains a typical Greco-Roman household code. Such codes contained instructions addressed to specific groups found within a typical household (other examples in the New Testament include Col 3:18–4:1; Eph 5:21–6:9). The household codes were very important in ancient Greco-Roman culture because it was a common belief that the structure of the household was divinely ordained and provided the basis for a strong, orderly, and prosperous society. Thus, the well-ordered household and every individual's responsibilities in it was understood as a fundamental part of one's sociopolitical duty. The disordered home led to the disordered city.

The material in this passage is arranged in the form of a chiasm, with mirrored sections forming half of the Greek letter χ. Thus, 1 Peter 2:13-17 mirrors 1 Peter 3:8-12 as instructions to the entire community, and 1 Peter 1:18-20 mirrors 1 Peter 3:1-7 pairing instructions to household slaves with instructions to wives, leaving 1 Peter 2:21-25 as the centerpiece of the chiasm:

> 1 Peter 2:13-17: instruction for everyone
>   1 Peter 2:18-20: instructions for slaves
>   1 Peter 2:21-25: the example of Christ
>   1 Peter 3:1-7: instructions for wives
> 1 Peter 3:8-12: instructions for everyone[17]

It is noteworthy that, at least by means of this structure, Peter associates household slaves with wives and connects their experience of and response to innocent suffering with that of Christ. Peter depicts his audience as people without power and privilege in society at large, the very thing we would expect of a people characterized as aliens and strangers (1 Pet 1:1, 17; 2:11). At the same time, Peter uses the household code to encourage his socially powerless readers to submit to the social structures within their cultural context.

Peter calls all Christians to live in submission to "governors." The first section of this larger unit 1 Peter 2:13–3:12 addresses subordination in the civil sphere. Though Christians are commanded to be subordinate to human authorities (for example, the emperor, 1 Pet 2:13, 17; or governors,

---

[17]Joel B. Green, *1 Peter*, THNTC (Grand Rapids, MI: Eerdmans, 2007), 72.

1 Pet 2:14), *hypotassō* does not necessarily entail loyalty to the governing powers or the individuals wielding the power of the state. Peter instructs the entire community that they should be subject to all people in appropriate ways and therefore engaged in their place within society. This is a way of doing what is right (1 Pet 2:15) in the public context. To be clear, in context, doing good is not merely private acts of Christian piety, but rather deeds that would also be generally acknowledged by (even nonreligious) society as good. Though Peter's Christian audience and the people in the surrounding culture are living out strikingly different values, nonetheless Peter implicitly acknowledges that there is enough common ground that both can agree on a limited shared set of goods, as seen in 1 Peter 2:12. Jobes comments, "This thought fits quite well with the Diaspora motif in which the letter is framed, for it follows Jeremiah's instructions: 'Seek the welfare of the city where I have sent you into exile, and pray to the Lord on its behalf; for in this welfare you will have welfare' (Jer 29:7 NASB)."[18]

Peter then clarifies that such civic participation must be done as "free people, not using your freedom as a cover-up for evil, but as God's slaves" (1 Pet 2:16). Christian freedom, rather than complete liberation from responsibility within the civic sphere, requires subordination to human authority, yet as those who are God's slaves. This remarkable notion picks up on Israel's experience of liberation from Egypt, which was immediately followed by their enslavement to God through the covenant at Sinai. So too, Christians are to experience their freedom in their somewhat paradoxical status as slaves to God—and this all within the civic context.

Though similar to Paul's teaching regarding Christian relationship to civil authority in Romans 13:1-7, 1 Peter 2:13-17 makes no assertion that civil authorities are servants of God who represent God's authority. The Petrine conception of civil authority's function is a simple utilitarian one devoid of divine warrant. The point of this passage is not to discourage resistance to authorities established by God, as appears to be the case in Romans 13:2, but to encourage doing what is right as a sign

---

[18]Jobes, *1 Peter*, 176.

of subordination to God's will, which in turn is a means to silence detractors (1 Pet 2:15). The passage ends by reemphasizing the command to "honor everyone," yet with the contrast between honoring the emperor (one's civic duty) and fearing God (the ultimate posture of reverence and devotion).

In the second section of the household code Peter points to the slave, who was most vulnerable in Greco-Roman society, as a paradigm of submission for the Christian community. Strikingly, Peter commands household slaves (*oiketai*) to be subject not only to good masters but also to unjust masters, to the point of "suffering unjustly" (1 Pet 2:19). The idea of innocent suffering is especially important to Peter (1 Pet 3:16-17; 4:12-19; and Jesus' innocent suffering in 1 Pet 2:21-25). That slaves are mentioned first is unique in the New Testament, for in the sequence of household instructions found in Ephesians and Colossians, slaves (*douloi*) are addressed after wives-husbands and children-parents (Eph 5:21–6:9; Col 3:21–4:1). Thus, Peter gives slaves pride of place—they are paradigms for all believers facing unjust suffering. Peter argues, "When you do what is good and suffer, if you endure it, this brings favor with God" (1 Pet 2:20). Suffering while doing good is the key here—innocent suffering glorifies God and provides a gospel witness to the watching world. The idea of doing good even in the face of unjust suffering is a major theme of the letter and is perfectly exemplified in the innocent suffering of Christ.

In 1 Peter 2:21-25, Peter offers the supreme example of and motivation for unjust suffering, Christ the ultimate innocent sufferer. Peter transitions from the unjust suffering of slaves to that of Christ by saying his readers are all (not just slaves) called to follow Christ's example. In Christ's own suffering, Peter says he has left you "an example, that you should follow in his steps" (1 Pet 2:21).

The character of Christ's example is expressed largely through the words of Isaiah:

> He did not commit sin, and no deceit was found in his mouth [Is 53:9];
> when he was being insulted, he persisted in not insulting in return;

when he was suffering, he persisted in not threatening [Is 53:7], but continued to entrust himself to him who judges justly. He himself bore our sins [Is 53:4, 12] in his body on the tree, that having died to sins, we might live to righteousness. By his wounds you have been healed [Is 53:5]. (1 Pet 2:22-24, my translation)

Christ is the perfect example of innocent suffering. He was neither sinful nor deceitful, yet even in his suffering, Christ did not defend himself or fight for a hearing before a human court. Rather, he entrusted himself to God's own judgment. Therefore, Christ's suffering becomes the example to all Christians who follow in his footsteps.

Whereas Jesus serves as the example par excellence of innocent suffering for Christians to follow ("you were called to this"), the passage then focuses on the unique redemptive value and purpose of Christ's death. Switching from "you" (second person) to "our" (first person), Peter highlights what only Christ could do. Jesus "himself bore our sins in his body." Christ bore or carried sin to the cross (or here "on the tree," Deut 21:22-23), so that Christians might "live for righteousness" (1 Pet 2:24). Christ, cast as Isaiah's Suffering Servant, submitted himself to unjust suffering in order to serve God's plan of redemption. Continuing with the imagery of Isaiah 53, Peter reminds his audience of their past: "You were like sheep going astray [Is 53:6]." But, again stressing the unique work of Christ, now they have "returned to the Shepherd and Overseer." This well-known shepherd imagery is frequently used of Yahweh in the Old Testament (see especially Ps 23), yet here is applied to Jesus Christ, who is the supreme pastor and overseer of the church (see 1 Pet 5:1-4).

Peter next addresses wives within the household. First Peter 3:1-7 begins with the connecting phrase "In the same way" or "likewise," which at once connects back to the instructions given to household slaves (1 Pet 2:18) and forward to the brief instructions given to husbands (1 Pet 3:7). Beyond the parallel struck between household slaves and wives in the overall chiastic structure of the section (see above), both passages share a basic flow of thought: first, an instruction to submit (1 Pet 2:18; 3:1); second, emphasis on the conduct that is pleasing to (or finds favor with) God (1 Pet 2:19-20; 3:2-4); and third, Peter offers an example and motivation for such behavior (1 Pet 2:21-25; 3:5-6).

The opening command to be subordinate to "your own husbands" is for a missionary purpose, "if some disobey the word, they may be won over" (1 Pet 3:1). Like the witness of household slaves, wives are to win over their unbelieving husbands "without a word." Two comments are necessary to understand this command in context. First, it would be an extremely precarious social situation for a Christian woman to be married to a non-Christian husband. Women in the ancient world were "not allowed to vote or hold office, could not take an oath or plead a case in court, could not be the legal guardian of their own minor children, and were legally dependent on either their father or a guardian."[19] In this situation wives and slaves who converted to Christianity were particularly vulnerable to suffering and unjust treatment at the hands of their nonbelieving husbands or masters. Thus, it is particularly in these contexts that the patient suffering of slaves and wives both emulates the example of Jesus and ultimately witnesses to his redemptive suffering.

Second, it would be a mistake to assume that all, or even most, husbands were disobedient to the word (as 1 Pet 3:7 makes clear). Horrell notes that the "instructions to husbands which follow in 3.7 shows that in many cases they can be addressed as believers too, and the instructions given to wives applies to them all, whether their husbands are Christian or not."[20] For all wives, it is inner beauty, rather than external adornment, that is pleasing to God. Though quietness is a virtue applicable to all Christians (2 Thess 3:12; 1 Tim 2:2), it was often especially applied to women (1 Cor 14:34-35; 1 Tim 2:11-15; Titus 2:4-5). Peter then offers as an example of submission and obedience with the experience of Sarah (Gen 18:12).

It is noteworthy to point out Peter's encouragement to "not fear any intimidation" (1 Pet 3:6). This phrase may indicate a recognition that,

---

[19]Achtemeier, *1 Peter*, 206.
[20]Horrell, *Epistles of Peter and Jude*, 56.

even when acting in submission and good conduct, Christian wives might still suffer. Horrell notes,

> By telling them not to fear such human threats the author implicitly reiterates his belief that God alone is to be feared and that commitment to God is the ultimate motivation for all Christian conduct. Furthermore, unlike in much moral instruction of the time, wives are here addressed directly, as subjects who can and must take their own moral responsibility. Their commitment to God must stand firm, even when accusation and suffering result.[21]

"In the same way," husbands are instructed to live with their wives in understanding (1 Pet 3:7). As in the section to slaves and wives, there is an address, "husbands," followed by an imperative ("live with your wives in an understanding way"), and then the purpose for the instruction ("so that your prayers may not be hindered"). Living in understanding includes, first, knowing that the wife is "weaker" ("weaker partner"), where it is most likely that Peter is thinking of the weakness of the physical body (weaker *skeuos*, or "vessel," implies this; see 1 Thess 4:4). Second, the husband is to understand that his wife is a coheir or equal participant in "the grace of life." Women, just as much as men, are recipients of the inheritance of eternal life promised by God (see 1 Pet 1:4). Thus, husbands are to show their wives honor, rather than using their physical or social strength to abuse or marginalize them. The point is clear: one's relational conduct toward others is of consequence for right standing before God—only when a husband honors his wife in these ways can he pray with integrity.

The final section taking up submission again addresses the entire community rather than individual groups within the household (1 Pet 3:8-12). First Peter 3:8 opens with "Finally, all of you," which notes the return to addressing the entire community (as in 1 Pet 2:13). Here Peter outlines the qualities of Christian character and actions needed to sustain the community both as Christians relate internally to fellow believers and as they respond to the hostility of a nonbelieving society. Within the Christian community especially, Peter's readers are instructed to maintain

---

[21]Horrell, *Epistles of Peter and Jude*, 59.

like-mindedness and sympathy toward one another, with compassion and humility. Yet, when facing insult from nonbelievers, they are to return such "evil" with a blessing, "since you were called for this, so that you may inherit a blessing" (1 Pet 3:9). Returning a blessing in response to evil is to respond in the opposite spirit when confronted by the nonbelieving world, and this is a kind of silent witness to the transforming power of the gospel (not unlike the response of the slaves and wives). Responding in the opposite spirit, returning blessing for insult, is the Christian teaching of nonretaliation that is rooted in Jesus' Sermon on the Mount (Mt 5:44; Lk 6:28) and is supported further by Jewish tradition, which cautions against revenge (Lev 19:18; Prov 20:22; 24:29).

The extensive citation of Psalm 34:12-16 in 1 Peter 3:10-12 ends this section and provides the basis for the instruction on nonretaliation. Those who want to "inherit a blessing" (1 Pet 3:9), to "see good days," must, according to the psalm, "keep his tongue from evil and his lips from speaking deceit." Like the example of Jesus (1 Pet 2:23), the psalm calls God's people not to engage in slander and deceit, even when pressed with the evil of the surrounding society. Rather, the psalm reassures Peter's audience that the Lord sees their suffering and he hears their cries. God knows and will act. Christians can follow the path of nonretaliation, the path Jesus took, because "the face of the Lord is against those who do what is evil." As Christ entrusted himself to "the judge who judges justly" (1 Pet 2:23), Psalm 34 urges Peter's readers to do the same.

DOING WHAT IS RIGHT IN THE MIDST OF OPPOSITION (1 PETER 3:13-17). Peter's readers are not to fear suffering, because God himself not only sees and hears their innocent suffering, but he also punishes the wicked (Ps 34:13-16, quoted in 1 Pet 3:10-12). The quotation of Psalm 34 serves as both a summary of the household code in 1 Peter 2:13–4:12 and transition to the themes of suffering and vindication (of both Christ and the audience) featured in the rest of the chapter. The exhortation to persevere through innocent suffering (1 Pet 3:13-17) is supported by the model of Christ's innocent suffering—which Peter turns to next in 1 Peter 3:18-22. We have seen this kind of exhortation-model strategy from Peter before:

household slaves (1 Pet 2:18-20) are encouraged to submit and suffer based on the example of Christ (1 Pet 2:21-25).

Reflecting back on the psalm, 1 Peter 3:13 asks, "Who then will harm you if you are devoted to what is good?" Of course, God himself sees and hears the one who is devoted to good, and God himself is his protection; therefore Peter, reiterating his point, quotes Isaiah 8:12: "Do not fear what they fear or be intimidated" (1 Pet 3:14). The phrase from Isaiah is to encourage Peter's audience not to fear other people, namely, the people who persecute and abuse them for their Christian faith. Rather than fear, Peter's readers are to "regard Christ the Lord as holy" and be ready to "give a defense" for the hope they have. Though it is possible that the technical term *defense* (*apologia*) could imply a legal or judicial context where Christians would have to defend the faith before a local magistrate, it is most likely that Peter has in mind a more informal context where believers are slandered and marginalized personally. In any case, the defense of the faith here is one where patient and loving nonretaliation in the face of persecution witnesses to the power of the gospel. Peter's central point in the entire letter is emphasized both at the beginning ("if you should suffer for righteousness, you are blessed") and the ending ("it is better to suffer for doing good . . . than for doing evil") of the passage. And, of course, not only is Jesus' innocent suffering the ultimate example and motivation for suffering for doing good, but ultimately Christ's suffering and triumph accomplishes redemption.

THE SUFFERING AND TRIUMPH OF CHRIST (1 PETER 3:18-22). It is clear that Christians ought not fear suffering when they suffer for doing good because God himself is their protection—this is the gist of Peter's quotation from Psalm 34. In this passage, once again, Peter encourages his audience to a certain character and conduct motivated by the example of Christ. Though perhaps the most difficult passage in 1 Peter to understand, there is little doubt that, along with 1 Peter 1:18-21; 2:21-25, this is the third major christological section of the letter. This passage further supports the assertion that Christians should not fear suffering for doing good because of the victorious death and triumph of Christ.

First Peter 3:18 begins the christological reason for why Peter's readers can suffer for doing good. "For" (which indicates cause) "Christ also suffered for sins . . . the righteous for the unrighteous, that he might bring you to God." Rather than merely a moral example, Peter uses sacrificial language to describe how Christ is the one who suffered with reference to human sin; he is the righteous substitute on behalf of unrighteous humanity. Further, the purpose of Christ's suffering is that "he might bring you to God." The events of Christ's suffering are recounted in the remainder of the verse: "he was put to death in the flesh, but made alive by the Spirit." The phrases "in the flesh" and "in the spirit" or "by the Spirit" should not be understood as driving a wedge between the natures of Christ—human and divine. Rather, from the earthly perspective, Jesus was judged according to human standards by being put to death. However, according to God's plan (1 Pet 1:2, 20), Jesus was vindicated by the power of the Spirit in resurrection.

Though 1 Peter 3:19 continues the sentence started in the previous verse, there are several difficulties regarding how this next phrase connects to what has come before. The basic questions are: When and where did Jesus go, what did he proclaim, and to whom? Answering the question of when Jesus went is directly connected to how one interprets the first phrase of 1 Peter 3:19, which begins with a relative pronoun *en hō*. Rather than going "in the spirit" before his incarnation, or between his death and his resurrection, it was after his resurrection, made alive by the Spirit, that Christ went and proclaimed. So, Christ went sometime after his resurrection. The participle in 1 Peter 3:19, translated "went" (*poreutheis*), makes this clear, as it is linked with the two previous participles, forming the series "Christ was put to death, he was made alive, he went." But where did he go? It is important to note that none of the major translations render the verb "descended." Rather, in context, this same verb is used in 1 Peter 3:22 to refer to Christ's ascension ("who has gone into heaven"). Furthermore, elsewhere in the New Testament this particular verb is used to refer to the ascension specifically (Acts 1:10-11) or to Christ's going to God (Jn 14:2-3, 12, 28; 16:7, 28). Christ, therefore, is not going down but up, which describes his ascension into heaven—and this especially in light of 1 Peter 3:22.

The next two questions can be answered together: What did he proclaim, and to whom? The "spirits in prison" are further qualified as those "who . . . were disobedient . . . in the days of Noah." It is likely, then, that these are the rebellious angels or spirits awaiting judgment. In our passage, this is supported in light of the reference to "angels, authorities, and powers" in 1 Peter 3:22. Some important background context that helps shed light on what Jesus proclaimed is provided by the narrative found in Genesis 6:1-4, along with the traditional Jewish interpretation of this narrative found in 1 Enoch. Rather than the spirits of deceased humans, these spirits are the evil supernatural beings who were understood to be the offspring of the disobedient angels, who, in the time of Noah, cohabited with the daughters of men. According to the tradition found in 1 Enoch 10, these disobedient spirits were locked in prison, held for God's future judgment. A further detail of importance is the verb describing what Jesus says. Rather than using the specific verb *euangelizō*, which is most often translated "preach the good news" with the message of salvation in view, here Peter uses the verb *kēryssō*, to "proclaim" or "announce" a message that could be positive (for example, the annunciation of the gospel of Jesus) or negative (announcing judgment).

Flood Traditions in 1-2 Peter and Jude

1 Peter, 2 Peter, and Jude all use the flood traditions of Genesis 6-7 to highlight God's judgment (see 1 Pet 3:20-21; 2 Pet 2:5; Jude 6). Whereas 1 Peter and Jude filter this tradition through Second Temple tradition (especially 1 Enoch 6-19), 2 Peter does not refer to this tradition directly.

Thus, the announcement Christ makes to these disobedient spirits concerns not the proclamation of the good news of their salvation but a word of their condemnation and subordination to the power of the exalted Christ. Because Jesus is victor over the evil spiritual powers (he is "at the right hand of God with angels, authorities, and powers subject to him," 1 Pet 3:22), believers can take courage in their present suffering, because they know that in Christ they share in his victory.

A final issue to address is the reason Peter mentions Noah, the flood, and baptism. Jobes notes, "Noah's flood was an Old Testament event that displayed God's salvation of the righteous few and his judgment on, and destruction of, an entire society that refused to repent."[22] In 1 Peter 3:21, Peter associates the Christian gospel that his readers have received with Noah by arguing for a typological connection between the flood and Christian baptism. When Jesus taught about the coming of the Son of Man, he too used the Noah story (Mt 24:37-39; Lk 17:26-27, 30).

Jobes concludes, "Peter's readers will be among those who escape the second 'flood' of judgment because they have already passed through the waters of Christian baptism, which saves them by virtue of the vindicating resurrection of Jesus Christ" and not by baptism itself.[23] This last point is reinforced by the parallel phrases "saved through [*dia*] water" (1 Pet 3:20, referring to Noah and his family) and salvation "through [*dia*] the resurrection of Jesus Christ" (1 Pet 3:21; see also 1 Pet 1:3). Jobes offers table 3.1 to present the relevant parallels:[24]

Table 3.1. Parallels between 1 Peter 3:20 and 1 Peter 3:21

3:20	3:21
a few	you
were saved	baptism now saves
through water	*through* the resurrection of Jesus Christ

For Peter, baptism itself is not the agent that removes moral dirt from the body, as if the ceremony of baptism could excuse Christians from living a moral life. Rather, it is through the power of Jesus' resurrection (1 Pet 1:3) that Christians have a good conscience before God. Finally, Wayne Grudem notes in the list below that the parallel between Noah and Peter's audience offers several implications:

◆ Noah and his family were a minority surrounded by hostile unbelievers; so are Peter's readers (3:13-14; 4:4, 12-13).

---

[22]Jobes, *1 Peter*, 252.
[23]Jobes, *1 Peter*, 252.
[24]Jobes, *1 Peter*, 252.

- Noah was righteous in the midst of a wicked world. Peter exhorts his readers to be righteous in the midst of wicked unbelievers (3:13-14, 16-17; 4:3-4).

- Noah witnessed boldly to those around him by believing God and building the ark. Peter encourages his readers to be good witnesses to unbelievers around them (3:14, 16-17).

- Noah realized that judgment was soon to come on the world. Peter reminds his readers that God's judgment is certainly coming, perhaps soon (4:5, 7).

- At the time of Noah, God patiently waited for repentance from unbelievers before he brought judgment. So it is also in the situation of Peter's readers.

- Noah was finally saved with only a few others. Peter thus encourages his readers that, though perhaps few, they too will certainly finally be saved, for Christ has triumphed and has all things subject to him (3:22; 4:13, 19; 5:10).[25]

In drawing out these parallels, Peter once again sets his present readers within the story line of the Old Testament and helps reshape their identity theologically.

DOING WHAT IS RIGHT IN THE MIDST OF OUTSIDERS (1 PETER 4:1-6). The previous section argued for a particular view of 1 Peter 3:18-22, that rather than descending into hell to preach the gospel to the deceased, Jesus actually proclaimed ultimate victory over the spiritual powers at his ascension after the resurrection. Now Peter turns in 1 Peter 4 to exhort his readers to live out Christ's triumph over the powers, first among an unbelieving world (1 Pet 4:1-6) and second in the midst of the Christian community (1 Pet 4:7-11).

In light of Christ's suffering and vindication, Peter's audience is to adopt the same attitude because "the one who suffers in the flesh is finished with sin." The conjunction *therefore* picks up the thought of 1 Peter 3:18, where

---

[25]Wayne Grudem, *1 Peter*, TNTC (repr., Grand Rapids, MI: Eerdmans, 2007), 160-61.

Christ suffered once for all to deal with sin, so that he might bring Peter's audience to God. Because of Christ's redemptive suffering, believers are to arm themselves with the same resolve that Jesus himself had. The conjunction *because* likely gives the content of the resolve, namely, that Jesus entrusted himself to God (1 Pet 1:23) while suffering at the hands of sinful people, and in doing so he finished with sin, dealing with it once and for all. So too, when believers suffer like Christ, it marks their break with sin; that is, that they suffer like Christ indicates their turning from sin to a new life of hope.

Armed with Christ's disposition, Peter's readers are "to live the remaining time in the flesh no longer for human desires" (1 Pet 4:2). This is a theme that has already surfaced in the letter (1 Pet 2:11-12, "abstain from sinful desires") and is expanded in the next verse with a list of empty, sinful behaviors that the audience has given up. The elect status of the audience has led to a new lifestyle, which is incomprehensible to their pagan neighbors: "They are surprised that you don't join them," which ultimately leads to outright social conflict (as a result, "they slander you"). In light of this conflict and suffering, Peter consoles and encourages his readers that their pagan neighbors will answer to "the one who stands ready to judge the living and the dead" (1 Pet 4:5). This assurance echoes back once again to the quotation of Psalm 34 in 1 Peter 2, where God himself is the one ready to vindicate the righteous and judge the wicked. The phrase "the living and the dead" refers to the universal scope of God's judgment (Acts 10:42; 2 Tim 4:1) and importantly asserts that God's judgment is not limited by physical death—that is, those who have died are not exempt from God's judgment.

The claim that those who have died are not exempt from God's judgment is a key starting point for understanding the next verse. Peter's comments in 1 Peter 4:6 are "meant to provide justification for the assertions in v. 5."[26] Because the audience's pagan neighbors will give an account, it is "For this reason the gospel was preached to those who are

---

[26] Actemeier, *1 Peter*, 286.

now dead" (1 Pet 4:6). The main questions arising from this phrase are, Who are the dead? and, When was the gospel preached to them?

In contrast to the "spirits in prison" (1 Pet 3:19), here the dead are clearly human beings, and whereas the proclamation in 1 Peter 3:19 was a general message (of defeat), 1 Peter 4:6 uses the verb "preach good news" (*euangelizō*), specifically referring to preaching the gospel. Yet, when was the gospel preached to these deceased people? Recent English commentaries and a few translations indicate that the dead in 1 Peter 4:6 are Christian believers who received the gospel message while alive but who have since died (both the NIV and CSB add the word *now*). The flow of thought is as follows: because death was, in general, a sign of condemnation and futility, pagan neighbors would have understood the death of Christians as proof that following Jesus was, in the end, pointless. If everyone dies anyway, why not enjoy fulfilling one's desires with drink, sex, and idolatry now? In the face of this, Peter argues that "although they [Christians] might be judged in the flesh according to human standards, they might live in the spirit according to God's standards" (1 Pet 4:6). That is, though from a human perspective followers of Jesus die, they will be vindicated (like Christ) and live again "in the spirit." In contrast to the human perspective that understands death as nullifying Christian faith, Peter encourages his readers that the decisive break with sin and its accompanying sufferings is in keeping with the living hope into which they have been born.

Love one another: Maintaining unity to God's glory (1 Peter 4:7-11). Whereas 1 Peter 4:1-6 anticipated objections that outsiders may have toward righteous suffering, 1 Peter 4:7-11 encourages believers to live out their new Christian character in community. Recalling themes announced in 1 Peter 3:8-9, especially compassion, humility, and blessing, this passage emphasizes love (1 Pet 4:8), hospitality (1 Pet 4:9), and service (1 Pet 4:10-11) within the Christian community.

Because God's final judgment is no remote contingency, Christians must live with the end or culmination of all things in mind. Though the worldly powers and institutions generating abuse against the church may seem inevitable in the context of pagan hostility, emphasizing the end challenges a secular narrative and reorients readers to expect God's final purposes to come to pass. Therefore, the fitting response is to be alert and sober-minded (a common refrain in 1 Peter; see 1 Pet 1:13; 5:8) and in an attitude of prayer. Followers of Christ should always live in light of God's reality. Both verbs (be alert and sober-minded) are directed to the purpose of prayer and connect back to the assertion that God himself is listening to the cries of the righteous (Ps 34, quoted in 1 Pet 2).

In 1 Peter 4:8-10, three parallel phrases map out in broad terms what actions should characterize the Christian community as they live in light of the end. It is in maintaining love, practicing hospitality, and serving that the community born into a living hope expresses its new identity in Christ. First, Peter argues that above all they are to love one another because "love covers a multitude of sins" (a quotation of Prov 10:12). Such mutual love overlooks the sins of others and maintains (perhaps at times restores; see Jas 5:20, where Prov 10:12 is also echoed) Christian fellowship by avoiding strife and conflict produced by sin and resentment.

Second, Peter encourages hospitality. The original language may actually stress that one be hospitable rather than just show hospitality. The significance is that Peter may not be thinking about a limited number of hospitable actions, but rather a general disposition that is always looking for ways to make room for others. Importantly, such hospitality is to be given "without complaining," which suggests that such practices are uncalculated and without resentment. Jesus' teaching, according to Luke, stressed taking opportunity to offer hospitality especially to those who cannot repay (Lk 14:12).

Finally, Peter stresses the need to serve one another according to the gifts received by God. Rather than considering God's gifts as an index of levels of spiritual status, these gifts are to be used in service toward others, and such service seems to be the responsibility of the entire community ("each one has received") rather than just the leaders. In 1 Peter 4:11, both speaking and serving should be seen as supplied by God for the purpose of caring for the community to the glory of Christ. The climax of the passage is a short doxology: "To him be the glory and the power forever and ever. Amen."

Christian endurance and persecution (1 Peter 4:12–5:11). According to the outline presented above, 1 Peter 4:12–5:11 functions along with 1 Peter 2:13–4:11 to stress living out the new identity as those born into a living hope.

SUFFERING AS FELLOWSHIP WITH CHRIST (1 PETER 4:12-19). Rejoicing in the midst of suffering is a theme introduced as an indicative reality in 1 Peter 1:6-9, yet here, Peter intensifies this idea by commanding the community to rejoice. Furthermore, 1 Peter 4:12-19 also reflects back to the instruction of 1 Peter 3:13-17, which stresses patient endurance in the face of persecution.

In 1 Peter 4:12, Peter claims that unjust suffering should not come as a surprise to his readers because as followers of Christ, who suffered innocently, they should rather expect to experience the same treatment he experienced.[27] Such innocent suffering is not a sign of God's rejection or anger, but rather suffering for Christ is a blessing, not merely because of the suffering itself but because following in the footsteps of Jesus' own suffering (1 Pet 2:21-25) is proof of the presence of the Spirit and of God in one's life (1 Pet 4:14). It is important to note that suffering for Christ is beneficial not because it builds character or virtue (though it may do that in other contexts) but because suffering for the name of Christ is evidence of genuine faith. Therefore, the Christian response to suffering is to "rejoice as you share in the sufferings of Christ . . . because the Spirit of glory and of God rests on you" (1 Pet 4:13-14).

As in the example of slaves (1 Pet 2:18-20), Peter stresses in 1 Peter 4:15-16 that not all who suffer receive a blessing: "Let none of you suffer as a murderer, a thief, an evildoer, or a meddler." Peter is quick to note the difference between suffering for one's own wicked behavior and for the sake of Christ. Of course, it is particularly Christian suffering in view (1 Pet 4:16).

---

[27]Note connections between 1 Pet 4:12 and previous material: the fiery ordeal echoes the refining fire of 1 Pet 1:7; rejoicing amid trials in 1 Pet 4:13 is anticipated in 1 Pet 1:6-7; the presence of the Spirit with suffering believers in 1 Pet 4:14 fills in the sanctifying work of the Spirit in 1 Pet 1:2; and finally, the idea of appointed times in 1 Pet 4:17 (and 1 Pet 5:6) echoes wording in 1 Pet 1:5, 11.

First Peter 4:17-19 offer further explanation of the time of suffering experienced by the Christian community. Echoing "the end is near" in 1 Peter 4:7, here Peter argues that the trials his audience are suffering stand as an indication that the "time [*kairos*] has come for judgment to begin" (1 Pet 4:17). As is typical of other New Testament writings, throughout 1 Peter the author expresses a view that the end of the age is imminent and that final judgment has already begun. The promise of judgment beginning with God's house recalls prophecies in Ezekiel, Zechariah, and Malachi, where God pronounces judgment on his people for violating the covenant. Yet, in the context of 1 Peter, the readers are suffering not because they have abandoned God but because they are living for Christ. Though they are experiencing part of God's eschatological judgment, which all humans must face, because of their faith in Christ Peter's readers need not fear this judgment. Jobes understands Peter's point as "eschatological judgment, understood as the sorting out of humanity, begins with God's house,"[28] and the people of God are to take courage that God sees and hears their cries (Ps 34) and that they can entrust themselves into the hands of God (1 Pet 2:23; 4:19).

After once again citing an Old Testament passage (Prov 11:31) to reinforce the point made in 1 Peter 4:17, Peter draws the section to a conclusion: "So then, let those who suffer . . . entrust themselves to a faithful Creator" (1 Pet 4:19). The encouragement to the persecuted community to endure hardships not only concludes this section but also connects back to the major theme of innocent suffering noted in 1 Peter 3:17 and the example of Christ entrusting himself to the just judgment of God (1 Pet 2:23; notice the parallelism between "just judge" and "faithful Creator").

UNITY IN COMMUNITY: LEADERSHIP IN SERVICE TO THE COMMUNITY (1 PETER 5:1-5A). Peter draws his letter to a close with instructions to the elders (1 Pet 5:1-4) and to "you who are younger" (1 Pet 5:5), and then exhorts the entire community to humble themselves. He cautions his readers once again to think clearly so they may not be caught unawares

---

[28]Jobes, *1 Peter*, 293.

by their adversary, the devil. The presence of "therefore" or "now" (*oun*) joins the argument regarding patience in the face of suffering at the end of 1 Peter 4 to the context of church leadership.

This passage begins with an appeal to the elders "among you" (1 Pet 5:1). Significantly Peter describes himself as a *sympresbyteros* ("fellow elder"), which draws together in solidarity the local church leadership with Peter's leadership from afar. Peter further describes himself as a "witness of the sufferings of Christ." Though Peter himself was an eyewitness to the life and resurrection of Christ, at the same time it is the responsibility of every elder to witness to the sufferings of Christ. It is noteworthy that Peter exhorts the elders to testify to the sufferings of Christ, which, in the context of the letter, implies that the elders themselves must follow in the footsteps of Jesus (1 Pet 2:21) and share in his sufferings (1 Pet 4:13) for the sake of leading the church.

Peter goes on to give specific instruction to the local elders. They are to "shepherd God's flock among you . . . overseeing" (1 Pet 5:2). It is interesting to see the term *presbyteroi* ("elders," 1 Pet 5:1) and *episkopountes* ("overseeing," a term otherwise understood as describing a "bishop," 1 Pet 5:2) communicate the same function within the church (note that *presbyteroi*, "elders," and *episkopoi*, "overseers" or "bishops," are used interchangeably in Acts 20:17, 28). The way in which the elders are to shepherd the flock is outlined by a series of three negative-then-positive phrases. First, an elder is not to shepherd the flock under compulsion, but willingly, according to God's will. Elders in the church should not be coerced into leadership. Second, an elder must not shepherd "out of greed for money," but rather out of eagerness to be of service. Though elders were given financial remuneration in the early church and likely were charged with oversight of money (1 Tim 5:17-18; Mt 10:10; 1 Cor 9:3-14), this should never be the motivation for service. Finally, an elder must not be domineering in his shepherding but rather focus on being a model and example to the flock. The primary way in which elders would serve as an example to the church would be in humility and willingness to be first to suffer like Christ.

Rather than power ("lording it over") or money, the reward for faithful shepherding is the "unfading crown of glory," which is given "when the chief Shepherd appears" (1 Pet 5:4). The image of the crown, usually referring to the eschatological inheritance of believers (see Jas 1:12; Rev 2:10), is connected to the image of Christ, the chief shepherd. This last image suggests that elders, along with the apostles, exercise their responsibility of shepherding the flock as those under the authority of and ultimately answerable to Jesus Christ, the head of the church.

Then, in 1 Peter 5:5, Peter turns to instruct "you who are younger." In this context, *younger* and *elder* refer to individuals who hold the office of elder and those who do not. As in 1 Peter 5:1, the term *elder* marks out one who is responsible for the oversight of the Christian community, while at the same time one who is also senior in terms of age and in faith. The term *younger* most likely refers to the rest of the community, those who are younger in age and faith. With the same verb used in the household code section (1 Pet 2:13–3:12), Peter instructs those who are younger to be subject to the elders. Then Peter concludes with a charge to both groups. As an entire community, they are to clothe themselves "with humility toward one another." Humility is to be expressed in leadership and in the congregation, all of which builds the unity of the church in the face of external pressure. And, once again, the basis of Peter's instruction is the Old Testament. Humility is the proper response toward one another because "He mocks those who mock but gives grace to the humble" (Prov 3:34).

FINAL EXHORTATION: MUTUAL HUMILITY—RESISTING THE DEVIL AND TRUSTING GOD (1 PETER 5:5B-11). Because God gives grace to the humble, Peter instructs his readers to humble themselves "under the mighty hand of God," which is a reference to God's deliverance of Israel from slavery in Egypt (Ex 3:19; 6:1; Jer 21:5; Ezek 20:33-34). This command is then supported by the promise that God exalts the humble "at the proper time." First Peter 5:7 continues the flow of thought by describing how humility is enacted. The phrase "casting all your cares on him" describes how believers are to humble themselves and once again emphasizes entrusting one's care and justice to God.

While looking to God's justice in humility, Peter challenges his audience to "Be sober-minded, be alert," and this because the devil is looking to devour those depending on God. Throughout the letter, Peter has focused on the hostility and slander of their pagan neighbors, but here (as implicitly in 1 Pet 3:18-22) he references the ultimate supernatural power behind such persecution, the devil himself. Peter's audience is to "resist him, firm in faith." Taking a stand against the devil is accomplished by standing firm in the faith despite suffering and persecution.

The main body of the letter ends with an assurance that amid opposition and suffering, God himself will "restore, establish, strengthen, and support you after you have suffered" (1 Pet 5:10). This closing affirmation of God's help recalls the opening assertions of God's action on behalf of Peter's audience: he has given new birth into a living hope, into an inheritance that will not pass away, and they are guarded by God's power until the "last time" (1 Pet 1:3-5). Finally, the encouragement of God's promised victory and care is rounded off with a short doxology.

COMMENTARY | CONCLUSION OF THE LETTER | 1 PETER 5:12-14

The final section marks the formal conclusion of the letter. The phrase "Through Silvanus . . . I have written" may indicate Silas was either the secretary or letter carrier, or perhaps both. At the same time, Peter describes his purpose for writing: "in order to encourage you and to testify that this is the true grace of God." Throughout the letter, Peter urges his readers to endure hardship and opposition with grace and great patience, as people who hope in the gospel of Jesus Christ. This is the truth, Peter argues, and he once again commands them to "Stand firm in it!"

The meaning of "She who is in Babylon . . . sends you greetings" most likely refers to the church in Rome. Finally, Peter ends the letter as he started it, with a blessing of peace: "Peace to all of you who are in Christ" (1 Pet 5:14), which echoes 1 Peter 1:2: "May grace and peace be multiplied to you." In between these two verses the reader has been made aware how this peace has been made possible even amid suffering and the constant challenge of a pagan society. The source of such peace is to be found only in sharing in the sufferings of Christ.

FURTHER READING | 1 PETER COMMENTARIES AND MONOGRAPHS

T: technical; ★: recommended; ★★: highly recommended

T★ Achtemeier, Paul J. *1 Peter: A Commentary on 1 Peter*. Hermeneia. Minneapolis: Fortress, 1996.

Balch, D. L. *Let Wives Be Submissive: The Domestic Code in 1 Peter*. Society of Biblical Literature Monograph Series 26. Atlanta: Scholars Press, 1981.

Best, Ernest. *1 Peter*. NCBC. Grand Rapids, MI: Eerdmans, 1983.

T★★ Elliott, John H. *1 Peter: A New Translation with Introduction and Commentary*. AB. New York: Doubleday, 2000.

———. *A Home for the Homeless: A Sociological Exegesis of 1 Peter, Its Situation and Strategy*. Philadelphia: Fortress, 1981.

★ Green, Joel B. *1 Peter*. THNTC. Grand Rapids, MI: Eerdmans, 2007.

Grudem, Wayne. *The First Epistle of Peter: An Introduction and Commentary*. TNTC. Repr., Grand Rapids, MI: Eerdmans, 2007.

Horrell, David. *The Epistles of Peter and Jude*. Peterborough, UK: Epworth, 1998.

★★ Jobes, Karen H. *1 Peter*. BECNT. Grand Rapids, MI: Baker, 2005.

Kelly, J. N. D. *A Commentary on the Epistles of Peter and Jude*. Grand Rapids, MI: Baker, 1996.

T Michaels, J. Ramsey. *1 Peter*. WBC. Waco, TX: Word Books, 1988.

T Schutter, William L. *Hermeneutic and Composition in 1 Peter*. WUNT. Tübingen: Mohr, 1989.

CHAPTER THREE

The Letter of 2 Peter

FOR SEVERAL REASONS CONSIDERED BELOW, scholars have argued that 1 Peter and 2 Peter are not from the same author and thus are not directly related. Because so much of the material found in Jude 4-18 surfaces in 2 Peter 2:1–3:3, Jude and 2 Peter are treated together (most major commentaries treat Jude and 2 Peter together rather than 1 Peter and 2 Peter). Thus, most current scholarship treats 2 Peter as if it were 2 Jude, emphasizing the literary-historical connection between Jude and 2 Peter over the canonical connection between 1 and 2 Peter.

There is reason, however, to note key connections between the two letters, such that the early church read them together as originating from the same author. For example, each letter is addressed from Peter, who is identified as an apostle (1 Pet 1:1-2, 2 Pet 1:1-2). The concern for apostolic authority surfaces again in Peter's discussion of leadership at the end of 1 Peter (1 Pet 5:1-4), and the eyewitness experience of Jesus' transfiguration plays a key role in the first chapter of 2 Peter (2 Pet 1:16). The opening of 1 Peter (1 Pet 1:1-2) names the recipients as elect exiles, yet their elect status is first "according to the foreknowledge of God the Father." In an opening prayer, 2 Peter notes: "May grace and peace be multiplied to you through the knowledge of God and of Jesus our Lord." As 1 Peter stresses God's special (fore)knowledge, 2 Peter stresses the corresponding human knowledge of God, both of which are necessary for saving relationship with God. First Peter identifies his readers as the "elect" (1 Pet 1:1), and 2 Peter likewise instructs his readers to "confirm your call and election" (2 Pet 1:10).

Furthermore, whereas reading the two letters independently leads to a somewhat limited Christology, when reading them together as a coherent narrative, readers come to appreciate a distinctive Petrine Christology that emphasizes the revelation of Jesus' eschatological glory at the transfiguration and his second coming (2 Peter) alongside the atoning nature of Christ's suffering, death, and resurrection (1 Peter). Even though there are questions regarding the authorship of 2 Peter, on the surface of the text 2 Peter refers to 1 Peter such that readers are encouraged to consider 1–2 Peter together as a twofold witness to Peter's teaching. The author of 2 Peter indicates not only that the teaching contained in 1–2 Peter is similar but also that it was not new to his readers.

OCCASION AND SETTING

The letter portrays a time of writing at the very end of Peter's life—either just before or after his death (2 Pet 1:14). As will be considered below, many have doubted both this setting and the attribution of Petrine authorship, not least because of the stylistic differences with 1 Peter. There has been much scholarly discussion over whether 2 Peter was composed during the apostolic period (the time in which the letter purports to have been written) or a later, postapostolic period. Some of these issues will be addressed below.

Author. The letter names the author as "Simeon Peter, a servant and apostle of Jesus Christ" (2 Pet 1:1) and refers to the author's presence at the transfiguration of Jesus Christ (2 Pet 1:18). This can be none other than Simon Peter, one of Jesus' earliest followers and a member of the Twelve. There is some question regarding the actual wording of the Greek text of 2 Peter 1:1. A few but important manuscripts replace "Simeon Peter" (*Symeōn Petros*) with "Simon Peter" (*Simōn Petros*). The reading of "Simeon Peter" is well attested in the manuscripts, and the change to

"Simon" can be explained by the fact that it is the more common spelling of the name, and thus a scribe could have "corrected" Simeon to Simon. If "Simeon" is the original wording, this could indicate a Palestinian setting for the letter (James calls Peter "Simeon" in another Palestinian setting, Acts 15:14) and thus may support the authenticity of Petrine authorship.

A majority of contemporary scholars argue that the letter was written by someone else in Peter's name. Church historian Eusebius classified 2 Peter as one of the *antilegomena* (a "disputed" book) and personally questioned its canonicity: "Of the disputed books which are nevertheless known to most are the letter called James, that of Jude, the second letter of Peter, and the so-called second and third letters of John" (*Hist. eccl.* 3.25.3). Earlier in the same chapter, Eusebius notes: "But the so-called second letter [of Peter] we have not received as canonical, but nevertheless it has appeared useful to many, and has been studied with other scriptures" (*Hist. eccl.* 3.3.1; see also 3.3.4.). The doubts regarding 2 Peter's canonical status were due to the fact that the letter was not quoted by the "ancient elders," unlike 1 Peter. Furthermore, Origen (as quoted by Eusebius, *Hist. eccl.* 6.25.8) registered doubt over Petrine authorship of 2 Peter: "And Peter, on whom the church of Christ is built, against which the gates of Hades shall not prevail, has left one acknowledged epistle, and, it may be, a second also, for it is doubted." In the early church discussion of 2 Peter, both the letter's authorship and authenticity were questioned. At the risk of oversimplification of the quite complex evidence, however, eventually these questions were overcome, and the epistle was accepted into the New Testament canon alongside 1 Peter.

Along with the concerns of the early church, there has been much modern skepticism over 2 Peter's authenticity as well. Sharp differences between the style and vocabulary of 1 Peter and 2 Peter have been noted by both ancient and modern interpreters. For many, the two letters contain such discrepancies in vocabulary and style that they cannot share the same author. For example, with respect to vocabulary, 2 Peter contains fifty-seven *hapax legomena* (words occurring only once in the New Testament), the largest percentage of any writing in the New Testament.

Only twenty-five of these occur in the Greek translation of the Old Testament, which indicates 2 Peter uses many words (thirty-two) that do not appear in any other biblical text. Because 1 Peter does not have near the number of nonbiblical terms, many have drawn the conclusion that this is evidence that 2 Peter could not have been written by the same author as 1 Peter. The two letters are also different with respect to style. Unlike 1 Peter, the Greek of 2 Peter is more complicated, repetitive, and somewhat grandiose. Interpreters as early as Jerome noted the stylistic differences: "He [Peter] wrote two epistles, which are called Catholic, the second of which, on account of its difference from the first in style, is considered by many not to be by him" (*Lives of Illustrious Men*).[1] Finally, beyond vocabulary and style, perhaps more significantly, the two letters differ in their use of the Old Testament. First Peter is heavily dependent on the Old Testament, either citing or alluding to the Old Testament some forty-six times. Second Peter, on the other hand, seems to hardly use the Old Testament at all, perhaps containing as few as five references.[2] This difference might be more significant than style or vocabulary because it could indicate different conclusions regarding the authority and theological place of the Old Testament. However, it is possible that scholars have overemphasized 2 Peter's lack of references to the Old Testament on account of how they track such references.

A traditional argument accounting for many of these differences, which finds its roots in the early church, is Jerome's argument that the one author (Peter) used two different secretaries. Yet, in order to account for the differences between the letters, one would have to assume that rather than merely taking down dictation, the secretary would be given a degree of freedom to compose all or part of the letter. In other words, one, or both, of the letters could have been composed by a secretary, with Peter approving the end product at some point in the process (see Cicero, *Letter to Atticus* 11.5, for

---

[1] *NPNF*[2] 3:3361.

[2] Many argue that 2 Peter alludes to the Old Testament only five times: Is 52:5 in 2 Pet 2:2; Prov 26:11 in 2 Pet 2:22; Ps 90:4 in 2 Pet 3:8; Is 34:4 in 2 Pet 3:12; and Is 65:17 in 2 Pet 3:13. See Richard J. Bauckham, *Jude, 2 Peter*, WBC (Nashville: Thomas Nelson, 2003), 138. However, references to the Old Testament might not be as sparse as some note.

an ancient example). A significant argument that considers how 2 Peter may both be written by someone other than Peter, while at the same time not intentionally deceiving readers, has been put forward by Richard Bauckham (see "Going Deeper: 2 Peter as Testamentary Literature" following).

Audience. The letter is addressed to all Christians in all places: "To those who have received a faith equal to ours through the righteousness of our God and Savior Jesus Christ" (2 Pet 1:1). This letter opening stresses the apostolic faith shared between the author and the audience. That such faith is apostolic, as opposed to the heretical "faith" of the letter's opponents, will be stressed throughout the letter. The author refers to the first letter (2 Pet 3:1), which most likely is a reference to 1 Peter; therefore, the letter associates its audience with that of 1 Peter. Those who reject authorship by Peter also call this reference to 1 Peter in 2 Peter 3:1 into question. Regardless of where the readers of 2 Peter live, 2 Peter 1:16 might imply that Peter knew his readers personally: "when we made known to you the power and coming of our Lord Jesus Christ." However, the pronoun *we* could refer to the apostles in general, and thus the author could be referring generally to the teachers or evangelists who instructed the readers. Furthermore, that the author mentions "our dear brother Paul has written to you" (2 Pet 3:15) suggests that the audience was somehow within the orbit of the Pauline mission—surely, they at least knew of or perhaps had a collection of Paul's letters.

Genre. Second Peter opens with the typical elements of a letter: a named author and audience, followed by a standard Christian greeting, "May grace and peace be multiplied to you" (2 Pet 1:2). Though the opening contains the letter form, both the main body and conclusion depart from this. The letter is silent regarding any personal greetings or references to a secretary or letter carrier at the end of the text; rather, 2 Peter ends with a final doxology (2 Pet 3:18). Much of 2 Peter's structure is crafted along the lines of a homily or speech. Duane Watson argues for the influence of classic Greco-Roman rhetoric, Doug Moo for the letter genre proper, and Bauckham for the particular genre of testamentary literature (see "Going Deeper: 2 Peter as Testamentary Literature").[3] Whether classified as a letter, speech, or testament (or some combination of these), the letter was composed to dissuade the audience of the opponents' dangerous teaching. This much is clear from the letter itself.

GOING DEEPER: 2 PETER AS TESTAMENTARY LITERATURE

Doubt regarding the authorship of 2 Peter has been problematic, especially in the Christian church. Stated succinctly, the question is: How can a particular text be viewed as inspired by God and, therefore truthful, if the attribution of authorship is deceitful? Richard Bauckham has made the argument that 2 Peter belongs to the particular genre of testamentary literature, a kind of writing where a text is written in the name of a famous person in order to pass that person's teaching on to the next generation. Bauckham argues that readers familiar with the genre would have understood that the claim of authorship by Peter was a thinly veiled fictional and therefore would not have been deceptive on the author's part.

In the intertestamental period, testamentary literature was popular and consisted of the parting words of Old Testament patriarchs. These were a kind of farewell speech. Examples of such testamentary literature survive as independent books (for example, Testament of Moses, Testaments of the Twelve Patriarchs, Testament of Job, 1 Enoch 91–104) or as part of a historical narrative (Tobit 14:3-11; 4 Ezra 14.28-36). Ethical instruction and future revelations are characteristic of testamentary literature. Key characteristics of testamentary literature include, first, the portrayal of a patriarch or Old Testament hero as giving ethical instruction to his children or intimate friends as a definitive summary of his teaching; and, second, the patriarch communicating this instruction so that his sons or followers can conduct themselves properly in future

---

[3]Duane Watson, *Invention, Arrangement, and Style: Rhetorical Criticism of Jude and 2 Peter*, Society of Biblical Literature Dissertation Series 104 (Atlanta: Scholars Press, 1988), 81-189; Douglas Moo, *2 Peter and Jude*, NIVAC (Grand Rapids, MI: Zondervan, 1996), 26.

circumstances. In fact, the communication conveys specific revelations of future events.

Bauckham argues that 2 Peter contains these key elements of testamentary literature: an ethical admonition in the form of a short summary of Peter's teaching (2 Pet 1:3-11); Peter's farewell speech, given with full knowledge of his impending death (2 Pet 1:12-15); and Peter's predictions of the rise of false teachers (2 Pet 2:1-3) and scoffers (2 Pet 3:1-4) following his death. Bauckham believes the entire letter is structured around these key passages, and as such the letter was composed in order to defend Peter's teaching in the face of the opposition of a future time (in which the readers now live).

This line of reasoning allows Bauckham to argue that 2 Peter is pseudonymous (not written by Peter), yet not deceitful and, therefore, canonical. If the letter's first readers correctly identified the genre of testamentary literature, his argument goes, then they would have understood that the letter was not actually written by Peter, even though the text claims Petrine authorship. In the end, Bauckham's argument offers an elegant way to understand how the pseudepigraphical letter is in no way fraudulent or deceptive.

STRUCTURE

After the letter opening (2 Pet 1:1-2), the body of the letter contains a sustained argument against the false teaching of the opponents (2 Pet 1:3–3:16). After an initial description of the theme and occasion of the letter (2 Pet 1:3-15) there are a series of responses to the false teachers' objections.

OUTLINE

    I. Letter greeting (2 Pet 1:1-2)

    II. Main body of the letter (2 Pet 1:3–3:16)

        A. Theme and occasion of the letter (2 Pet 1:3-15)

            1. Summary of Peter's teaching (ethical admonition; 2 Pet 1:3-11)

            2. Peter's "testament" (2 Pet 1:12-15)

    B. Responses to the "false teachers" (2 Pet 1:16–3:10)

        1. Reply to objection one (2 Pet 1:16-19)

        2. Reply to objection two (2 Pet 1:20-21)

        3. Peter's prediction of false teachers (2 Pet 2:1-3a)

        4. Reply to objection three (2 Pet 2:3b-10a)

        5. Denunciation of false teachers (2 Pet 2:10b-22)

        6. Peter's prediction of scoffers (objection four articulated)
           (2 Pet 3:1-4)

        7. Reply to objection four (2 Pet 3:5-10)

    C. Final exhortations (2 Pet 3:11-16)

  III. Conclusion and benediction (2 Pet 3:17-18)[4]

COMMENTARY | LETTER GREETING | 2 PETER 1:1-2

Second Peter begins with the necessary elements to make the text a letter: named sender, audience, and greeting. In general, the named author, "Simeon Peter," and audience are discussed above. A further characteristic of the author to note here is that he calls himself a "servant [*doulos*] and an apostle of Jesus Christ." The combination of both terms is natural enough, as the author notes his ministry role, an apostle in the church, as well as the supporting grounds for such a role, that he is first a servant of Christ. It is interesting that whereas James and Jude call themselves servants of Jesus Christ, and 1 Peter explicitly (and 1 John implicitly) claims to be an apostle, only the author of 2 Peter claims both titles.

The audience possesses the same precious faith as the apostolic author and shares in such faith "through the righteousness of our God and Savior Jesus Christ" (2 Pet 1:1). Though the phrase could be understood as referring separately to "our God" and "[our] Savior Jesus Christ," it is more likely that both phrases, "our God and Savior," refer to Jesus Christ (note the similar structure used by the author in 2 Pet 1:11, "our Lord and Savior Jesus Christ"). This is one of the few passages in the New Testament where Jesus is so directly called God. It certainly reflects the

---

[4]See Bauckham, *Jude, 2 Peter*, 135, for this outline.

closing doxology, where glory is given to Jesus because of his divine grace (2 Pet 3:18). This, indeed, is a very high Christology.

Finally, in what is a standard Christian greeting, "grace and peace be multiplied to you," the author includes a phrase important for the rest of the letter: "through the knowledge [*epignōsei*] of God and of Jesus our Lord." Knowledge, for the author, is an important way to describe coming to know God specifically through Jesus Christ; this is a conversion knowledge, not merely the knowing of facts.

Theme and occasion of the letter (2 Peter 1:3-15).

Summary of Peter's teaching (2 Peter 1:3-11). The opening section of the letter gives a summary of Peter's teaching, where he reminds his readers of God's saving acts (2 Pet 1:3-4), which establishes the basis for Christian living (2 Pet 1:5-10) that has final salvation in view (2 Pet 1:11).

In 2 Peter 1:3, the origin of "divine power" could be Jesus or God—"his" could refer back to either. Though a final distinction is difficult, the entire passage has a christological focus and likely refers back to Christ. The phrase "his divine power" (*theias dynameōs*) is standard in Greek literature and is an example of 2 Peter's use of Hellenistic religious vocabulary. The point of the phrase is that God's divine power gives everything necessary for life and godliness (or perhaps a "godly life"; see NIV). Everything a believer needs to live a pleasing life is already given by God, and these things are given "through the knowledge [*epignōseōs*] of him who called us by his own glory and goodness."

In 2 Peter 1:4, it is by these, that is, by Christ's glory and goodness (or "virtue," *aretē*), that believers have been given "great and precious promises." These promises most likely refer back to all that is given for life and godliness in 2 Peter 1:3. Second Peter 1:4 goes on to give the purpose of being given such gifts: "so that through them you may share in the divine nature, escaping the corruption that is in the world" (2 Pet 1:4).

The phrase "share" or "participate in the divine nature" has occupied much of the discussion regarding this passage. Many scholars have noted that this language was quite common in a Greek religious and philosophical context, and thus the language in 2 Peter 1:4 is a good example of the author's Hellenistic influence. The idea of corruption could mean either moral or physical corruption. Bauckham is likely correct in arguing that "the context demands the idea of physical corruption: decay, transitoriness, mortality."[5] The contrast between the "incorruptibility" (*aphtharsia*) of divine nature and the "corruptibility" (*phthora*) of the human body was a common theme in Hellenistic literature. The contrast between incorruptible and corruptible is found in Paul (1 Cor 9:25), who understands that the world is in bondage to "corruption" (*phthora*; see also Rom 8:21) and that Christians are awaiting the eschatological gift of "incorruptibility" (*aphtharsia*; see 1 Cor 15:42, 52-54; Gal 6:8). If this is correct, then the corruption from which believers escape is that of physical decay and mortality. This is the end-time, Christian hope of future resurrection from the ultimate physical decay experienced due to the fall. The resurrection is, of course, not a present experience, because in this life the Christian still experiences decay and mortality. In contrast to the Greek religious thought of the day, however, Peter argues that such decay is not because the world is material (the notion that the material world is inherently evil) but because of sin (or "evil desire"). Implicitly Peter is challenging a Greco-Roman worldview; corruption is due to sin, not because material existence is necessarily bad or evil.

The sharing in the divine nature, then, is not merely becoming moral or growing in godly character, nor can this mean that Christians participate in God's own essence. Rather, it refers to the immortal life followers of Christ will experience at the resurrection. By Christ's saving activity, he not only has given what is required for a godly life in the present but also promises resurrection life in the future. David Horrell sums up succinctly: "Here the author seems to be expressing the belief that after death (or the return of Christ), Christians will share the immortality and incorruptibility of God's nature."[6]

Because everything pertaining to life and godliness is freely given in Christ, Peter exhorts his readers to a new life of moral progress in 2 Peter 1:5-10. The phrase "For this very reason" at the beginning of 2 Peter 1:5

---

[5]Bauckham, *Jude, 2 Peter*, 182.
[6]David Horrell, *The Epistles of Peter and Jude* (Peterborough, UK: Epworth, 1998), 150.

marks the flow of thought from the knowledge and promises given in 2 Peter 1:3-4 to the ethical characteristics outlined in the next phrase.

The list of virtues in 2 Peter 1:5-7 contains terms drawn from Greek moral philosophy (specifically, "virtue," *aretē*; "self-control," *enkrateia*; "godliness," *eusebeia*). Though each element of the list comes from within the Hellenistic worldview, its framework is marked as particularly Christian by the first and last items—the only terms whose position in the list is significant. The first virtue in the list is "faith" (*pistis*, 2 Pet 1:5), and the final virtue in the list is "love" (*agapē*, 2 Pet 1:7). These two virtues bookend the others and effectively make this a Christian virtue list. It is noteworthy that the structure of the list emphasizes that each virtue is the basis for producing the next ("make every effort to supplement your faith with") until the list comes to a climax in love. Love is the climatic or the crowning virtue that encompasses all the previous virtues.

> **Enduring Trial**
>
> The concern for enduring trial as part of the Christian life appears in James 1:2-4 and in 1 Peter 1:6-9. Endurance is implicit in 2 Peter, 1 John, and Jude, which all were written to contexts where false teaching was a threat to the health of the church. Here Peter lists endurance as one of the virtues needed to live a godly life.

The result of the virtues listed in 2 Peter 1:5-7 is outlined in 2 Peter 1:8-10. The author argues that "if you possess these qualities" (2 Pet 1:8) and "if you do these things" (2 Pet 1:10), where both "these qualities" and "these things" refer back to the virtues in 2 Peter 1:5-7, then they will keep you "from being useless or unfruitful in the knowledge of our Lord Jesus Christ." The idea of knowledge in 2 Peter is a knowledge of Jesus gained at conversion. Therefore, 2 Peter 1:8-9 is connecting the new life of virtue, supplied by the great and precious promises of God, to the salvation of the readers. Because of this connection between conversion and moral transformation, the author urges his readers to "make every effort to confirm your calling and election" in 2 Peter 1:10. Horrell writes, "Living the right way (vv. 5-8), in the gracious provision which God has made (vv. 3-4), will ensure that *you never stumble*."[7]

---

[7]Horrell, *Epistles of Peter and Jude*, 152.

Finally, 2 Peter 1:11 describes one's entry into Christ's kingdom. Bauckham notes, "Despite the emphasis on moral effort in the second section (5-7), this concluding statement makes it clear that final salvation is not man's achievement but the gift of God's lavish generosity."[8] Thus, the author comes full circle again describing God's great and precious promises.

Peter's "testament" (2 Peter 1:12-15). The author communicates the reason for writing the letter: it is a reminder of "these things," which refers to the "great and precious promises" outlined in 2 Peter 1:3-11. Throughout the letter, Peter generally reminds his readers of the correct understanding of Christ's return. Beginning in 2 Peter 1:16, he begins an apologetic dialogue responding to the objections of the false teachers. In many ways, 2 Peter 1:12-15 is a transition section turning from a summary of Peter's teaching (2 Pet 1:3-11) to a defense of orthodox teaching, refuting a list of objections in the rest of the letter (2 Pet 1:12–3:10).

Some have argued that this section is Peter's "testament," one of the key features of the testamentary genre (see "Going Deeper" above). The author knows that his earthly life is almost over because "Jesus Christ had . . . made clear to me" (2 Pet 1:14). Reference to laying "aside my tent" is an indication that Peter knows his physical life is coming to an end. Knowing of his impending death, Peter makes every effort that his readers remember his teaching after his departure (*exodos*, 2 Pet 1:15). The letter itself is the means by which he reminds them of his teaching, and when the letter is read in the future, it will continue to be a reminder long after this death.

Peter's responses to the teaching of the "false teachers" (2 Peter 1:16–3:10). This major section running through the body of the letter is best outlined as a series of responses to the deceitful claims of the false teachers. Something that complicates tracing the flow of thought in this section is that direct statements from the false teachers are not recorded in the text. Rather, one must reconstruct their claims by paying attention to clues in the author's response to them. This is something like hearing

---

[8] Bauckham, *Jude, 2 Peter*, 193.

only one side of a phone conversation; though there are clues, they come from only one perspective.

Reply to objection one (2 Peter 1:16-19). In this passage the author defends apostolic teaching by replying to the first of several objections. Many of these objections are marked out in the text by a formal structure. The construction "not . . . but" (*ou . . . alla*, 2 Pet 1:16) contrasts the objection of the false teachers with the apostolic correction. The first objection directly challenges apostolic teaching about Jesus Christ, claiming that it consists of "cleverly contrived myths." Peter's apostolic reply (marked by "but") is that rather than clever myths, the apostles are in fact "eyewitnesses of his majesty [*megaleiotētos*]." The objection is that the apostles fabricated their teaching about Jesus' "power and coming," which was a specific claim regarding Jesus' second coming (*parousia*, a technical term in the New Testament for Jesus' second coming).

Peter's apostolic reply is that the apostles were in fact eyewitnesses of Jesus' power and coming. Rather than actually witnessing Jesus' second coming, the apostles witnessed Jesus' transfiguration, a moment where "he received honor and glory from God" (2 Pet 1:17). This is a reference to an episode in the Synoptic Gospels where Jesus goes up to a mountain to pray with Peter, James, and John, and on top of the mountain Jesus' appearance is visibly transformed, and the disciples hear the voice of God the Father expressing his approval of the Son: "This is my beloved Son, with whom I am well-pleased" (2 Pet 1:17, see Mt 17:1-8; Mk 9:2-8; Lk 9:28-36). The transfiguration is likely to be understood apocalyptically in the sense that Jesus revealed a glimpse of his power and glory, which anticipates the vision everyone will see at his second coming. That is, Jesus revealed for just a moment during his earthly ministry his true divine power, which will be revealed at his second coming. For Peter, this event, more than any other, serves as proof that Jesus is powerful and, therefore, that he is coming again. The experience of the transfiguration is the apostolic eyewitness proof of Jesus' future coming (*parousia*)— proof that the false teachers could not refute.

In 2 Peter 1:19, Peter continues to counter the objection that the apostles fabricated such a teaching. The verse opens with "So" (NRSV) or "We also" (CSB), which indicates further evidence offered against the false teacher's objection. In addition to the apostles' eyewitness testimony, "the prophetic word" corroborates the "power and coming" of Jesus. It is likely that when Peter refers to the prophetic word he is thinking not just of individual prophecies, or only the prophetic books, but rather the entire Old Testament, which witnesses alongside the transfiguration to the power and coming of Christ (see 1 Pet 1:10-12). The "prophetic word" is modified by an adjective phrase that could be translated "more sure" (or "more fully confirmed," as in ESV, NRSV). If the phrase has a comparative sense, the logic would be that the prophetic word is more sure than the transfiguration. Peter has just stressed, however, the importance of the transfiguration as apostolic proof of Jesus' coming. Rather, it seems that Peter is insisting that alongside apostolic eyewitness testimony, the prophetic message in the Old Testament is likewise "strongly confirmed" (CSB) or "altogether reliable" (NET). Thus, the events of the transfiguration, witnessed by the apostles, and the prophetic word stand side by side, both confirming that Jesus Christ will come again in power. To reiterate, there is no comparison between the relative strengths or merits of the apostolic witness (and by extension, the New Testament) over against the prophetic witness (the Old Testament); instead, both apostles and prophets serve together as a confirmation of Jesus' coming.

Protecting the Church from False Teaching

Second Peter, 1 John, and Jude were written in contexts where the church was threatened by false teaching. These letters become a key resource as the church confronts teaching and living that do not align with the gospel in any age.

Thus, Peter's response to the first objection contains two parts: first, as an apostle Peter himself was an eyewitness to the transfiguration, which anticipated Jesus' *parousia*; and second, the prophetic word of the Old Testament also stands as an altogether reliable confirmation regarding the power and coming of Christ. Peter concludes that "you will do well to pay attention to" these things because they (especially the prophetic word) are like a "lamp shining in a dark place."

Reply to objection two (2 Peter 1:20-21). The challenge to pay attention to the prophetic message of the Old Testament leads to a second objection. Again, the construction "not . . . but" (*ou . . . alla*, 1:21, where *ou* is translated as "no") marks the objection and the apostolic reply. The skeptic argues that the prophetic word is merely the "prophet's own interpretation" (2 Pet 1:20) and, therefore, is produced "by the will of man" (2 Pet 1:21). If the prophetic word originates from the human prophet's own subjective interpretation, then there is no divine warrant standing behind such prophecy—the entire Old Testament is founded on human impulse and not the power of God.

The apostolic response to this objection is that the prophets "spoke from God" because they were "carried along by the Holy Spirit" (2 Pet 1:21). In 2 Peter 1:20 Peter argues that no "prophecy of Scripture comes from the prophet's own interpretation." The Christian Standard Bible has made clear that the adjective "one's own" (*idias*) in 2 Peter 1:20 refers to "the prophet's own interpretation" rather than the readers' own or the prophecy's own interpretation. In other words, Peter is countering the argument that the prophets in the Old Testament gave their own interpretation to the visions and messages they were given by God and thus can be disregarded as mere human opinion. In contrast, the author argues that Old Testament prophecy was not initiated by human will but by God's will and initiative. Those human prophets "were carried along [*pheromenoi*] by the Holy Spirit" (2 Pet 1:21) and therefore spoke from God.

These first two objections and their corresponding replies go together. Faith and hope in the powerful coming of Jesus Christ do not arise from cleverly concocted myths but are based on the sure Word of God—the word announced by apostle and prophet, the one, sure Word of God. Later in the letter, Peter once again expresses confidence in this dual witness—apostolic and prophetic—encouraging his readers to remember these messages (2 Pet 3:2).

Peter's prediction of false teachers (2 Peter 2:1-3a). The first few phrases of 2 Peter 2 mark a transition from defense to attack. After predicting the rise of the false teachers (2 Pet 2:1-3a), the rest of the chapter offers a response to the third objection (2 Pet 2:3b-10a) and then mounts a strong attack against and condemnation of the false teachers (2 Pet 2:10b-22). The author skillfully transitions from the discussion of Old Testament prophets in 2 Peter 1:19-21 to the presence of false prophets in the Old Testament in 2 Peter 2:1. This transition effectively contrasts the apostolic testimony (2 Pet 1:16-18) with the rise of the false teachers in 2 Peter 2:1-3. The chiastic structure helps highlight this contrast and progression of thought:

> *apostles* (2 Pet 1:16-18)
>   Old Testament prophets (2 Pet 1:19-21)
>   Old Testament false prophets (2 Pet 2:1a)
> *false teachers* (2 Pet 2:1b-3a)[9]

Identifying this chiastic structure helps to see the contrast between Old Testament prophets and Old Testament false prophets, and ultimately the sharp contrast between the apostles and the false teachers. Just as the Old Testament prophets had to contend against Israel's false prophets, so too the apostles must stand against the false teachers—both false prophets and false teachers are responsible for leading God's people astray. Peter warns that the false teachers will "bring in destructive heresies" specifically: first, they deny Jesus and his redemptive work (denying the "Master who bought them"), and second, they teach that in Christ they are free to act on their desires any way they wish ("many will follow their sensuality [ESV] or "depraved ways" [CSB]). In this summary and transition, Peter argues that, just like false prophets arose in Israel, so also false teachers now are appearing in the last days, leading people astray through their abhorrent teaching and sensual conduct.

Reply to objection three (2 Peter 2:3b-10a). After predicting the rise of the false teachers and identifying two "destructive heresies" they bring with them, Peter replies to a third objection. Though the form observed

---

[9]Bauckham, *Jude, 2 Peter*, 236.

previously ("not . . . but," *ou . . . alla*) is missing here, the objection of the false teachers is marked by the second sentence in 2 Peter 2:3: "Their condemnation, pronounced long ago, is not idle." All we have in the text is Peter's reply, and therefore we must reconstruct the exact objection in 2 Peter 2:3. The false teachers must have argued that condemnation against the wicked is idle. In other words, because the teaching of Jesus' second coming is a myth and the prophetic word is subjective, then there is no future divine judgment. This highlights how the first three objections are interrelated.

The apostolic reply to this objection can be seen in 2 Peter 2:4-10 through a series of "if" statements (notice the "if . . . if . . . if . . . then" structure). Peter addresses the rejection of God's judgment but does not tackle the problem head-on, nor does he attempt to address the problem of the alleged delay of future judgment. Rather, on the basis of past events, Peter argues for the certainty of God's coming judgment. The past events are from Israel's history, and it is clear, by the examples he chooses, that the author of 2 Peter has used material from Jude 6-8 to construct his argument. He cites three of the best-known examples of divine judgment from the Old Testament: the judgment of the disobedient angels in 2 Peter 2:4 (Gen 6:1-4), the judgment of the flood in 2 Peter 2:5 (Gen 6–8), and the destruction of Sodom and Gomorrah by fire in 2 Peter 2:6-8 (Gen 19). In addition to these references to judgment, he also mentions the righteous, who are rescued by God. Amid God's judgment during the flood, "Noah . . . and seven others" were protected by God, and, in the midst of reducing Sodom and Gomorrah to ashes, God "rescued righteous Lot." Though 2 Peter and Jude share references to the disobedient angels (Jude 6) and Sodom and Gomorrah (Jude 7), 2 Peter, unlike Jude, adds positive examples of the righteous being delivered (Noah and Lot).

Peter concludes his reply by saying, "then the Lord knows how to rescue the godly from trials and to keep the unrighteous under punishment for the day of judgment" (2 Pet 2:9). So, Peter replies to the objection against the certainty of future judgment by pointing to past events of judgment and rescue. The Lord is able to rescue and to punish. Furthermore, there is a hint that as the angels who sinned are kept for future judgment, so too are the false teachers (we will see this notion reinforced later in the chapter).

Denunciation of the false teachers (2 Peter 2:10b-22). In the previous section Peter responded to the false teachers' denial of future judgment by appealing to past events of the Lord's judgment and rescue. In this section, the author gives a loosely constructed list of denunciations against the false teachers. Second Peter 2:10b-18 is based in part on Jude 8-16, whereas 2 Pet 2:19-22 relies on a series of proverbs to round out the section.

There is a clear break in the flow of thought halfway through 2 Peter 2:10, where the second part of the verse argues that the false teachers reject the cosmic order designed by God. The false teachers are arrogant, "not afraid to slander the glorious ones," but, in contrast to their presumptuous boldness, even angels "who are greater in might and power, do not bring a slanderous charge against them." The glorious ones, as 2 Peter 2:11 clarifies, are angelic beings (whether good or bad is unclear, though likely referring to fallen angels), over whom the false teachers inappropriately claim power and authority. They show their disregard for God's order by speaking contemptuously about these spiritual powers and thus fail to register the proper understanding of their power and influence.

In view of their presumptuous disregard of such spiritual powers, Peter compares the false teachers to "irrational animals" who "slander what they do not understand," which results in their own destruction. The slander here is likely referring back to 2 Peter 2:10 (slander against angels) and, in an ironic twist, the false teachers will share in the judgment of the very fallen angels they now slander. The destruction here refers not to the fate of the animals, born to be destroyed, but to the future destruction of the fallen angels.

The next verse announces that they "will be paid back" (2 Pet 2:13), which further indicates the false teachers will experience future judgment "for the harm they have done." The next two phrases mark out the brazen immorality (they "carouse in broad daylight") and shameless polluting of public worship (they "are spots and blemishes . . . while they feast with you"). Feasting is likely a reference to the community meal shared during Christian worship (a love feast; see Jude 12), which indicates the false teachers have metastasized to the central organ of the church, the communion meal. It is here that they delight "in their deceptions." The relentless denunciation of the false teachers continues in 2 Peter 2:14 with the vivid expression, "They have eyes full of adultery" (or perhaps more woodenly, "They have eyes full of an adulteress"), which suggests their eyes are always on the lookout for a woman with whom to commit adultery.[10]

Showing dependence on Jude 11, Peter describes the false teachers "abandoning the straight path" and following the way of Balaam (though Jude also refers to Cain and Korah in addition to Balaam; see Judg 11). Balaam is a fitting example because he was a false prophet who offered his services at a price because he was greedy for gain. Balaam specifically expected to receive money from Balak for cursing Israel (Num 22). Later in the story, Balaam's journey is interrupted by his reluctant donkey not wanting to proceed because the donkey can see the angel of the Lord (unseen by Balaam). Balaam beats his donkey for refusing to continue, only to have the Lord open the donkey's mouth to speak ("a speechless donkey spoke," 2 Pet 2:16). The Old Testament story, as understood in 2 Peter, is that the donkey rebukes Balaam for his disobedience in selling his prophetic ability for financial gain. This interpretation of Balaam's story is very much in keeping with Jewish tradition after the closing of the Old Testament canon. So, for Peter, Balaam represents the arrogance of one who thought he could succeed in opposing God's will. Through the allusion to Numbers, Peter identifies this as the attitude of the false teachers as well.

Though there is a paragraph break between 2 Peter 2:16 and 2 Peter 2:17, this only indicates a slight pause in the continued denunciation of the false teachers. They are "springs without water" (2 Pet 2:17), having the appearance of a productive resource, only to be found empty and

---

[10]See Bauckham, *Jude, 2 Peter*, 266, for this translation.

worthless. Once again referring to the future judgment reserved especially for the fallen angels (2 Pet 2:4, 12), Peter notes that the "gloom of
darkness has been reserved for them" (2 Pet 2:17). Like empty springs,
the false teachers utter "empty words," and with these words they attempt
to seduce others who are especially vulnerable to such errors (namely,
"people who have barely escaped"). The final phrase, "escaped from those
who live in error," was a typical way of referring to the pagan neighbors
by whom the readers were surrounded (see 1 Pet 1:14).

Up to this point Peter shows his dependence on both the images and
ordering of Jude 8-16, yet in 2 Peter 2:19-22, the author diverges from
Jude and sums up the denunciation of the false teachers with a series
of proverbs.

First, the false teachers promise freedom, likely freedom from future
judgment. Such a notion of freedom was directly connected to a life free
from any moral restraint. Though this seemed like freedom, the one
boasting of liberation from cultural mores in the end becomes enslaved
to desire, trading one master (morality) for another (desire). Thus, the
freedom peddled by the false teachers is no freedom at all but rather
slavery to human desire. Peter illustrates this truth by providing a proverbial summary: "For whatever overcomes a person, to that he is enslaved" (2 Pet 2:19 ESV).

Marked by the opening phrase "For if," the flow of thought continues,
moving from the emptiness and self-deception of moral freedom to a
conditional statement. The "if" phrase of the conditional uses 2 Peter's
distinctive vocabulary for conversion, "having escaped the world's impurity" (note the connection to 2 Pet 1:4, escaping corruption), "through
the knowledge of the Lord and Savior Jesus Christ" (knowledge again
suggesting conversion). If they are "again entangled . . . and defeated, the
last state is worse. . . . It would have been better . . . not to have known"
(2 Pet 2:20-21). This phrase is very similar to the words of Jesus in
Matthew 12:45 and Luke 11:26, which highlight the danger of apostasy. It
is not immediately clear whether the "they/them" in this passage refers
only to the false teachers or, more broadly, to the Christian community

who are influenced by them. It is possible that both are intended. It is interesting that they are described as turning "back from the holy command delivered to them." This command could possibly refer to the love command, which, rather than viewed as a single command, stood as the embodiment and central focus of the Jewish law.

The precarious situation of the one turning back from the command of God is then illustrated with two proverbs, one focusing on a dog returning to its vomit

> ## The Love Command
>
> The command to love the neighbor (Lev 19:18) runs through all the Catholic Epistles. James quotes the command (Jas 2:8), and 1 Peter alludes to it (1 Pet 1:22). Second Peter warns those turning back from the "holy command," which is likely the command to love the neighbor, and love for one's believing neighbor is a central theme of 1 John.

(Prov 26:11) and the second on a pig returning to the mire. Both animals, a dog and a pig, presumably after being washed or otherwise being whole (or healthy), return to their sickness and filth. Both memorably illustrate the moral and spiritual danger of turning away from the faith. This is a bleak and sharp denunciation of the false teachers and is designed to communicate that, though they deny the accountability of any future judgment on their present actions and attitudes, such a judgment is certainly waiting for them.

Peter's prediction of the scoffers (2 Peter 3:1-4). This section echoes 2 Peter 2:1-3, where the author predicted the coming of false teachers who will arise within the community. There is a clear parallel in 2 Peter 3:3, where, again shifting from present to future tense (just like in 2 Pet 2:1-3), Peter warns of scoffers coming in the future. Like the false teachers' "depraved ways" (2 Pet 2:2), the scoffers follow "their own evil desires" (2 Pet 3:3). These parallel passages predict the rise of the same group, called either false teachers or scoffers, who, from the perspective of Peter's deathbed (2 Pet 1:12-15), pose a threat to the community in the future. Yet, from the perspective of the audience reading the letter in the present, these false teachers or scoffers are now misleading the community.

Transitioning from the sharp denunciation of the false teachers in the previous passage and back to his defense of apostolic teaching, Peter addresses his audience directly as "dear friends" (2 Pet 3:1). He once again situates himself as an apostle through emphasizing that this is the "second letter" he has written. This is most likely a reference to 1 Peter and therefore a reference to the author's apostleship. With this reference, the author assumes the audience is familiar with the existence if not the content of 1 Peter. It is clear that the author intends a connection between the two letters because the author suggests that the letters function in the same way, namely, as a reminder (note the parallel with 2 Pet 1:12 in stating the purpose of 2 Peter, "I intend always to remind you of these things"). Specifically, Peter wants his readers to "recall the words previously spoken by the holy prophets and the command . . . given through your apostles" (2 Pet 3:2). This echoes Peter's defense of apostolic and prophetic authority, addressed in his first reply to the false teachers (see 2 Pet 1:16-21). Again, prophet and apostle are not pitted against each other but rather together constitute the message the audience is to remember and obey.

Reply to objection four (2 Peter 3:5-10). In 2 Peter 3:4 Peter moves to the false teachers' fourth objection. Unlike the previous objections, this time Peter reports their very words: "Where is his 'coming' that he promised?" (2 Pet 3:4). Here the "scoffers" openly mock the idea of Christ's return, implicitly pointing at the delay of Jesus' second coming as an excuse to doubt. This time Peter also provides the rationale for such skepticism. The false teachers point to the world around them and say, "All things continue as they have been since the beginning of creation" (2 Pet 3:4). The phrase "since our ancestors fell asleep" could refer to the first generation of Christians, who have begun to die without seeing Christ's return, or to the deaths of the Old Testament fathers. If it refers to the death of the first generation of Christians, the objection could reflect a crucial moment at the end of the first century when the Lord had not returned despite the promise of the apostles. This, of course, assumes a later date of composition of 2 Peter. Another view is that "our ancestors" refers to the Old Testament patriarchs, a view that would work well with an early date of composition for 2 Peter. Either way, the false teachers claim that there is no sign that God will intervene in the world because nothing has changed since the beginning of creation.

Like the twofold reply to the first objection (2 Pet 1:16-19), Peter once again offers a two-step response. In 2 Peter 3:5-7 Peter draws attention to the true account of creation in God's Word. Peter addresses the grounds of their objection (in 2 Pet 3:4), and then in 2 Peter 3:8-10 he focuses on the forbearance of God.

As the false teachers appeal to the beginning of creation, so Peter responds with an argument that addresses the facts of creation. The first clause, "they deliberately overlook this" (2 Pet 3:5), can mean either that the false teachers deliberately ignore the facts about creation or that the facts of creation have escaped their notice. The Greek phrase is difficult, but the former is most likely. First, they "forget" ("suppress this fact," NET) that heavens and the earth were formed long ago "by the word of God . . . from water and through water" (2 Pet 3:5). This, of course, is an allusion to the creative activity of God in Genesis 1 where creation is described, in part, as the separation of the earth from the waters above and below. In the ancient world, people thought that the earth and air were surrounded by water. The earth was brought about from water, since it was by separating and gathering water that the land was formed. The point is that creation was a result of God's word, and water was the instrument God used in creation. Thus, the first step in Peter's response is reminding them that all things were made through the word of God and through water.

The second thing that the false teachers deliberately forget is that through the water and the word of God the "world of that time perished when it was flooded" (2 Pet 3:6). The phrase "through these" in 2 Peter 3:6 specifically refers back to both water and the word of God in 2 Peter 3:5. The same cause (the word of God) and instrument (water) of creation (2 Pet 3:5) also brought about the judgment through destruction of that same world, "when it was flooded" (2 Pet 3:6). Peter insists that God's judgment in the flood is proof of his intervention in the world.

Third and finally, the false teachers forget that "By the same word," that is, the same word of God responsible for creation and the flood, "the present heavens and earth" will be judged by fire (2 Pet 3:7). God has executed judgment through his word and by means of water in the past (the flood); therefore, the same holds true for the future, with the only difference being that judgment will be accomplished through fire.

Table 4.1

Creation	Flood	Consummation
word of God creates (Gen 1:1; Ps 33:6)	word of God judges	"same word" stores up
heaven and earth formed out of water (Gen 1:2, 9-10; Ps 33:7)	existing world (kosmos) destroyed by water (Gen 6–9)	heaven and earth destroyed by "fire"

After addressing the second part of the false teachers' objection, Peter now returns to the gist of the fourth objection: "Where is his 'coming' that he promised?" (2 Pet 3:4).

In 2 Peter 3:5 the false teachers deliberately "forget" or "overlook" (*lanthanō*), yet Peter urges his readers not to "forget" or "overlook" (*lanthanō*; 2 Pet 3:8). The audience is encouraged not to forget that "With the Lord one day is like a thousand years, and a thousand years like one day" (2 Pet 3:8), which is an allusion to Psalm 90:4. The point is that God's perspective on time is not limited by a human lifespan. God's perspective is vastly more comprehensive than that of men and women, who, accustomed to short-term expectations, are impatient to see the coming (*parousia*) of Christ in their own lifetime.[11]

From God's perspective, what seems like a long delay is but a short time. Peter argues that the "Lord does not delay his promise" (2 Pet 3:9). Rather than seeing the passage of time as a delay of Christ's coming, or worse, as proof that he will never return, the passage of time puts God's patient forbearance on full display. Forbearance is the quality of God by which "he bears with sinners, holds back his wrath, refrains from intervening in judgment as soon as the sinner's deeds deserve it."[12]

---

[11]This language is from Bauckham, *Jude, 2 Peter*, 321.
[12]Bauckham, *Jude, 2 Peter*, 312.

Rather, he "is patient with you," the Christian readers of the letter, "not wanting any to perish but all to come to repentance" (2 Pet 3:9). The author is likely referring to those of the audience who are tempted by the false teachers to go astray and oppose the faith.

Though God's forbearance is on display in the duration of time passing before Christ's coming, the future judgment will certainly come. God is merciful, "not wanting any to perish," and he is just, "the day of the Lord will come." The day of the Lord refers to the coming day of God's judgment announced long ago in the messages of the prophets (Amos 5:18-20; Joel 1:15; 2:11), which will come at an unexpected time, like a thief in the night. At the judgment, "the heavens will pass away . . . the elements will burn and be dissolved" (2 Pet 3:10). Both of these phrases refer to the fact that the whole of creation, the heavens and the earth (and everything in between), will pass away. However one understands the exact way in which the heavens and earth will pass away, it is certainly related to the coming judgment by fire in 2 Peter 3:7. The final phrase, "and the earth and the works on it will be disclosed," is very difficult because the final verb (*heurethēsetai*) normally means "be found," which does not make sense here. Horrell notes, "Although a somewhat unusual sense for the word, it is best taken as a divine passive, meaning, 'will be discovered by God,' or revealed, uncovered, brought to light. . . . All the deeds and works of human beings will be laid bare before God, and vv. 11-14 focus on the moral implications of the coming day."[13]

Final exhortations (2 Peter 3:11-16). Having replied to all the false teachers' objections, the author now turns to the moral implications of his teaching. Peter returns to some of the key ideas from the opening of the letter in 2 Peter 1:3-11, especially the moral characteristics flowing from God's "great and precious promises."

Because future judgment is coming ("Since all these things are to be dissolved in this way," 2 Pet 3:11) the readers are challenged to live a

---

[13]Horrell, *Epistles of Peter and Jude*, 181.

certain way. In light of the coming judgment, "it is clear what sort of people you should be," and Peter clarifies this by urging his audience to be "in holy conduct and godliness" (note the connection to godliness in 2 Pet 1:7). The spiritual and moral transformation for which the audience is to strive is based both on the coming day of judgment ("as you wait for the day of God") and on the promise of "new heavens and a new earth" (2 Pet 3:13). The idea of waiting or expecting is a reoccurring theme in 2 Peter 3:12-14 and connects to the frequent New Testament theme of eager waiting and expectation for Christ's return (see especially Jude 21). This, of course, is connected to one of the main objections addressed by the letter, namely, the delay of Christ's coming. As seen earlier in the letter, confident expectation of Christ's return is based on God's promises expressed in the prophetic word. The promise of "new heavens and a new earth" (2 Pet 3:13) recalls the prophetic announcement of God's restoration of all things (Is 65:17; 66:22; see also Rev 21:1). In contrast to the corruption in the world they currently experience (recall 2 Pet 1:4), Peter's readers are to live life now in light of restored creation, for which they hope. The new heavens and earth will be a place "where righteousness dwells."

In 2 Peter 3:14 a new paragraph opens, encouraging the audience to be found spotless while they wait for God to make all things right once again. They are to wait for "these things," referring back to God's coming judgment and hope of new heavens and earth. While waiting in hope for judgment and restoration, believers live in holiness. In the next two verses, Peter briefly refers back to God's forbearance (2 Pet 3:9), saying, "Regard the patience of our Lord as salvation," and then reinforces this perspective by connecting it to the writings of Paul. In contrast to the false teachers, Peter's rebuttal represents the unified apostolic (2 Pet 1:16-18) and prophetic (2 Pet 1:19-21) message. That "Paul has written to you" is a fascinating suggestion that the audience of this letter received copies of Paul's correspondence. In the next verse, the author refers to Paul speaking "about these things in all his letters," suggesting that it was a collection of Paul's writings that the audience either possessed or of which they had some specific knowledge. As a fellow apostolic witness,

Peter expresses confidence in this collection of Paul's letters, both describing how they were written "according to the wisdom given to him" and, strikingly, warning that Paul's letters are abused and twisted by the "untaught" as they do "the rest of the Scriptures." Though the exact content of the collection is speculation, it is important to note this early attestation to an authoritative group of Pauline letters circulating among early Christian communities and its significance for understanding the early development of smaller canonical collections within the New Testament.

COMMENTARY | CONCLUSION AND BENEDICTION | 2 PETER 3:17-18

A final transition to the conclusion of the letter is marked by the phrase "Therefore, dear friends" (2 Pet 3:17). The purpose of the letter has been to remind the readers of the apostolic teaching they knew and received (2 Pet 1:12; 3:1), and now, "since you know this," Peter urges his readers to be on guard so as not to be "led away by the error of lawless people," clearly a reference to the deceptive influence of the false teachers. The "stable position" to which they are to hold is the apostolic teaching represented by Peter throughout the letter. The final encouragement and benediction once again recall themes from 2 Peter 1:2-11, exhorting the audience to "grow in the grace and knowledge of our Lord and Savior Jesus Christ" (note once again the key term *knowledge*). Rather than closing the letter with a salutation or final greetings, the last phrase contains a doxology, expressing the praise of glory of Jesus Christ. Though not the usual way to close a letter in the New Testament, other Catholic Epistles conclude with a doxology or with such a passage near the end of the letter (Jude 24-25; 1 Pet 4:11; 5:11). A somewhat unique feature of 2 Peter's closing doxology is that it is addressed to Jesus Christ (see elsewhere in the New Testament 2 Tim 4:18; Rev 1:5-6). The glory now declared over Christ echoes God's own proclamation of glory and honor on Jesus at the transfiguration (2 Pet 1:17). That such glory is both "now and to the day of eternity" resonates with the theme of the coming day of the Lord woven throughout the letter.

FURTHER READING | 2 PETER COMMENTARIES AND MONOGRAPHS

T: technical; ★: recommended; ★★: highly recommended

T★★ Bauckham, Richard, J. *Jude, 2 Peter.* WBC. Nashville: Thomas Nelson, 2003.

★ Davids, Peter H. *The Letters of 2 Peter and Jude.* PNTC. Grand Rapids, MI: Eerdmans, 2006.

T Green, Gene L. *Jude and 2 Peter.* BECNT. Grand Rapids, MI: Baker, 2008.

Kelly, J. N. D. *A Commentary on the Epistles of Peter and Jude.* Grand Rapids, MI: Baker, 1996.

Moo, Douglas. *2 Peter and Jude.* NIVAC. Grand Rapids, MI: Zondervan, 1996.

Neyrey, Jerome H. *2 Peter, Jude: A New Translation with Introduction and Commentary.* AB. New York: Doubleday, 1993.

Reese, Ruth Ann. *2 Peter and Jude.* THNTC; Grand Rapids, MI: Eerdmans, 2007.

★ Schreiner, Thomas R. *1-2 Peter and Jude.* CSC. Nashville: Holman, 2020.

CHAPTER FOUR

The Letter of I John

THOUGH IT IS VERY COMMON to consider the letters of John together with the Gospel of John (and Revelation), from early on 1–3 John were collected and associated within the Catholic Epistles rather than with other Johannine writings. Within their context in the Catholic Epistles, there are key connections associating 2 Peter with 1 John. Both letters emphasize the idea of knowledge or the understanding gained at conversion: 2 Peter insists a godly life comes "through the knowledge of God" (2 Pet 1:3) and the "knowledge of our Lord Jesus Christ" (2 Pet 1:8, see also 2 Pet 1:3; 2:20). Likewise, 1 John emphasizes the assurance of knowing: "This is how we know that we know him: if we keep his commands" (1 Jn 2:3); "I have written these things to you who believe . . . so that you may know that you have eternal life" (1 Jn 5:13; see also 1 Jn 3:19; 4:7, 13).

Another connection between 2 Peter and 1 John is that in 2 Peter's warning against scoffers the author notes the heretical claim will include an appeal that all things have continued as they were "from the beginning [*ap' archēs*] of creation" (2 Pet 3:4).[1] Soon after these words 1 John opens by declaring (*apangellomen*) that which "was from the beginning [*ap' archēs*] . . . concerning the word of life" (1 Jn 1:1). In addition to a shared

---

[1]David R. Nienhuis and Robert W. Wall, *Reading the Epistles of James, Peter, John and Jude as Scripture: The Shaping and Shape of a Canonical Collection* (Grand Rapids, MI: Eerdmans, 2013), 256.

concern for knowing that comes from conversion, both 2 Peter and 1 John contend against those who threaten the integrity of the apostolic faith, with both authors calling these dangerous people "false prophets." The word *pseudoprophētēs* only appears in 2 Peter and 1 John, and in both letters the "false prophets are identified as teachers (2 Pet. 2:1; 1 John 2:27) who 'deny' (*arneomai*) a key Christological claim (2 Pet. 2:1; 1 John 2:22-23)."[2] Finally, supporting both the content of such conversion knowledge and opposition of false teaching stands the apostolic faith. The authors of both 2 Peter and 1 John ground the authority of their message in their status as eyewitnesses of Jesus' life and ministry (2 Pet 1:16, 18; 1 Jn 1:1-4).[3] Though seldom considered together, these significant connections are consistent with how the early church collected the Catholic Epistles together, where 2 Peter is followed by 1 John. The two letters read in close canonical succession would highlight these links.

OCCASION AND SETTING

Authorship. First John does not open like a typical letter, and the author never identifies himself, either at the beginning of the letter or anywhere else. Whereas previous scholarship held to common authorship of the Gospel of John, the letters of John, and Revelation, it is now more widely thought that different authors wrote the letters of John and the Gospel. However, both the significant similarities of style and language shared between 1 John and the Gospel of John and the testimony of the early church suggest that both were written by John the apostle, the son of Zebedee.

Regarding the relationship between 1 John and the Gospel of John, Raymond Brown famously concluded "that in the NT it is difficult to find

---

[2]Nienhuis and Wall, *Reading the Epistles*, 256.
[3]David Nienhuis notes: "Strikingly, the claim presented here is closely corroborated in the only place John gets a speaking role in Acts, when Peter and John respond to their persecutors in a unified voice, 'We cannot keep from speaking about what we have seen and heard' (Acts 4.19)." See Nienhuis, "'From the Beginning': The Formation of an Apostolic Christian Identity in 2 Peter and 1–3 John," in *Muted Voices of the New Testament: Readings in the Catholic Epistles and Hebrews*, ed. K. M. Hockey, M. N. Pierce, and F. Watson, Library of New Testament Studies 565 (London: Bloomsbury T&T Clark, 2017), 70-85, here 81.

two works more similar in expression."[4] They both have a Greek style characterized by repetition and a somewhat limited vocabulary. They share development of similar themes: light (Jn 1:4-9; 3:19-21; 5:35; 8:12; 9:5; 11:9-10; 12:35-36, 46; 1 Jn 1:5-6; 5:13), darkness (Jn 1:5; 3:19; 8:12; 12:35, 46; 1 Jn 1:5-6; 2:8-9, 11), life (Jn 1:4; 5:26; 6:33, 35, 48; 8:12; 11:25; 14:6; 1 Jn 1:2; 5:12), and truth (Jn 3:21; 14:6, 16-17; 15:26; 1 Jn 1:6, 8; 2:21; 3:19; 4:6; 2 Jn 1, 4; 3 Jn 3). Significantly, these ideas are developed in both texts as contrasting pairs or as dualisms: light and darkness, truth and error, God and the devil, love and hate. Furthermore, the two works have several clauses and phrases that are nearly identical, for example, "We testify to what we have seen" (Jn 3:11; 1 Jn 1:2); "so that your joy may be complete" (Jn 16:24; 1 Jn 1:4); and "The one who walks in the darkness" (Jn 12:35; 1 Jn 1:6). Both 1 John and the Gospel of John begin with a prologue focusing on the *logos*. The Gospel of John opens with "in the beginning was the word" (see Jn 1:1-18), and 1 John unpacks "the word of life" (see 1 Jn 1:1-4). It must be noted that there are differences of language between the two texts along with the conspicuous absence of any reference to the Old Testament in 1 John, both of which suggest to some that 1 John and the Gospel of John could not have been written by the same person. Although these and other similarities are not irrefutable proof of the same author, it is the traditional position that the letters and the Gospel were written by John the son of Zebedee.

In addition to the similarities between 1 John and the Gospel of John, early church evidence uniformly points to John the apostle as the author of 1 John. Irenaeus uses 1 John and then notes that it belongs to John the author of the Fourth Gospel (*Haer.* 3.16.5, 8). The author of the Muratorian canon (perhaps late second century) lists among the received books "The Letter of Jude and two bearing the name of John are accepted in the universal church." It is clear that the author has 1 John in mind as he quotes 1 John 1:1, 3-4. Both Clement of Alexandria (*Stromateis* 2.15.66; 3.4.32; 3.5.42, 44; 4.16.110) and Tertullian (*Against Marcion* 5.16; *Against Praxeas* 28;

---

[4]Raymond E. Brown, *The Epistles of John*, AB (New York: Doubleday, 1982), 21.

Antidote for the Scorpion's Sting 12) both understood that 1 John was written by John the apostle. Furthermore, Dionysius of Alexandria specifically notes the shared vocabulary between the Gospel of John and 1 John suggests common authorship (*Hist. eccl.* 7.25.17-21).

Audience. With no letter opening or salutation, there is only indirect evidence for the identity of the intended readers. They are addressed as believers in Jesus who are experiencing the repercussions of a schism (1 Jn 2:19). A group has left the original community, and the author indicates: "I have written these things to you concerning those who are trying to deceive you" (1 Jn 2:26). The letters of John in general depict the persistent presence of deceivers (2 Jn 7) who cause friction between individuals and particular churches they are associated with (3 Jn 9).

It is possible that the readers make up the membership of several churches in fellowship with the author's church. It seems clear that the author wishes to protect the readers from the influence of "false prophets" (1 Jn 4:1) who are likely associated with those who have left the community (1 Jn 2:19-20). Rather than being influenced by those who have left the church, the author writes "so that you may also have fellowship with us" (1 Jn 1:3) so that "our joy may be complete" (1 Jn 1:4). The audience is portrayed as living in a world that does not know them because it did not know Christ (1 Jn 3:1) and because it is under the influence of the evil one (1 Jn 5:19). The world, then, is seen as in direct opposition to God; therefore, the audience is challenged to love God rather than the world (1 Jn 2:15-17).

The letter ends with an admonition: "Little children, guard yourselves from idols" (1 Jn 5:21). This is a curious way to end a letter. Perhaps the charge to keep themselves from idols implies that the readers were Gentiles—Jews would likely not need this command. However, this view depends on understanding the warning against idolatry as a more literal command. Some would understand this to be a warning against metaphorical idolatry, and thus it would tell us little about the historical audience. On the other hand, the letter refers to the well-known Jewish command to love the neighbor (1 Jn 2:7-8), which could indicate a Jewish audience. It is likely that John wrote to churches in and around Ephesus (see Eusebius, *Hist. eccl.* 3.3.1).

Genre. First John does not have the typical characteristics of a Greco-Roman letter. The expected letter opening, which includes the formula of parties ("person *x* to person/group *y*") and a salutation ("greetings"), is absent. Furthermore, 1 John does not contain any personal greetings and has no thanksgiving section, and the text ends abruptly without any letter closing. Though 1 John stands out as having none of these common features of a letter, the text was clearly written by an individual (1 Jn 2:1, 7, 12-14) to a specific group (or groups). There seems to have been a specific situation that called forth the letter (1 Jn 2:18-19).

Some have suggested that the content of 1 John originated as a sermon or homily that had now been written down and passed along for reading in other situations. Several times the author mentions that "I have written," which, perhaps, suggests this was a written document and not a sermon. Raymond Brown has argued that 1 John was written as a kind of commentary on the Gospel of John, specifically refuting the opponents' false teaching based on their misinterpretation of the Gospel. Perhaps most convincing is the view that 1 John was a circular letter written for a group of specific communities facing similar issues. Perhaps this view can account for the absence of a letter opening, because the specific greetings could have been conveyed by a letter carrier (this idea will be explored further in the discussion of how John's three letters are related in the next chapter).

STRUCTURE

Tracing the structure and flow of thought through 1 John is notoriously difficult because of the repetition of key vocabulary and the author's stylistic choice to return to and expand on subjects already addressed. Scholars generally identify either two or three sections between the prologue and conclusion of the letter. The twofold structure is perhaps slightly more plausible because John makes two clear claims regarding the gospel: "God is light" (1 Jn 1:5) and "God is love" (1 Jn 4:8), with the dividing line between the two marked by the repeated phrase "this is the message we/you have heard" (1 Jn 1:5; 3:11).[5]

OUTLINE

I. Prologue concerning "the word of life" (1 Jn 1:1-4)

II. Part one: "God is light"—and we should walk accordingly: "This is the message we have heard from him and declare to you" (1 Jn 1:5–3:10)

1. Thesis: "God is light" (1 Jn 1:5)

2. First command: Ethical implications of "God is light" (1 Jn 1:6–2:2)

3. Second command: Obey God's commands (1 Jn 2:3-11)

4. Third command: Defy the world and its allure (1 Jn 2:12-17)

5. Fourth command: Renounce those who distort the truth (1 Jn 2:18-27)

6. Fifth command: Live like God's children (1 Jn 2:28–3:10)

III. Part two: "God is love"—and we should walk accordingly: "For this the message you have heard from the beginning: We should love one another" (1 Jn 3:11–5:12)

1. Love one another in practical ways (1 Jn 3:11-24)

2. Beware of false prophets who would deceive you (1 Jn 4:1-6)

3. Love one another as God loves us in Christ (1 Jn 4:7–5:4a)

4. Never compromise your testimony (1 Jn 5:4b-12)

IV. Conclusion: The boldness and confidence of those who walk in God's light and love (1 Jn 5:13-21)[6]

---

[5]Brown argues that 1 John mirrors the structure of the Gospel of John in opening with a prologue (Jn 1:1-18; 1 Jn 1:1-4), then progressing in two distinct sections (Jn 1:19–12:50, the book of signs; Jn 13:1–20:29, the book of glory; 1 Jn 1:5–3:10, "God is light"; 1 Jn 3:11–5:12, "God is love"), and finally concluding with an epilogue (Jn 21; 1 Jn 5:13-21).
[6]Brown, *Epistles of John*, 124.

COMMENTARY | PROLOGUE CONCERNING
"THE WORD OF LIFE" | 1 JOHN 1:1-4

First John does not begin like a letter; rather, in the opening verses, much like the Gospel of John, we find a prologue concerning "the word of life" (1 Jn 1:1). It is noteworthy that, whereas later, in 1 John 2:19, we learn of the pressing situation of schism facing the readers, here in the opening verses there is no direct hint at such a difficult situation. Perhaps we should understand the rhetorical strategy of the author as opening with the solution rather than the problem. The solution is the word of life, which is the foundation of fellowship between believers and God as well as between believers themselves.

In an unusual, yet attention-catching way, the letter opens with four relative clauses, each fronted by a relative pronoun ("that which"; 1 Jn 1:1). Each of the relative pronouns introduces a dependent clause, which must be connected to a main sentence for its meaning. Both the use of relative pronouns and the dependent relative clauses catch the readers' attention and hold them in suspense, waiting for the main verbal idea, which does not come until 1 John 1:3.

The verbal ideas in three of these relative clauses focus on perception: "heard," "seen," "touched" (1 Jn 1:1). In addition to these verbs of perception, the author writes as part of a group ("we") that claims a particular kind of knowing or perceiving. This is likely a claim to eyewitness experience of Jesus' life and ministry. The author writes as representative of the apostles, who physically encountered the life and ministry of Jesus Christ (note the very same kind of eyewitness testimony in 2 Pet 1:18). This apostolic witness in terms of sense perception is "concerning the word of life"—the central theme of the entire section.

But what exactly does the phrase "word of life" refer to? It could either refer to Jesus himself, as the living word (*logos*) of God (compare Jn 1:14), or to the life-giving message, the word preached *about* Jesus (namely, the gospel). The parallel between 1 John 1:1-4 and the opening prologue of the Gospel of John (Jn 1:1-18) and the verbs of perception both suggest that John is referring to something more than a spoken message (how does one touch a message with one's hands?). The word of life most likely refers to Jesus Christ and the entire message of his life and teaching. This is a "message that has been embodied in a person—the person of Jesus Christ."[7]

If the word of life is Jesus himself, then "from the beginning" in the first relative clause could refer to the historical beginning of the gospel, namely, the beginning of Jesus' ministry. Yet it is possible, especially in light of the prologue of the Gospel of John, that the first relative clause ("what was from the beginning") could refer to the preincarnate *logos*, and thus the beginning might refer to the beginning of all creation, when the *logos* was present (Jn 1:2-3). If that is the case, the last three clauses in 1 John 1:1 could then refer to the incarnate *logos* (specifically, the beginning of Jesus' earthly ministry). Though it is only later in the letter that we discover that the readers were facing stiff opposition to the doctrine of the incarnation, specifically a denial that "Jesus Christ has come in the flesh" (1 Jn 4:2; see also 1 Jn 2:22; 2 Jn 7), a refutation of such a denial seems to underlie the letter's prologue. In other words, rather than specifically stating the theological problem of denying the incarnation, John's opening prologue starts with the answer—Jesus, the "word of life," the "eternal life that was with the Father" (1 Jn 1:2), is now revealed in time and space.

Finally, in 1 John 1:3, after a repetition of "what we have seen and heard," we reach the main sentence (the main subject-verb)—"we are announcing to you" (my translation). Note the present tense, "we are announcing." The very act of writing the letter is the announcement of what the apostles saw and heard "concerning the word of life." This is their written testimony and declaration. Here also, we find the reason for the declaration, "so that you may also have fellowship with us" (1 Jn 1:3). Not only does John write so that the readers have a sense of partnership or fellowship with the apostles, but at the same time John

---

[7]Colin G. Kruse, *The Letters of John*, PNTC (Grand Rapids, MI: Eerdmans, 2000), 53.

notes that "our fellowship is with the Father and with his Son, Jesus Christ" (1 Jn 1:3). John stresses that the fellowship enjoyed between believers (here the apostles and the readers) is in direct relationship with the fellowship human beings can enjoy with the Father through the Son. Stated in the opposite way, fellowship with God is directly related to fellowship with God's people. This is a key theme announced here and subsequently developed throughout the letter. Though the first recipients of the letter were not themselves witnesses to the life and ministry of Jesus, they are nonetheless able to fellowship with the apostolic generation through receiving their message—which leads to fellowship with the Father through the Son.

In 1 John 1:4 the prologue is drawn to a close with a connection between "we proclaim" and "we write." The proclamation is accomplished in the writing of this letter, and the content of the proclamation is the apostolic message about the word of life. Just as a reason is given for the proclamation ("so that you may also have fellowship") here too a reason is given for writing, "so that our joy may be complete." Joy is the ultimate end of the process of proclaiming the word of life, and this joy looks forward to future fulfillment, when believers are finally united together with God.

COMMENTARY | PART ONE "GOD IS LIGHT" | 1 JOHN 1:5–3:10

The two major divisions of 1 John can be seen in the repeated phrases, "This is the message we have heard from him and declare to you" (1 Jn 1:5) and "For this is the message you have heard from the beginning" (1 Jn 3:11). These two parallel phrases indicate the two loosely related halves of the letter. Brown describes this first major section of the letter as focusing on the "obligation of walking in light in response to the gospel of God as light. The response to this gospel divides the secessionist Antichrists from the author's Little Children."[8]

---

[8]Brown, *Epistles of John*, 189.

Thesis: "God is light" (1 John 1:5). In the prologue John proclaims a message about the word of life; here he makes clear the content of that message. In 1 John 1:3 of the prologue, John notes "we are proclaiming [*apangellomen*]" (my translation) to you what we have seen and heard. Now, in 1 John 1:5, John notes that this is the "message [*angelia*] we have heard from him and declare [*anangellomen*] to you." Despite the different verbal prefix (*ap-* in 1 Jn 2:3 and *an-* in 1 Jn 2:5), the same idea is communicated by both verbs: a declaration of the message the apostles received from Jesus to all those coming after them. The content of what is announced is "God is light."

The claim that "God is light, and there is absolutely no darkness in him" is not a reply to an objection but a reminder of what Christians confess about God (not apologetics but dogmatics). To call God light implies something central about God's character. God is absolute in his glory, in truth, and in holiness. Whereas in 1 John God is light, in the Gospel of John Jesus is consistently described as light: Jesus is "the true light that gives light to everyone" (Jn 1:9), and he has "come as light into the world, so that everyone who believes in me would not remain in darkness" (Jn 12:46). Jesus is the preexistent light that has come into the world (Jn 1:4-5, 9). With 1 John now stressing that God is light, there is an implicit parallel between God and Jesus Christ such that we can see the overall logic of 1 John and the Gospel of John teaching that God's identity was truly and fully revealed in the divinity of Jesus Christ.

First command: Ethical implications of "God is light" (1 John 1:6–2:2). Directly connected to the claim in 1 John 1:5 that God is light, the next section works out the moral implications flowing from the fact that God is light. The structure of John's argument in this section consists of a series of three conditional sentences, each of which contrasts a false claim with a correct counterclaim. Each of these opening statements should be read with hypothetical force: "If we claim" (NIV). It is likely that the opening false claim of each sentence represents the position of the opponents in 1 John, all of whom articulate a false understanding of walking in the light.

Table 5.1

False Claims	Correcting Counterclaims
1 John 1:6: "if"	1 John 1:7: "but if"
1 John 1:8: "if"	1 John 1:9: "but if"
1 John 1:10: "if"	1 John 2:2: "but if"

The first conditional sentence is made up of 1 John 1:6-7, where the initial claim is that "We have fellowship with him." Connecting back to 1 John 1:3, this is a claim to have fellowship with God the Father through the Son, the same God whose character is unmitigated light. It is possible that, along with the general claim to have fellowship with him (God), there is an implicit claim to participate along with the apostles in proclaiming the message as well.

The claim to have fellowship with God is shown to be false by behavior, because one continues to "walk in darkness." The idea of walking conveys a complete lifestyle, including all of one's actions. To walk in darkness is to live in full rejection of God, who is light. It is a bold hypocrisy to claim fellowship with the God of light at the very same time as continuing to walk in the darkness. John's final verdict is that such people "are lying and are not practicing the truth."

First John 1:7 offers the counterclaim: "If we walk in the light as he himself is in the light, we have fellowship." Thus, if one's behavior is consistent with "God is light" (1 Jn 1:5), then the implicit claim to have fellowship is true. To know and have fellowship with God requires a corresponding conduct that reflects, though imperfectly, God's own light. The two consequences of walking in the light are that "we have fellowship with one another" and "the blood of Jesus . . . cleanses us from all sin" (1 Jn 1:7). The first consequence stresses what was already announced in 1 John 1:3, namely, that fellowship with God entails fellowship with other Christians. The one walking in the light is also one whose sin has been cleansed or purified by Jesus' blood. Perhaps the present tense of the verbs (*walk* and *cleanse*) suggests that both are ongoing activities. That is, the decision to follow Jesus is an ongoing process of faith, surrender, trust, and obedience.

The second conditional sentence is made up of 1 John 1:8-9, where the initial false claim is "We have no sin" (1 Jn 1:8). It is significant to note that the claim is that one does not continue in sin (this is suggested in the tense of the verb). This is likely the perspective of John's opponents, who have the wrong idea of what the Christian life is like. If we are to understand this perspective as that of John's opponents, he is clearly stating that they are self-deceived and do not have the truth within them—charges that resurface later in the letter.

The corresponding counterclaim contends, "If we confess our sins, he is faithful and righteous to forgive . . . and to cleanse" (1 Jn 1:9). The antidote to self-deception is confession of sin. Once again, the present tense of the verb seems to suggest that such confession is an ongoing characteristic of the one who truly walks in the light. God's response to human confession of sin is that, in his character as "faithful and righteous," he forgives. Yet, that God forgives the sins of those who are unrighteous and guilty does not impinge on his fidelity or justice.

The third and final conditional sentence contains a similar claim to that in 1 John 1:8, yet here the verb appears in the perfect tense: "We have not sinned." Even as voiced by John's opponents, this could not be a claim to never have sinned at all. Rather, as in the case of 1 John 1:6, 8, this is most likely a claim by John's opponents that since their (so-called) conversation they have not sinned. This wrong understanding of the Christian life not merely leads to self-deception (1 Jn 1:8), but it actually makes "him [God] a liar," with the result that "his word is not in us" (1 Jn 1:10).

Rather than directly providing a counterclaim, as in the previous conditional sentences, John turns to address his readers directly. In 1 John 2:1 he explains exactly why he is writing: "I am writing you these things so that you may not sin." It is important to note that when John writes "so that you may not sin," he is in no way agreeing with the perspective criticized in 1 John 1:8, 10. This is clear because in the next phrase he argues, "if anyone does sin, we have an advocate with the Father—Jesus Christ the righteous one." This phrase is somewhat a rebuttal to the entire perspective of 1 John 1:6-10. Those who are children of God can and do continue to sin, yet they have an "advocate" (*paraklēton*) with the Father. The advocate, or one who speaks on behalf of the accused, here is Jesus Christ, the one who is himself righteous. It is noteworthy that the word *paraklētos* appears only here and in the Gospel of John (Jn 14:16, 26; 15:26; 16:7), where the term refers to the Holy Spirit. In 1 John 2:1, Jesus stands in the presence of the Father and advocates on behalf of those who are sinful.

Furthermore, in 1 John 2:2 we learn that Jesus' advocacy on behalf of sinners extends to the point of his atoning death: "He himself is the atoning sacrifice [*hilasmos*] for our sins." Not only does Jesus the advocate speak a word on the sinner's behalf, but he also removes the guilt of sin and God's anger toward it. The meaning of *hilasmos* ("atoning sacrifice" or "propitiation") has been the focus of a great deal of discussion. Are we to understand an angry God placated (or propitiated) by the sacrifice of Jesus, or should we understand that it is the sinner's offense that is wiped away ("expiated") by Jesus' blood? Or perhaps the one sacrifice of Jesus accomplishes both? The term *hilasmos* appears in the New Testament only here and in 1 John 4:10, both in the context of a sinner receiving cleansing from transgressions. The majority of contexts in the Greek Old Testament where this term is used refer to the removal of guilt through sacrifice; thus the translation "atoning sacrifice" is to be preferred.

John continues in 1 John 2:2 by asserting that Jesus' sacrifice is "not only for ours, but also for the sins of the whole world" (NIV). To be clear, John is arguing that Jesus' atoning sacrifice is not just for "our" sins, or the sins of his Christian readers, but it is also for the sins of the whole world. Such a sentiment appears elsewhere in 1 John ("the Father has sent his Son as the world's savior," 1 Jn 4:14) and in the Gospel of John (where John the Baptist announces "the Lamb of God who takes away the sin of the world!" Jn 1:29). But the fact that Jesus' atoning sacrifice is for the sins of the whole world cannot mean that all people's sins are forgiven and thus all are granted salvation. Later in the letter, John rules this out, arguing, "The one who does not have the Son of God does not have life" (1 Jn 5:12). It is clear throughout 1 John for one to have the Son requires believing in Jesus Christ, come in the flesh (1 Jn 4:2; 2 Jn 7). Rather than everyone in the world being redeemed by Christ's atoning sacrifice, we might rather suggest "that Jesus Christ is the atoning sacrifice for the sins of the whole world because his death was sufficient to deal with the sins of the whole world, but that his sacrifice does not become effective until people believe in him."[9]

Second command: Obey God's commands (1 John 2:3-11). The rebuttal of false claims articulated in the "if" statements in 1 John 1:6–2:2 continues in the next section (1 Jn 2:3-11), yet with greater focus on the opponents' claims to having true knowledge of God. The most important difference between the two sections is the grammatical form in which the corrections are presented.

This section focuses on how the readers can be sure they know God by keeping his commandments. John argues, "This is how we know [*ginōskomen*] that we have come to know [*egnōkamen*] him; if we keep his commandments" (my translation). John uses the verb *know* in several ways throughout his letter, but often as a description of this conversion knowledge of God (1 Jn 2:3, 5, 29; 3:19, 24; 4:6, 13; 5:2). This is a positive statement of assurance given to encourage John's readers that they can know for sure that they have a transformational knowledge of God.

Such assurance is confirmed by action. John writes that it is by keeping his commandments that his readers can know they truly know God. But what commandments does John have in mind? The term *command* or *commands* appears frequently in 1 John. Every time it occurs in the singular (1 Jn 2:7 [3×], 8; 3:23 [2×]; 4:21), it refers to the command of Christ that his followers love one another. Later in the letter, John explicitly states, "This is his command: that we believe in the name of his Son, Jesus Christ, and love one another as he commanded us" (1 Jn 3:23). This should inform our understanding of what command John has in mind here in 1 John 2:3.

After an encouraging word of assurance to his readers, John then turns to a series of false claims regarding knowledge of God. The first claim, in 1 John 2:4-5, picks up from the previous verse: one who claims

---

[9]Kruse, *Letters of John*, 75.

to know God, "and yet doesn't keep his commands, is a liar, and the truth is not in him" (1 Jn 2:4). Using the present tense in the phrase "yet doesn't keep" likely stresses not the one-time failure to keep God's commands but ongoing disobedience. In 1 John 2:5, John offers the antithesis: "Whoever keeps his word, truly in him the love of God is made complete." Note that the command John's readers are to keep is the love command, and it is in this person that the love of God has been made complete.

John addresses the second false claim in 1 John 2:6-8. Flowing from the assurance John wants to give to his readers that they are "in him," here the concern is that the opponents might make the same claim, to be in him. But John once again reinforces the necessary connection between saying and doing: "The one who says he remains in him should walk just as he [Jesus] walked" (1 Jn 2:6). A claim to remaining in God must be supported by a life (walk) that is patterned after Jesus' own life.

Dealing with the list of false claims is temporarily interrupted by 1 John 2:7-8 as John again directly addresses his audience. John insists that the command he is writing about is not new but "an old command that you have had from the beginning" (1 Jn 2:7). The "beginning" could refer back to the Torah, where Israel is commanded to love their neighbor (Lev 19:18), or it could refer to the ministry of Jesus, where the disciples heard the command of Christ to love one another (Jn 13:34). Either way, this is "the word you have heard."

This makes sense of how the command is old and from the beginning in 1 John 2:7, but how, then, is the command also new? John says, "Yet I am writing you a new command" (1 Jn 2:8). Jesus himself gave his disciples the command to love one another, and, in John 13:34, Jesus calls this a new command. So, the command to love one another is the new command that, at the time of writing for John, was well in the past (whether given in Jesus' ministry or at Sinai), so it was an old command that they already knew and had from the beginning. The next two phrases continue to hint at the newness of the command, that the command is "true in him and in you." The command to love is made true in how Jesus loved; he is the command's truest expression. The command's being "true . . . in you" refers to the believing community to which John writes. John also notes that the command is true "because the darkness is passing away and the true light is already shining." The light that is already shining can be none other than Jesus Christ himself, who is the "true light . . . coming into the world" (Jn 1:9; see also Jn 1:4-8; 8:12; 9:5; 12:35-36, 46). The result of Christ, the light, coming into the world is that the darkness, the world in all of its opposition to Christ, is passing away. It is significant that the darkness of the world order, which is opposed to God, passes away in the light of Jesus' supreme expression of love—not through violence but through the supreme love of Jesus is the darkness of the present world order undone.

John addresses the third and final false claim in 1 John 2:9-11. Following from the very end of the previous section, John addresses "the one who says he is in the light" (1 Jn 2:9). Like the previous claim to know God, this final claim to be in the light is a claim to closeness to God. However, the claim is falsified because of the failure to love. One cannot be in the light while at the same time hating "his brother or sister," but rather, that one is "in the darkness until now" (1 Jn 2:9). Stated positively, the one who remains in God "loves his brother or sister [and] remains in the light" (1 Jn 2:10). It is not that loving results in one being in the light, but rather it is being in the light that enables one to love because God first loved us (1 Jn 4:19). John notes that in this person "there is no cause for stumbling," or there is nothing that causes him to fall into sin.

The Love Command

The command to love other Christians is pervasive throughout John's letters (1 Jn 2:7-11; 3:10-11, 14, 23; 4:7, 11, 20-21; 5:1-2; 2 Jn 5-6; 3 Jn 6). This theme runs through all the Catholic Epistles (see for example, Jas 2:8; 1 Pet 1:22).

Finally, in 1 John 2:11 John restates and expands on the negative assessment of 1 John 2:9: not only is the "one who hates his brother and sister in the darkness" but he "walks in the darkness" and "the darkness has blinded his eyes" (1 Jn 2:11). This expanded description of the one who fails to love emphatically associates him with the darkness, both the sinful behavior that rejects the light and the realm that produces such behavior. The one who fails to love is part of the darkness that is passing away.

Third command: Defy the world and its allure (1 John 2:12-17). Within this larger section there are two subsections, both of which are structured around sets of three. First, in 1 John 2:12-14, there are three sets of three: in 1 John 2:12-13 the phrase "I am writing to you" is addressed to three groups, "little children" (*teknia*), "fathers," and "young men"; in 1 John 2:14, the phrase "I have written to you" appears three times, addressing "children" (*paideia*), "fathers," and "young men"; and finally in the last part of 1 John 2:14 there are three coordinate clauses ("you are strong," "God's word remains in you," and "you have conquered the evil one"). Furthermore, 1 John 2:15-17 contain two sets of three: each of the three verses contains a contrast (love for the world versus love for the Father, 1 Jn 2:15; what comes from the world versus what belongs to the Father, 1 Jn 2:16; and the world passes away versus God, who remains forever, 1 Jn 2:17); and 1 John 2:16 lists three specific things that belong to the world.

Though alternating between present ("I am writing") and aorist ("I wrote"), it is most likely that in both cases John is talking about his present letter. "Little children" is the way John has addressed his readers in general throughout the letter, where, in the style of wisdom writing, an authority figure speaks to his followers with family affection. Therefore, in 1 John 2:12, 14, when John speaks to the children he is likely referring to the entire community (or communities) to which he has addressed the letter. John assures his entire audience that "your sins have been forgiven on account of his name" (1 Jn 2:12).

When John addresses fathers and young men, it is likely that he makes some kind of distinction within the Christian community, perhaps along the lines of mature Christian elders (fathers) and newer Christians (young people). In 1 John 2:13, John encourages the fathers because "you have come to know the one who is from the beginning." Jesus Christ is more than likely this one who was from the beginning, and perhaps in light of 1 John 1:1 this is the beginning of Jesus' public ministry—with John this could also be hinting at the preexistence of Jesus as well. The young men are encouraged because they have "conquered the evil one." Yet, in what way could younger Christians be understood as having conquered the evil one? Later in the letter John uses this term "conquer" (*nikaō*) in reference to the world (or the antichrists in the world, 1 Jn 4:4), and in 1 John 5:4-5 those born of God their father conquer the world through their faith in Christ. So perhaps it is through their faith in Christ that they have conquered the evil one.

In 1 John 2:14, the same three groups are addressed. John addresses the children this time as those who "have come to know the Father." The fathers are addressed again as knowing "the one who was from the beginning." And finally, the young men are addressed because "you are strong, God's word remains in you, and you have conquered the evil one." This final threefold encouragement brings the section to a close.

As the previous section concluded with a note about conquering the evil one, in a similar way this next section warns against the world and its influence.

First John 2:15 opens with the letter's first command, "Do not love [*mē agapate*] the world." The word *world* occurs twenty-three times throughout 1 John. John uses this word to refer to the natural world (1 Jn 3:17) and, in a locative sense, of where people live (1 Jn 4:1, 4, 9, 14, 17); however, most often it refers to the worldview of the world in opposition to God (1 Jn 2:15-17 [6×]; 5:4 [2×], 5) or the world of people under the power of the evil one, who are also opposed to God (1 Jn 3:1, 13; 4:5 [3×]; 5:19). Therefore, John warns against loving the world itself (the world in opposition to God) or the things in the world (namely, the things that are supportive of world in opposition to God). Later in the letter John argues that those who remain in the world are under the influence of the evil one and do not belong to God (1 Jn 5:19).

John then offers a set of three contrasts in 1 John 2:15-17:

Table 5.2

Verse	"the world"	vs	"the Father"
1 John 2:15	love of world	vs	love of Father
1 John 2:16	comes from the world	vs	comes from the Father
1 John 2:17	world passes away	vs	the one who obeys God remains forever

The first contrast between love of the world and the love of the Father communicates a fundamental incompatibility between the two loves. One cannot love both the world and the Father at the same time. First John 2:16 introduces a threefold description of the things in the world. The first two, the "lust of the flesh" and the "lust of the eyes," describe the base, morally corrupt desires within one, which are intensified by what one sees. The third description, "the pride in one's possessions [*biou*]," refers to the hope or confidence that comes from having material possessions. These are the basic elements that make up the world, and John strikes the contrast that "everything in the world . . . is not from the Father, but is from the world," and as such will never satisfy. The final contrast, posed in 1 John 2:17, is between the "world with its lust," which "is passing away" (like the darkness, 1 Jn 2:8), and "the one who does the will of God," who "remains forever."

Fourth command: Renounce those who distort the truth (1 John 2:18-27).

First John 2:18 starts a new section as marked both by the repetition of "children" (*paideia*) as a direct address to his readers, and the shift in subject, from encouragement to warning. The warning is framed as "the last hour," where John understands the last days spoken of in the prophets and in Jesus' teaching as now unfolding. He specifi-

God and the World as Incompatible Allegiances

Throughout the Catholic Epistles the world is understood as in fundamental conflict with God's purposes. James warns against being stained by (Jas 1:27) or in friendship with the world (Jas 4:4), and 1 Peter calls Christians to do right as they face suffering at the hands of the "pagans," those in the world (1 Pet 1:14-18; 4:1-4). Similarly, 1 John consistently warns that the world didn't know God (1 Jn 3:1) and that the world hates followers of Christ (1 Jn 3:13; see also 1 Jn 4:1-9, 17; 5:4-5, 19; 2 Jn 7).

cally notes, "The antichrist is coming, even now many antichrists have come," and "by this we know that it is the last hour" (1 Jn 2:18). Much could be said regarding the end-time figure opposed to God, who is called the antichrist (1 Jn 2:18 [2×], 22; 4:3; 2 Jn 7). Other passages in the New Testament refer to a "man of lawlessness" (1 Thess 2:3), those falsely claiming to be Messiah (Mt 24; Mk 13), or the beast (Rev 13). Either a false Christ or an antichrist, the term describes a counterfeit Messiah, one who opposes the true Christ. Here John uses the term *antichrist* to label the opponents of the communities to whom he writes.

John says the antichrists "went out from us, but they did not belong to us; for if they had belonged to us, they would have remained with us" (1 Jn 2:19). Because John does not elaborate on the details of the schism, it seems clear that his readers already knew both about the event and the group that left. John does, however, clarify that those who left are antichrists, helping his readers identify the influence and danger this group poses. We will call this group the secessionists because they quit the true Christian community, and, by leaving, they demonstrated that they never really belonged. Though the verb "they went out" (*exēlthan*) could suggest expulsion (as in Mk 1:26), the context suggests they chose to leave without coercion. Though John does not explain why they left, the context of the letter suggests they left because of a very different understanding of the identity and nature of Christ. Later in the passage we find that not only did those who left the community (the secessionists) deny that Jesus is the Christ (1 Jn 2:22), but also that they were actively attempting to lead John's readers astray (1 Jn 2:26). Furthermore, later in the letter John makes it clear that his readers are God's children (1 Jn 3:1); the secessionists are children of the devil (1 Jn 3:10). It seems that they have formed a countercommunity claiming to be the true church.

At the beginning of 1 John 2:20 John directly addresses his readers ("But you"). In sharp contrast to the secessionists, who left the community, John's audience has received an "anointing from the Holy One" (1 Jn 2:20). This anointing (*chrisma*) remains or abides in them (1 Jn 2:27), and therefore he can say, "All of you know the truth." Later in the passage John further discusses the anointing his readers have received, yet first he further unmasks the secessionists. To this point in the letter John has described the opponents as walking in the darkness, as not keeping the commandments, as not loving brothers or sisters, as claiming to be without sin, to know God, and to abide with him. In this passage, John more clearly identifies their wrong understanding of Christ—aberrant Christology. In 1 John 2:21, John encourages his readers because they do not need anyone (especially the secessionists) to teach them the truth, "because no lie comes from the truth" (1 Jn 2:21). Here the truth certainly refers to the truth about Jesus, that he is the Christ and that he came in the flesh (1 Jn 4:2; 2 Jn 7).

John makes two statements that both apply to the secessionists: "the liar" is the "one who denies that Jesus is the Christ," and the antichrist is "the one who denies the Father and the Son" (1 Jn 2:22). First, because the secessionists were once part of the Christian community, this denial that Jesus is the Christ was likely not an outright rejection of Jesus as Messiah, but rather they likely denied a key component of orthodox Christology. Later in the letter, components of this aberrant Christology surface more clearly, most especially that they deny Jesus Christ has come in the flesh (1 Jn 4:2-3, 15; 5:1, 6-8). Perhaps viewed along with the opening prologue, which stresses the apostolic perception of Jesus' physical existence, this could be a denial or weakening of the human nature of Jesus.

Second, John claims this defective Christology leads to a denial of the person of the Father and of the Son. John further articulates the dangerous implications of this defective Christology: "No one who denies the Son has the Father" (1 Jn 2:23). Though John does not detail the exact relationship between the Father and the Son, there are hints later in the letter. John asserts that the Father sent the Son (1 Jn 4:10) and that the Father testifies concerning his Son (1 Jn 5:9-10). Therefore, the secessionists' claim to have fellowship with God (1 Jn 1:5), to know God (1 Jn 2:3), or remain in him (1 Jn 2:6) are false claims because of their denial that Jesus came in the flesh. Balancing this negative statement, John states, "He who confesses the Son has the Father as well" (1 Jn 2:23). John's readers hold to a correct Christology, and therefore they truly know and remain in the Father. John, of course, writes to warn his readers away from the corrupt moral and doctrinal influence of the secessionists.

John again directly addresses his audience and encourages them that "What you have heard from the beginning is to remain in you" (1 Jn 2:24).

"What you have heard" refers to the original gospel message announced to John's readers at their conversion, and this is the message (1 Jn 1:5) about which John now writes in order to reinforce and encourage his audience. John promises that by remaining in the original gospel message, his readers will therefore "remain in the Son and in the Father" (1 Jn 2:24). Furthermore, he says in 1 John 2:25, "this is the promise he himself made to us: eternal life." Then, shifting back to warning, John makes clear what has been implicit all along, that he has written the letter because of "those who are trying to deceive you."

Finally, in 1 John 2:27, John turns to encourage his readers, reminding them that "the anointing you received from him remains in you, and you don't need anyone to teach you." But what is this anointing (*chrisma*)? The anointing John's readers received, which "teaches you about all things," is the Holy Spirit. This is confirmed in the similar function between the Spirit in the Gospel of John and the anointing in 1 John:

Table 5.3

	John 14–16: The Holy Spirit	1 John 2:20-27: The anointing
Teaches	John 14:17	1 John 2:27
Leads to truth	John 14:26	1 John 2:27
Gives knowledge	John 14:17	1 John 2:20
Abides in us	John 14:17	1 John 2:27

Though the secessionists likely received baptism and thus were initiated into the community, John implies that they never received the anointing and therefore do not have true knowledge, and thus they ultimately did not remain in the true church. John's readers, by contrast, received baptism and the anointing, which remains in them. For this reason they do not need anyone, especially the secessionist, to teach them. Therefore, the greatest defense against the deception of the secessionists is the Holy Spirit, who teaches and remains in the Christian community. John's written encouragement and warning via the letter is not, then, designed to teach his readers something new but rather to strengthen what they already know by the Spirit, "because you do know [the truth]" (1 Jn 2:21). Thus, the final exhortation of the section is that "just as it has taught you, remain in him" (1 Jn 2:27).

Fifth command: Live like God's children (1 John 2:28–3:10). First John 2:28 seems to draw the previous section to a close as well as begin the next. The exhortation to remain in him is echoed from the previous section, especially as the last refrain in 1 John 2:27, yet at the same time the idea of having confidence "at his coming" and "when he appears" (1 Jn 2:28) anticipates the discussion of when he appears in 1 John 3:2. As we have seen before, the direct address to "little children" suggests a new section starting in 1 John 2:28. Finally, the shared themes linking 1 John 2:28-29 with 1 John 3:9-10 (namely, the idea of revelation, remaining, and being born of God) suggest a coherent unit of thought.

John encourages his readers to remain in Christ, "so that when he appears we may have confidence and not be ashamed before him at his coming" (1 Jn 2:28). Though John's use of "revelation" or "appearing" (*phaneroō*) can refer to Jesus' incarnation (1 Jn 1:1-2; 3:5, 8), here and in 1 John 3:2 the term clearly speaks of Christ's future appearing "at his coming [*parousia*]." John uses what becomes the technical term for Jesus' second coming (*parousia*), the time when the works of the evil one and the antichrist will finally be destroyed. John's readers are to have confidence, not being ashamed, at this promised coming, and such confidence is only possible based on their remaining in Christ. First John 2:29, then, furthers this encouragement and introduces the connection between knowing God and righteous action that is outlined in 1 John 3:4-10. John argues that everyone who does what is right has been born of him. It is important to note the logic. Righteous deeds are not the cause of being born of God but rather the result. In what becomes a theme running through the rest of the letter, John insists that those born of God will enact righteous deeds. The entire second half of the letter stresses that God is Father and that those born of the Father will live in the righteousness that comes from him.

With the sequence of the argument started in 1 John 2:28 resuming in 1 John 3:4, all of 1 John 3:1-3 stands as a parenthesis within John's reflection on what it means to be fathered by God. Before moving on to unpack how John's readers are to live as children, we will examine 1 John 3:1-3.

This brief exclamation of God's fatherly love brings together the themes of new birth and the coming of Jesus. Revealing some of the intensity of emotion, John says, "See what great love the Father has given us." That John qualifies it as great (*potapēn*) stresses both the quantity and quality of the Father's love for us—both how much love and what amazing love. Furthermore, John stresses that God's love renders a new status on his readers: "that we should be called God's children—and we are!" (1 Jn 3:1). Thus, the readers are not children of God in name only but in fact and with all the privileges and position this entails. Importantly, the issue of *being* the children of God and *doing* what the children of God should do is addressed in the next verse. Yet before moving on, John highlights the resulting conflict of this status as God's children: "The reason the world does not know us is that it didn't know him." That the world does not recognize this new identity as God's children should not discourage the audience because, later in the letter, John argues that they overcome or conquer the world through "our faith" (1 Jn 5:3-4; see also 1 Jn 4:4-5).

In the next verse John says, "We are God's children now" (1 Jn 3:2). Previously, John has discussed how the secessionists were revealed as antichrists "now" (1 Jn 2:18), yet in contrast he says of his audience, you are "God's children now" (1 Jn 3:2). While this contrast is clear, the final character of John's audience is not yet fully formed. The next phrase further describes this tension: "and what we will be has not yet been revealed." Whereas the identity as a child is conferred and settled, the transformation of character remains yet future. However, even though such transformation has not yet taken place, John encourages hope by connecting such transformation to the coming of Christ: "We know that when he appears, we will be like him." This emphasizes the contrast between the present state or experience of childhood (which has not yet been revealed) and the future state or experience of childhood (which shall be revealed). Or stated another way, what God has already made true of the readers' status now will be true in their character and action in the future ("we will be like him"). Though the audience would have felt this tension, there is "continuity between the present and future status of God's children."[10] And this is true "because we will see him as he is." This seeing at Christ's coming will not merely be a seeing of his earthly body or public ministry (1 Jn 1:1) but seeing his heavenly glory. John encourages his readers, saying, "Everyone who has this hope in him purifies himself just as he is pure" (1 Jn 3:3). The hope of seeing and being like Jesus when he comes starts to work itself out in the readers' lives at present.

After the brief parenthesis of 1 John 3:1-3, John returns to the kind of righteous life characteristic of the child of God. There are several parallels between 1 John 1:6–2:2 and 1 John 3:4-10. In both sections the theological statements "God is light" (1 Jn 1:5) and "God is Father" (1 Jn 3:1-2) are balanced by an appeal for ethical behavior. The primary difference of course is the imagery: the language of living in the light is replaced by living as God's children. First John 3:4-9 forms six lines, each of which divides roughly in half—the first phrase or sentence makes a claim, and the second either develops further (1 Jn 3:4, 5, 7, 9) or provides a contrast (1 Jn 3:6, 8, similar to the structure of 1 Jn 1:6–2:2). Finally, 1 John 3:10 draws the section to a close by stating how to distinguish between the children of God and the children of the devil (or the secessionists).

Table 5.4

Claim	Development
1 John 3:4: "Everyone who commits sin practices lawlessness;	and sin is lawlessness."
1 John 3:5: "You know that he was revealed so that he might take away sins;	and there is no sin in him."
1 John 3:6: "Everyone who remains in him does not sin;	everyone who sins has not seen him or known him."
1 John 3:7: "Children, let no one deceive you. The one who does what is right is righteous,	just as he is righteous."
1 John 3:8: "The one who commits sin is of the devil, for the devil has sinned from the beginning.	The Son of God was revealed for this purpose; to destroy the devil's works."
1 John 3:9: "Everyone who has been born of God does not sin, because his seed remains in him;	. . . he is not able to sin, because he has been born of God."

---

[10]Brown, *Epistles of John*, 423.

In 1 John 3:4-6, John's main concern is to set out the first (negative) condition for living as children of God: renunciation of sin. The greatest roadblock to meeting Christ with confidence (1 Jn 2:28) and living into the identity of a child of God is a life of sin, which those who left the community have ignored as unimportant (1 Jn 1:8, 10). John describes the nature of sin as lawlessness (*anomia*), yet this is not merely a definition of sin, as if sin equals lawlessness, full stop. Rather, the sin John's readers must avoid is the very sin of the secessionists, the apocalyptic sin of lawlessness or rejection of doctrine (that Christ has come in the flesh) and ethics (loving brothers and sisters). In the next verse, John restates that Jesus is both sinless and the one who takes away sin (compare with 1 Jn 1:9; 2:1-2). Therefore, everyone "who remains in him does not sin" (1 Jn 3:6). The child of God must renounce sin as a habit, because "everyone who sins has not seen him or known him" (1 Jn 3:6). The verb *sins* is in the present tense and likely indicates not just the fact of sinning but the ongoing nature of sinning. John is clear that children of God deceive themselves if they claim to be without sin (1 Jn 1:8) and that the letter itself was written in the inevitable event that children of God sin (1 Jn 2:1-2).

First John 3:7-9 distinguishes between the children of God and the children of the devil. John warns, "Children, let no one deceive you," and this likely indicates that the letter is intended to keep his readers from being deceived by the secessionists themselves. What will keep them from deception is to observe their actions: "the one who does what is right is righteous" (1 Jn 3:7). Actions matter, and even though what the children of God will be (1 Jn 3:2) has not yet appeared, the future hope of seeing Christ starts to transform behavior now. The only way John's readers know what is right or pure is to see Christ's righteousness and purity (1 Jn 3:3, 7). The one who loses sight of such hope of righteousness and purity—the one giving in to the habit of sin and deception (1 Jn 3:7)—is "of the devil" (1 Jn 3:8). In order to encourage his readers, John argues that the "Son of God was revealed . . . to destroy the devil's works" (1 Jn 3:8). Finally, 1 John 3:9 insists that anyone "who has been born of God does not sin, because his seed remains in him." Again, the present tense of the verb suggests the child of God does not practice or continue in sin because the new identity as a child of God (the seed) is true of them (1 Jn 3:1-2).

The section is drawn to a close by John's statement in 1 John 3:10: "This is how God's children and the devil's children become obvious." Though it is possible the phrase "this is" could point forward to loving brother or sister as the distinguishing mark between the children of God and the children of the devil, it seems more likely that it refers back to 1 John 3:4-9 as a subsection. Thus, sinning is the point of distinction, and the reference to not doing what is right, especially failing to love one's brother or sister, anticipates the next section (1 Jn 3:11-24).

COMMENTARY | PART TWO "GOD IS LOVE" | 1 JOHN 3:11-5:12

Here we come to the second major section of the letter. The two major sections are marked out by the repeated phrases "*This is the message we have heard* from him and declare to you" (1 Jn 1:5) and "For *this the message you have heard* from the beginning" (1 Jn 3:11). Whereas the first half of the letter loosely revolved around the key theological claim that God is light, Raymond Brown describes this second major section of the letter as focusing on the "gospel that we must love one another as God has loved us in Jesus Christ; only then can we love God and believe in Jesus as His Son."[11]

Love one another in practical ways (1 John 3:11-24). The ending of the previous passage, distinguishing the children of God from the children of the devil, anticipates this section in the phrase "especially the one who does not love his brother or sister" (1 Jn 3:10). As we saw a parallel between 1 John 1:6–2:2 and 1 John 3:4-10 above, there is another parallel here between 1 John 2:3-11, where obedience ("keeping the command") is described as a condition for living in the light of God, and 1 John 3:11-24, where the necessity of loving one's brothers and sisters is a condition of being a child of God.

---

[11]Brown, *Epistles of John*, 437.

The prime example of obedience is expressed in the love command: "For this is the message you have heard from the beginning: We should love one another" (1 Jn 3:11). The message "you have heard from the beginning," like the new/old command discussed in 1 John 2:7-8, is likely the gospel message the audience heard at their conversion. A substantial portion of that message was the command to love one another, given by Jesus (see Jn 13:34; 15:12, 17). In the next verse, John offers perhaps the most famous counterexample to loving one's brother. Rather than loving his brother, Cain, "who was of the evil one," murdered his brother because "his [Cain's] deeds were evil, and his brother's were righteous." The story of Cain and Abel (Gen 4:1-25) provides the background of John's reference here and constitutes the only allusion to the Old Testament in all of 1 John. Cain symbolizes the antithesis of brotherly love, exemplified in the self-giving of Jesus Christ. John reminds his readers of the message they already received "from the beginning, that we should love one another" (1 Jn 3:11). Cain is offered as the prototype of one who hates one's brother, to the point of murder (1 Jn 3:12). It is interesting that John's comment that Cain was of the evil one is not an idea present in the Genesis account; rather, it is reflected in several postbiblical Jewish sources.[12]

Just as Cain is the prototype for hating one's brother, and the secessionists by implication walk in the way of Cain, now John contrasts his believing audience with the world. Rather than seeing the secessionists and the world as two different groups, John unites them. He urges his readers, "Do not be surprised . . . if the world hates you" (1 Jn 3:13). In the next verse the readers are encouraged because "we know that we have passed from death to life because we love our brothers and sisters" (1 Jn 3:14). John insists that the act of loving fellow believers is what differentiates them from the world. For John, those who do not love, such as Cain, remain in death. This final phrase of 1 John 3:14, then, transitions to the next verse, where John makes the implicit connection between Cain as a murderer and the one who does not love one's brother or sister:

---

[12]For example, Philo, *On the Posterity and Exile of Cain* 11.38; *On the Migration of Abraham* 12.74; Josephus, *Ant.* 1.65; Jubilees 4.15; *1 Clement* 4.7.

"Everyone who hates his brother or sister is a murderer" (1 Jn 3:15, an idea very similar to Jesus' teaching in Mt 5:21). John concludes, "You know that no murderer has eternal life residing in him."

In 1 John 3:16, John turns from the negative example of Cain to the positive example of Christ, who "laid down his life for us" (1 Jn 3:16). He argues that the only way we know love is that Jesus laid down his life. According to Hall Harris, the verb "laid down" (a form of *tithēmi*) is "unique to the Gospel of John (10:11, 15, 17, 18; 13:37, 38; 15:13) and 1 John (only here). From John's perspective Jesus' act in giving up his life was a voluntary one; Jesus was always completely in control of the situation surrounding his arrest, trials, and crucifixion (see Jn 10:18)."[13] Thus, rather than having his life taken from him, Jesus willingly laid it down for others. Thus, as Jesus laid down his life, John argues that true followers of Jesus should "lay down our lives for our brothers and sisters" (1 Jn 3:16). Jesus' sacrificial death is the ultimate example of loving the neighbor. Jesus' followers, therefore, should give toward the needs of others, and thus 1 John 3:17 asks, if anyone withholds material goods from a fellow believer, "How does God's love reside in him?"

Faith and Works

The necessary unity of confession and ethics—or faith and works—is a central concern in this section. It is also a central concern of James 2. The connection between faith and works is implicit throughout 1 Peter (where the good works of Christians are on display for nonbelievers).

Though still part of the same section (1 Jn 3:11-24), the direct address "little children" marks a soft transition from considering the command to love in the negative context of the secessionists (in the example of Cain), to the more positive context of describing how the command to love should characterize the believing community. In 1 John 3:18, John notes that believers should "not love in word or speech, but in action and in truth." More than calling for sincerity or genuineness, it is love demonstrated in actions that John calls loving in truth.

---

[13]W. Hall Harris, *1, 2, 3, John: Comfort and Counsel for a Church in Crisis* (Dallas: Biblical Studies Press, 2003), 159.

First John 3:19-22 reads at first like a digression away from John's main point concerning loving one another. Referring back to love in action, 1 John 3:19 claims, "This is how we will know that we belong to the truth," namely, when love for brothers and sisters finds expression beyond words. Such action, and the knowledge or assurance it brings, "will reassure our hearts before him" (1 Jn 3:19). Love in action is a sign that one is God's child, and knowing this gives assurance.

In the next two verses, John speaks to assuring one's heart in two possible contexts: when our hearts condemn us, and when they do not. John argues that love in action should assure us "whenever our hearts condemn us; for God is greater than our hearts, and knows all things" (1 Jn 3:20). In 1 John 2:1-2, Jesus stands as the advocate for the one who acknowledges sin, which leads to assurance. Here in 1 John 3:20, John argues that God "knows all things"; he knows the degree of human brokenness and sin, and yet he still forgives. When the heart of a conscientious person brings up condemnation and thoughts that God cannot truly be a forgiving God, John argues that "God is greater than our hearts" (1 Jn 3:20). So, Christians must adopt a life of confession (1 Jn 1:6–2:2) while at the same time not losing heart. John goes on to say that if "our hearts don't condemn us, we have confidence before God" (1 Jn 3:21). Here John addresses the hope that God's child actually begins to see transformed character take root, which should lead to confidence. The point is that whether sinning and repenting (with the heart condemning, 1 Jn 3:20) or living victoriously over sin (with the heart not condemning, 1 Jn 3:21), God's children should have confident assurance of God's love and forgiveness. First John 3:22 continues this thought, connecting such confidence to receiving "whatever we ask from him because we keep his commands and do what is pleasing in his sight."

The beginning and ending of this section are connected through the parallel phrases "This is the message" (1 Jn 3:11) and "Now this is his command" (1 Jn 3:23). Stress on his command draws 1 John 3:11-24 to a close while at the same time introducing key themes appearing in the next section (believing in 1 Jn 4:1-6 and loving in 1 Jn 4:7-21). Articulating a central concern of the letter, John argues that God's command is first "that we believe in the name of his Son Jesus Christ" and second that we "love one another as he commanded us" (1 Jn 3:23). Though John has emphasized belief in Jesus' incarnation already (1 Jn 1:1-4), he will go on to say more about what to believe regarding Jesus Christ (1 Jn 4:2, 14). As for the second command, we have already seen the instruction to love one another woven through the fabric of 1 John 1–3. In the historical context of the letter, the secessionists deny both of these commands, whether verbally or through their actions.

Finally, the central concern in 1 John 3:11-24 is summarized in 1 John 3:24: "The one who keeps his commands remains in him, and he in him." Loving others functions as reassurance that one is a child of God. Yet, John extends this insight by adding that assurance also comes "from the Spirit he has given us." The work of the Holy Spirit has already been introduced implicitly in John's discussion of the anointing (1 Jn 2:20, 27) and anticipates the need to distinguish between the Holy Spirit and false spirits, whose goal is to deceive.

Beware of false prophets who would deceive you (1 John 4:1-6). Those who believe and love (1 Jn 3:23) are challenged now to discern the Spirit of God from the spirit of antichrist. As noted above, 1 John 4:1-6 discusses further what we should believe: "Dear friends, do not believe every spirit" (1 Jn 4:1), and 1 John 4:7-21 once again takes up how we are to love: "Dear friends, let us love one another" (1 Jn 4:7). This section concerning the need to test the spirits has a clear connection to the previous section. In 1 John 3:2 John mentioned "the Spirit he has given us," which anticipates the instruction to discern between "the Spirit of truth and the spirit of deception" (1 Jn 4:6). This transition and connection between opening ("test the spirits," 1 Jn 4:1) and closing ("know the Spirit of truth and the spirit of deception," 1 Jn 4:6) clearly mark off the limits of the passage.

The end of the passage offers a helpful lens through which to view the opening exhortation. First John 4:6 draws the conclusion, "This is how we know the Spirit of truth and the spirit of deception" (1 Jn 4:6). With this insight in place, 1 John 4:1 does not challenge readers to test or discern between any number of various spirits but rather to make a clear distinction between just two: the Holy Spirit and the spirit of error. John warns his readers not to "believe every spirit" because not all of them are from God; rather, they are to "test [*dokimazete*] the spirits to see if they are from God" (1 Jn 4:1). Any child of God can evaluate whether a spirit is from God because each one has the "anointing" that enables them to know "all things" (1 Jn 2:20, 27). The test is spelled out in greater detail in the following verse, but here it is important to make a few observations. First, John goes on to give the reason the test is necessary, "because many false prophets have gone out into the world" (1 Jn 4:1). These false prophets are most likely the secessionists who went out from the Christian community and aligned themselves with the world (1 Jn 2:18-19; 2 Jn 7). They are false prophets because of what they deny about Christ. This leads to a second and very important observation: the test is not given to spirits, as if John's readers are being told to speak directly to spiritual powers. Rather, the readers are to evaluate what the false prophets, those very human secessionists, say about Christ.

In 1 John 4:2 John explains how the test works: "Every spirit that confesses that Jesus Christ has come in the flesh is from God." This is clearly a christological test focusing on the crucial importance of Jesus' incarnation. If one denies that Jesus came in the flesh, as the secessionists do, this anti-confession is animated by the spirit of error. Here *spirit* signifies the animating force behind the person making the claim. Therefore, the correct christological claim that Jesus is the Son of God come in the flesh is in fact animated by the Holy Spirit. On the other hand, denying this claim is motivated by the spirit of error. John's readers are challenged to distinguish between the two by means of this christological test.

The confession animated by the spirit of error is summarized in 1 John 4:3: "Every spirit who does not confess Jesus is not from God." Furthermore, to deny Jesus as incarnate Lord is an activity animated by the spirit of antichrist, and John's readers know this spirit is coming and "even now it is already in the world" because the secessionists have gone into the world. Note how well John's theology here anticipates a trinitarian understanding of God: the true child of the Father confirms her status as a child by confessing the incarnation of Jesus Christ as the Son of God (see 1 Jn 4:9-10, 14-15; 5:10-13) through the Spirit of truth.

Having discussed the two spirits, the Spirit of truth (or the one that is from God) and the spirit of deceit (or the spirit of antichrist), 1 John 4:4 turns to discuss the two groups of people who manifest those two spirits. John says, "You are from God, little children," implicitly because they make the right confession about Jesus come in the flesh through the guidance of the Spirit of truth. And because of this, "you have conquered them, because the one who is in you is greater than the one who is in the world" (1 Jn 4:4). "Them" refers to the secessionist opponents, called false prophets in 1 John 4:1, and the "one who is in you" is the Spirit of truth (the anointing of 1 Jn 2:20, 27), who is greater than the spirit of antichrist, "who is in the world."

By contrast, they (the secessionists) "are from the world," and therefore "what they say is from the world, and the world listens to them" (1 Jn 4:5). John has already connected the secessionists to the false prophets who have gone into the world, and here he reiterates that point—they are at home in the world more than in the believing community. Finally, in 1 John 4:6, John assures his readers that they are from God because "anyone who knows God listens to us," which is a contrast with the secessionists, who are in conversation with the world. Also, listening "to us" is likely a reference to the apostolic witness regarding Jesus' incarnation in keeping with John's use of *we* in the prologue (1 Jn 1:1-4). John claims that, under the guidance of the Holy Spirit, the faithful tradition concerning Jesus Christ—right teaching about Christology—was handed down by apostolic witness and now is recorded in this letter. By means of this faithful apostolic witness, John's readers can "know the Spirit of truth and the spirit of deception."

Love one another as God loves us in Christ (1 John 4:7–5:4a). John returns to the theme of loving one another announced in 1 John 3:23: "This is his command: that we . . . love one another as he commanded us." Here he instructs his readers to love: "Dear friends, let us love one another" (1 Jn 4:7). The phrase "dear friends" indicates the beginning of a new section, where John once again identifies mutual love for one another as the key characteristic marking out those "from God" (1 Jn 4:6). This is in implicit contrast to the secessionists, who, hating brothers and sisters (1 Jn 3:13), are influenced by the spirit of the antichrist.

The precise way in which love is from God finds more detail later in the passage (1 Jn 4:9-10), but here John states once again that the one who loves is a child of God ("has been born of God and knows God," 1 Jn 4:7). As noted previously, it is not the act of loving that makes one a child, but the fact of being God's child leads to the act of loving one another. Thus, John can state the same truth negatively in the next verse: "The one who does not love does not know God, because God is love" (1 Jn 4:8). Of course, "his commands" refers ultimately to the instruction to love one another, and in both 1 John 2:4 and 1 John 4:8 loving one's brothers and sisters is connected to truly knowing God—the one who loves knows God. For John, knowing entails both confession ("Christ came in the flesh") and a transformation of character ("love one another"). Like the similar claims "God is light" (1 Jn 1:5) and implicitly that God is Father (1 Jn 3:1), the claim that God is love is not merely stating that God loves, "for loving is not just another action of God, like ruling. Rather, all God's activity is loving activity. Nor does the author say, 'Love is God'; for he is interested in the loving activity of a person, not in abstract definitions."[14]

The way in which God has loved is revealed in 1 John 4:9-10. It is important to note that immediately after claiming that God is love, John describes the way in which God's love was revealed to the world, in his sending "his one and only Son into the world" (1 Jn 4:9). The revelation of God's love is not a secret truth only accessible by those with special initiation; rather, this is a public display of God's love through the sending of the Son. The mission of God's Son was to be sent into the world "so that we might live through him," and this act of sending entails an important

---

[14]Brown, *Epistles of John*, 515.

relationship between the Father and the Son. Furthermore, John continues in the next verse to describe what God's love consists of: "not that we loved God, but that he loved us and sent his Son to be the atoning sacrifice for our sins" (1 Jn 4:10). Again, the character of God's love is revealed in the Father sending the Son, and the purpose of the Father sending the Son was so that he would "be the atoning sacrifice [*hilasmon*] for our sins." This phrase at the end of 1 John 4:10 describes further how, by the Son's being sent into the world, "we might live through him." John's readers live by means of the atoning sacrifice of Christ on behalf of sin.

The next step in the discussion is that, if the love of God incarnate in Jesus is revealed *to* us (1 Jn 4:7-10), then that same love must be incarnate *in* us (1 Jn 4:11-16). First John 4:11 argues that because God greatly loved his readers, they in turn must also love one another. Part of the principle here is that discipleship (being loved by God, knowing God, growing in holiness before God) cannot be separated from mission. The connection between God's love for his children and their love for others is further implied in 1 John 4:12. Though God is not seen, John argues, "If we love one another, God remains in us and his love is made complete in us." Thus, the invisible God is made visible in the love believers show toward one another. It is unclear whether the phrase "This is how we know" in 1 John 4:13 refers back to the act of loving one another or refers to what comes in the following verses regarding seeing and testifying about the Father sending the Son, because the activity of the Spirit is central in both loving (what comes before) and having faith (what comes next). Either way, John speaks of God's gift of the Spirit as giving assurance that "we remain in him and he in us" (1 Jn 4:13). Recalling the apostolic testimony that opened the letter (the *we* in 1 Jn 1:1-4), here John restates the content of that witness: "we have seen and we testify that the Father has sent his Son as the world's Savior" (1 Jn 4:14). And the confession arising out of this apostolic seeing and testifying is that "whoever confesses that Jesus is the Son of God—God remains in him and he in God" (1 Jn 4:15). Here a connection is drawn once again between the apostolic testimony and the correct christological confession regarding the Son. John then provides a subconclusion to this section, stating, "We have come to know and to believe the love that God has for us" (1 Jn 4:16).

In the middle of 1 John 4:16 there seems to be a shift within John's discussion of love. In the second half of the verse, John restates the premise of the section, "God is love," repeating the same claim of 1 John 4:8. Such repetition creates a degree of rhythm throughout the passage. One can distinguish the first claim that God is love in 1 John 4:8, which is followed by the revelation of God's love in the Father sending the Son into the world (1 Jn 4:9), and the second statement that God is love in 1 John 4:16, which is followed by a kind of result, stressing remaining or abiding in God: "God is love, and the one who remains in love remains in God." In the next verse, John reflects on two notions he has mentioned previously: (God's) love made complete (1 Jn 2:5; 4:12) and confidence in the day of judgment (1 Jn 2:28). It is God's love for us that is made complete, and the expression of love's completion (or "perfection," ESV) is seen especially in Christians loving one another. Attaining such love completed within us results in confidence at Jesus' coming "in the day of judgment" (1 Jn 4:17). John concludes that such confidence and love is "because as he is, so also are we in this world." This confusing phrase surely is translated more clearly in the NIV: "In this world we are like Jesus" (1 Jn 4:17). Therefore, "believers who love one another in this world, in the same way as Christ loved his disciples . . . when he was in the world, show that they live in God, and therefore they need have no fear as they face the day of judgment."[15]

Developing the theme of confidence and love, John argues, "There is no fear in love; instead, perfect love drives out fear" (1 Jn 4:18). Having mentioned confidence in the day of judgment, it is likely that John encourages his readers that future judgment should not provoke fear, especially from those who are living out the love displayed in the Son's atoning sacrifice toward one another. It is fear of judgment John has in mind as he clarifies "because fear involves punishment" (1 Jn 4:18). Within the logic of the passage, the one living in fear is necessarily one

---

[15]Kruse, *Letters of John*, 168.

who is not loving and thus lacking confidence at the coming judgment, and therefore this one is not complete in love (1 Jn 2:5; 4:12, 17). In 1 John 4:19 the theme of confidence continues, yet implicitly with a contrast. We do not fear; rather "we love, because he first loved us" (1 Jn 4:19). One should be confident knowing that God is the one who initiates love, which is a theme repeated throughout this section—"he loved us" (1 John 4:10); "the love that God has for us" (1 Jn 4:16).

The next two verses of this section restate themes related to love in the immediate passage. The claim "I love God," accompanied by hatred for one's brothers and sisters, is a false claim; "he is a liar" (1 Jn 4:20). This theme is pervasive throughout the letter (1 Jn 2:9-11; 3:11-24; 4:7-21; 5:2). The reason this claim is false is that failing to love one's brother or sister "whom he has seen" means he "cannot love God whom he has not seen" (1 Jn 4:20). Once again, John stresses the necessary connection between loving God and loving fellow believers, a connection he makes emphatic in the final verse of the section: "The one who loves God must also love his brother and sister" (1 Jn 4:21).

Whereas John reintroduces the theme of believing that Jesus is the Christ, 1 John 5:1-4 is a continuation of the larger discussion of love in 1 John 4:7–5:4. After reengaging the discussion of belief, the subject of loving those who are children of God continues the passage's main theme. The subunit of 1 John 5:1-4 draws to a close with a description of the victory God's children have over the world.

At the beginning of this section, John argued that the one who loves has been born of God (1 Jn 4:7), and here he claims that the one "who believes that Jesus is the Christ has been born of God" (1 Jn 5:1), restating the two themes announced together in 1 John 3:23. Furthermore, within the discussion of love (1 Jn 4:7–5:4), John has made reference to the necessity of confessing faith in Jesus Christ: "Whoever confesses that Jesus is the Son of God—God remains in him" (1 Jn 4:15). This reinforces the notion that both believing Jesus is the Christ, the Son of God come in the flesh, and loving one's brother or sister are necessary for the children of God. This is restated in the second half of the verse: "and everyone

who loves the Father also loves the one born of him" (1 Jn 5:1). To stress
the verbal expression in the original Greek, one might translate, as Brown
does, "Everyone who loves the parent loves the child begotten by him."[16]
This rendering stresses the necessary link between loving the Father and
loving fellow believers born of the Father.

How do John's readers know that they actually love the children of
God? John answers this question in 1 John 5:2, "when we love God and
obey his commands." Whereas earlier in the letter John has required that
claims to love God must be accompanied by genuine love for fellow believers, here he reverses that connection to offer assurance that believers
know they love fellow believers by loving God and keeping his commands. Rather than exposing a logical inconsistency, John seems merely
to be insisting that loving God and loving fellow believers cannot exist
apart from each other. Love for God is to keep his commands, and, as we
have seen throughout 1 John, God's primary command is to love one
another. The next sentence spans the end of 1 John 5:3 and the beginning
of 1 John 5:4: "And his commands are not a burden, because everyone
who has been born of God conquers the world." That God's commands
are not a burden to those who know him and have been born of God
makes sense because God remains in them. This has been an emphasis
throughout the letter, specifically the way God remains in the believer is
through the Holy Spirit (or the anointing). The final idea closing John's
long discussion of love (1 Jn 4:7–5:4) insists that the one born of God (the
one who loves and believes) conquers the world. This idea forms a link
with the following section, where the nature of this victory is discussed.

Never compromise your testimony (1 John 5:4b-12). The previous section
focused on the necessity of loving one another (1 Jn 4:7–5:4a) and concluded with the encouragement that "everyone who has been born of
God conquers [*nikē*] the world" (1 Jn 5:4). Here the world is not the earth,
or good creation, but the evil world order, which stands in opposition to
God. In the second half of 1 John 5:4, John clarifies: "This is the victory

---

[16]Brown, *Epistles of John*, 566.

[*nikē*] that has conquered [*nikēsasa*] the world: our faith." Faith in the context of 1 John is the specific confession that the Father sent his Son into the world, the Son of God, who, we will learn a few verses later, is the one who "came by water and blood" (1 Jn 5:6). It is by this faith, faith in Jesus Christ, that John's readers have conquered the world. The next verse outlines further the content of "our faith" by stating that the "one who conquers [*hē nikē*] the world . . . believes that Jesus is the Son of God" (1 Jn 5:5). The true children of God believe that Jesus is the Son of God, and by means of this faith they overcome the false teaching and resistance to the apostolic message represented by the world. What is, then, the conquering power that conquers the world? The Gospel of John says it is Jesus: "Be courageous! I have conquered the world" (Jn 16:33). Through faith, the children of God have a part in Christ's victory that overcomes the world. In the context of the letter, it is the conversion and baptism of John's readers that constituted a specific moment in the past where their faith conquered the world.

John now clarifies who this Jesus Christ is: "the one who came by water and blood" (1 Jn 5:6). That John is stressing the testimony to Jesus' identity is made clear by the reference to the Spirit testifying in 1 John 5:6, accompanied by a brief discussion of the three testifying—the water, blood, and Spirit—finally connecting the discussion of human versus divine testimony in 1 John 5:9-12 in the next section. It was not by water only, but by water and by blood that Jesus came, and the "Spirit is the one who testifies" about this truth. John's cryptic language here has proven difficult to understand with precision. It is clear that water, blood, and Spirit are all witnesses giving testimony concerning Jesus Christ. It is also clear that in John's immediate context the fact that Jesus came by water was not disputed (either by John's audience or presumably by the secessionists), but that he came by water and by blood is disputed, along with the Spirit's testimony. Perhaps the best way to understand the reference here is to the water and blood that flowed from Jesus' side at his crucifixion (Jn 19:34), and perhaps John is arguing that this was a clear testimony about who Jesus was—that he was the atoning sacrifice for the sins of the world.

GOING DEEPER: WATER AND BLOOD

What do the "water and blood" refer to? There are four major views:

1. That Jesus came by/in water and blood, for some, refers to the sacraments of baptism and the Eucharist (the Lord's Supper). Some early interpreters of 1 John (Ambrose, Augustine, Chrysostom, Cyril of Alexandria) argued that Christ came bringing the sacraments—water referring to baptism, and blood referring to the blood of Christ in the Lord's Supper. However, this would be an obscure way of referring to the sacraments (a reference to the body of Christ is missing), and there is no evidence in 1 John that the secessionists denied the sacraments.

2. Others argue that "came by/in water and blood" refers to the incarnation in general. In the Gospel of John, the verb *come* is used to refer to the entrance of the Word into the world (Jn 1:11; 16:28; 5:43), and in John's letters *come* plus the preposition *en* is used twice, both referring to Christ coming in the flesh (1 Jn 4:2; 2 Jn 7). Thus, because the secessionists denied that Jesus was fully human, John's statement about water and blood is understood as a statement about the reality of Jesus' body—stressing the corporal nature of the incarnation. The problem with this view is that it does not account for the Spirit—the Spirit is associated with Jesus' baptism and death but not the incarnation.

3. It is possible that "came by/in water and blood" refers to the baptism and the death of Jesus—the beginning and ending points of his ministry. Water of course was used at Jesus' baptism (Jn 1:26, 31, 33), and blood, then, refers to Jesus' death (Jn 19:34). That Jesus came by/in water and blood is perhaps, then, a statement about how Jesus' life and death contributed to his identity as Son of God—both water and blood testifying to that fact. Though this is a common way of understanding the passage, the Greek preposition "by" (*dia*) would be problematic, because it links water and blood grammatically, which would suggest that water and blood refer to one action, not two chronologically separate actions (like Jesus' baptism and death). Thus water and blood, on this view, more likely refers to one event rather than two events.

4. Finally, some ancient (Augustine) and modern (Raymond Brown) interpreters argue that "come by/in water and blood" refers only to the death of Jesus. Just after Jesus died, blood and water flowed from his

side (Jn 19:34). Significantly, this is the only other Johannine passage where the two elements are joined. Here the water and blood are together a powerful witness to the significance of Jesus' death. However, the question remains as to how is Jesus' death, marked by the witness of water and blood, also his "coming"? Though this seems like an obstacle, just before his death sentence Jesus says that "I have come into the world for this" (Jn 18:37). Perhaps, then, Jesus is announced as the Christ through his unique death, by the Spirit's power, when the water and blood poured out from his side at the crucifixion.

In the following verses (1 Jn 5:7-8), John claims that there are three that testify, and these three are the Spirit, water, and blood. It seems that John identifies three witnesses that testify to the truth of Jesus' identity as Son of God because Deuteronomy 19:15 states, "A fact must be established by the testimony of two or three witnesses." The testimony of the Spirit seems clear; he remains in John's readers, so they need no one to teach them (1 Jn 2:27), and it is by the Spirit of God they know Jesus Christ has come in the flesh (1 Jn 4:2). Yet it is less clear how the water and blood offer their testimony. John argues that "these three are in agreement" (1 Jn 5:8). With the unity of the three witnesses stated, John continues with the theme of witness in the next section.

Concluding his discussion of the Spirit, the water, and the blood, John turns to God's own testimony. It is likely that John was influenced by the pattern of ascending witnesses in John 5:31-40. In the Gospel, the first witness to Jesus is John the Baptist. The "greater testimony than John's" listed in John 5:36-44 includes Jesus' works given him by the Father, the Scriptures inspired by God, and the testimony of the Father himself. In a similar fashion, the witnesses of Spirit, water, and blood are sent from God to testify regarding the Son and are then followed by a witness from God himself. First John 5:9 sets out a lesser-to-greater argument: "If we accept human testimony, God's testimony is greater." That is, if we accept the human testimony in general, then we should certainly accept God's testimony, and this testimony is about his Son.

Furthermore, John argues, "The one who believes in the Son of God has this testimony within himself" (1 Jn 5:10). It is important to note that, whereas the Spirit's work is emphasized in 1 John, it is the testimony itself that is internalized here. Thus, the internalized testimony is most likely the witness concerning Jesus Christ, that he is the Son of God come in the flesh—the very message John's audience received from the apostolic testimony (1 Jn 1:1-4). Then, as characteristic in many instances, John restates the opposite: "The one who does not believe God has made him

GOING DEEPER: COMMA JOHANNEUM

One of the more famous examples of textual criticism in the New Testament is found in 1 John 5:6-8. Additional lines of text are preserved in 1 John 5:7-8 in some later manuscripts that the translators of the King James Version used in their work. The presentation of these extra lines in King James has been labeled the Comma Johanneum (or the Johannine Clause). The additional phrases are noted below in italics:

> Jesus Christ—he is the one who came by water and blood, not by water only, but by water and by blood. And the Spirit is the one who testifies, because the Spirit is the truth. For there are three that testify: [*in heaven: the Father, the Word, and the Holy Spirit, and these three are one. And there are three who bear witness on earth:*] the Spirit, the water, and the blood—and these three are in agreement. (1 Jn 5:6-8)

The evidence is decidedly against the authenticity of the extra phrases. Manuscript evidence shows the longer reading only appears in nine late manuscripts, and four of these only record extra words in the margin. The majority of these nine manuscripts date from the sixteenth century, with the earliest manuscript (Codex 221) only dating to the tenth century. But the marginal note in Codex 221 seems to be an addition to the original text and therefore likely is from a later date. The oldest manuscript with the added phrases in its main text (that is, not in the margin only) dates from the fourteenth century, which is quite late. All of this together constitutes a weak case for the authenticity of these phrases.

a liar, because he has not believed in the testimony God has given about his Son" (1 Jn 5:10). It is interesting to note that failing to acknowledge sin (1 Jn 1:10) and failing to believe God's testimony about his own Son (1 Jn 5:10) both result in making God a liar—"A wrong ethical stance and a wrong Christological stance have the same effect because both impugn what God did in sending His Son."[17]

Having emphasized receiving God's testimony, John now describes its content: "this is the testimony: God has given us eternal life, and this life is in his Son" (1 Jn 5:11). Kruse helpfully notes, "Up to this point the author has emphasized God's witness concerning the person (came in the flesh) and work (came by water and blood) of the historical Jesus, but here he emphasizes God's testimony concerning the benefit made available to believers through him."[18] The benefit is eternal life, which is Jesus himself (1 Jn 5:20), who has been with the Father from the beginning (1 Jn 1:2). Therefore, John concludes very simply, "The one who has the Son has life," but the one who "does not have the Son of God does not have life" (1 Jn 5:12).

COMMENTARY | CONCLUSION: THE BOLDNESS AND CONFIDENCE OF THOSE WHO WALK IN GOD'S LIGHT AND LOVE | 1 JOHN 5:13-21

John states the purpose for writing: "so that you may know that you have eternal life" (1 Jn 5:13). John drew his description of God's testimony to a conclusion in the previous section by stressing that God has given us eternal life and that we must have the Son in order to have this life. Now, in drawing the letter to a close, John offers those "who believe in the name of the Son of God" assurance of that eternal life. Here, John is clear about the aim and intention of his letter, which echoes the purpose of the Gospel of John as well: "These are written so that you may believe that Jesus is the Messiah, the Son of God, and that by believing you may have life in his name" (Jn 20:31).

---

[17]Brown, *Epistles of John*, 602.
[18]Kruse, *Letters of John*, 182.

Next, John focuses on an aspect of assurance, namely, that of confidence in actions flowing from being a child of God. This "confidence we have before him" or in his presence, comes first in the form of prayer: "If we ask anything according to his will, he hears us" (1 Jn 5:14). This notion surfaced previously in 1 John 3:22, where confidence before God (1 Jn 3:21) was directly connected to "keep[ing] his commands and do[ing] what is pleasing in his sight" (1 Jn 3:22). Here confidence is connected to having eternal life in the Son (1 Jn 5:12-13). This confidence in prayer is further amplified because "if we know that he hears whatever we ask, we know that we have what we have asked of him" (1 Jn 5:15), and all of this "according to his will" (1 Jn 5:14).

The general instruction regarding confidence in prayer then gives way to the specific example of praying about sin and especially praying for believers who fall into sin in 1 John 5:16-17. The condition is given in 1 John 5:16: "If anyone sees a fellow believer committing a sin that doesn't lead to death, he should ask, and God will give life to him" (1 Jn 5:16). John has already noted that "if anyone does sin, we have an advocate with the Father—Jesus Christ the righteous one" (1 Jn 2:1). If Jesus is the advocate for sinners, then the child of God can have "confidence . . . before him" or in his presence (1 Jn 5:14) and pray that "God will give life to him" (1 Jn 5:16), namely, the fellow believer who falls into sin. Thus, though a child of God falls into sin, through prayer and ultimately the atoning sacrifice of Jesus, the believer can continue in eternal life, the life given by God through Christ. Yet, John goes on to emphasize that prayers should be made and life is given to the one "committing a sin that doesn't lead to death," because "there is sin that leads to death. I am not saying he should pray about that" (1 Jn 5:16).

In the next verse, John summarizes his example of confidence in prayer over believers who sin by saying, "All unrighteousness is sin, and there is sin that doesn't lead to death" (1 Jn 5:17). Though once again this might lead us to ask what is the sin that leads to death, the key observation to make is that John is making an implicit distinction not between sins (that is, one that leads to death and one that does not), but rather between a believer who sins and a nonbeliever who sins. The result of the sin committed by a "brother" or fellow believer is not eschatological death; however, the sin committed by a nonbeliever of course does ultimately result in death. Throughout the letter John has had the secessionists in mind, the ones he calls antichrists who have gone into the world. The reason their sin leads to death is that they persistently deny Christ in what they believe (Jesus Christ did not come in the flesh) and their actions. Thus, it is in their "Christ-rejecting behavior evidenced by" their denial of "their own sinfulness, their need for atonement, and Christ's ability to provide that atonement" that results in their eschatological "death."[19]

John draws his instruction to a close by restating several key insights shared throughout the letter, all of which stress the assurance that all who are born of God have because "we know" (1 Jn 5:18-20). This threefold repeated phrase structures this final passage of the letter by naming the specific benefits of being a child of God (1 Jn 5:18), of belonging to God (1 Jn 5:19), and of knowing God (1 Jn 5:20).

In 1 John 5:18 John restates the character transformation that occurs in the life of a child of God: "We know that everyone who has been born of God does not sin." The verb *sin* appears in the present tense and likely indicates an ongoing disposition of sin (thus the ESV translates, "does not keep on sinning"). This claim John first made and expanded in 1 John 3:4-10 is now summarized. Yet, here he adds, "but the one who is born of God keeps him, and the evil one does not touch him" (1 Jn 5:18). Whereas throughout 1 John the phrase "the one born of God" usually refers to believers, here it must refer to Jesus as the Son because the one born of God is the one who keeps believers from the evil one (an idea reminiscent of Jn 17:12-15).

First John 5:19 restates the benefit of being from God, which places believers in a different position with respect to the world: "We know that we are of God, and the whole world is under the sway of the evil one."

---

[19]Tim Ward, "Sin 'Not unto Death' and Sin 'Unto Death' in 1 John 5:15," *Churchman* 109 (1995): 236.

The mark of distinction between John's readers and the world is that they are from God and therefore are no longer under the influence of the world. This underlines the distinction made between John's readers and the secessionists, which he has been making throughout the letter (1 Jn 2:18-19; 4:1-5 especially).

Finally, in 1 John 5:20 John reiterates the key role the Son of God has in giving his readers assurance that they know the true God: "the Son of God . . . has given us understanding so that we may know the true one" (1 Jn 5:20). Earlier in the letter, John assured his readers that the anointing teaches them all things (1 Jn 2:27), and earlier in 1 John 5 it was the testimony of God the Father that revealed the coming of the Son. Perhaps this is a reciprocal making known between the Father, the Son, and the Spirit at work in 1 John. The Son gives understanding about God and, more, assures us that "We are in the true one—that is, in his Son Jesus Christ. He is the true God and eternal life" (1 Jn 5:20). Thus, John's readers are assured that they are in Christ, which separates them from the world and unites them as the children born of God. Both God and Jesus Christ are called the true one, and John concludes 1 John 5:20 with the phrase "He is the true God and eternal life," which grammatically could refer either to God or to Jesus Christ. Brown notes: "Many commentators point out that surely the author does not yet mean what Nicaea means by 'true God of true God,' even though the reference in 5:20 to both Father and Son as 'true' may have led to that formula."[20] In the end, the phrase most likely refers to Jesus, and thus constitutes a strong claim to the divinity of Jesus Christ.

The final word of 1 John is a warning, which is somewhat the negative counterpart of the three positive words of assurance in 1 John 5:18-20. Absent from any formal salutation, John concludes by warning, "Little children, guard yourselves from idols" (1 Jn 5:21). In this warning John seems to assume a covenant context where there is a negative connection between the true God (1 Jn 5:20) and idols, or false gods (1 Jn 5:21). God's

---

[20]Brown, *Epistles of John*, 640.

covenant people were constantly warned not to leave the one true God and go after idols. It seems clear that John thinks of the secessionists as those who have abandoned the one true God and by implication have redirected their focus (and worship) to that which is not God—idols. As John understands that the secessionists are trying to seduce the readers, this warning summarizes much of the concern of the letter as a whole.

FURTHER READING | 1-3 JOHN COMMENTARIES AND MONOGRAPHS

T: technical; ★: recommended; ★★: highly recommended

T★★ Brown, Raymond E. *The Epistles of John.* AB. New York: Doubleday, 1982.

Dodd, C. H. *The Johannine Epistles.* MNTC. London: Hodder & Stoughton, 1947.

★★ Kruse, Colin G. *The Letters of John.* PNTC. Grand Rapids, MI: Eerdmans, 2000.

Lieu, Judith. *The Theology of the Johannine Epistles.* NTT. Cambridge: Cambridge University Press, 1991.

Marshall, I. Howard. *The Epistles of John.* NICNT. Grand Rapids, MI: Eerdmans, 1978.

Painter, John. *1, 2, and 3 John.* Sacra Pagina. Collegeville, MN: Liturgical Press, 2008.

T Smalley, Stephen S. *1, 2, 3, John.* WBC. Nashville: Thomas Nelson, 2007.

T Strecker, Georg. *The Johannine Letters: A Commentary on 1, 2, and 3 John.* Hermeneia. Translated by Linda M. Maloney. Minneapolis: Fortress, 1996.

★ Yarbrough, Robert W. *Johannine Epistles.* BECNT. Grand Rapids, MI: Baker, 2008.

CHAPTER FIVE

The Letters of 2-3 John

OFTEN THE LETTERS OF John, Revelation, and the Gospel of John are read or studied together as a collection of Johannine literature. The link connecting these texts, of course, is the historical author John. As noted in the previous chapter, the early church generally recognized that these texts shared common authorship by John, but what is interesting is that this did not lead to an early adaptation of a Johannine corpus—the publication of John's writings as an independent collection. In fact, there is no plausible indication in the manuscript evidence that a so-called Johannine corpus ever circulated. The Gospel of John usually circulated with the other Gospels, and Revelation was collected at the end of the New Testament as a kind of climax to the canon. The letters of John, being separated from the Gospel and Revelation, were finally set within the Catholic Epistles, interestingly enough separated from Revelation by Jude.

There are several similarities that draw 1–3 John together. First, 1 and 2 John both speak to the same situation, where a secessionist group "went out from us" and denied "the coming of Jesus Christ in the flesh" (1 Jn 2:19, 22-23; 2 Jn 7). Second, John labels the secessionists as antichrists in 1 John (1 Jn 2:18, 22), as does the Elder in 2 John (2 Jn 7). The centrality of the love command is notably shared between 1 John (1 Jn 3:11, 23; 4:7, 21; 5:1-4) and 2 John (2 Jn 4-6), along with the desire to see his children walking in the truth (1 Jn 1:3-4; 2 Jn 4). Thus, there is a clear and strong connection between 1 and 2 John.

There is an equally strong connection between 2 and 3 John. They share the same form; both follow the typical form of a Greco-Roman personal letter, including an introduction, main body, and conclusion. Both letters are written by the "Elder" (*presbyteros*; 2 Jn 1; 3 Jn 1) to those whom he loves in truth (2 Jn 1, to the "elect lady"; 3 Jn 1, to Gaius). Both letters express joy over "your children walking in truth" (2 Jn 4; 3 Jn 4), both implicitly warn of the antichrist (2 Jn 7; whom Diotrephes seems to embody, 3 Jn 9) and both letters conclude with a comment regarding wanting to talk face to face rather than to use paper and ink (2 Jn 12) or pen and ink (3 Jn 13).

In addition to this, there is one key term that draws all three letters together. The strongest connection in language shared between all three letters of John is the reoccurring term *truth* (*alētheia*). Not only does some form of *alētheia* appear in every chapter of 1 John (1 Jn 1:6, 8; 2:4, 21; 3:19; 4:6; 5:6), but the key term also stands in the opening and closing sections of the letter. After the prologue (1 Jn 1:1-4), the letter's opening set of contrasts in 1 John 1:5–2:2 articulates that those who fail to practice the truth (*poioumen tēn alētheian*; 1 Jn 1:6) will not have fellowship with God, and the one claiming to have no sin is deceived and does not have "the truth [*hē alētheia*]" (1 Jn 1:8). In 1 John 3:18 the author exhorts his readers to love "in action and in truth [*alētheia*]" and says that by such action they will know that they are of the truth (*ek tēs alētheias*; 1 Jn 3:19). Then, in 1 John 4–5, it is the "Spirit of truth [*alētheias*]" with whom John is concerned. Finally, 1 John concludes with the claim that "the Son of God has come," and therefore knowledge of "the true one," that is, Jesus Christ, and "the true God and eternal life" (1 Jn 5:20) is public. Thus, the theme and more importantly the term *alētheia* brackets the entire letter of 1 John.

The term *alētheia* in turn links 1 John to 2 and 3 John. In the opening verse of 2 John, the author qualifies his own love for the "elect lady and her children" as "in the truth [*en alētheia*]" and goes on to claim the same for "all who know the truth [tēn alētheian]." The term appears again in 2 John 2-4, where the author expresses joy over the fact that his readers have been walking the truth. Echoing 2 John 1, the term is used again in the opening verse of 3 John: "The elder: To my dear friend Gaius, whom I love in truth [en alētheia]." Then, echoing 1 John 1:6, 8; 3 John 3 expresses joy at the fact that "you are walking in truth" (en alētheia peripateis). The term also appears in 3 John 4, 8, 12.

Though all three letters share the key term *truth*, the strength and number of connections are greatest between 1 John and 2 John, and then between 2 John and 3 John. Thus, 2 John stands in close relationship to both 1 John and 3 John, while there are fewer connections between 1 John and 3 John. It seems, therefore, that 2 John is the crucial link holding the letters of John together as a complete collection.

OCCASION AND SETTING

Authorship. Both 2 and 3 John are personal letters in the typical style common of a Greco-Roman letter. Each opens with a clear letter opening that names the author and audience. Both letters are written by the "Elder" (*presbyteros*; 2 Jn 1; 3 Jn 1). Though *elder* can refer to an older person generally, it more likely refers to someone in a particular position of leadership in the early church; it also seems to be a title for an apostle. Papias refers to the apostles as elders, one of whom was John: "I inquired into the words of the elders, what Andrew or Peter or Philip or Thomas or James or John or Matthew or any other of the Lord's disciples had said" (recorded in Eusebius, *Hist. eccl.* 3.39.4).

There is little external evidence for the authorship of 2 and 3 John. The Muratorian canon refers to two epistles written by John, as does Clement of Alexandria (*Stromateis* 2.15.66). John Painter has argued that there is evidence that Irenaeus understood John as the author of both 1 and 2 John, because Irenaeus quotes 2 John 7-8 alongside 1 John 4:1-3; 5:1 not only as if they were authored by the same person, but even perhaps as if these passages came from the same text (*Haer.* 3.16.8). This could indicate that Irenaeus knew 1 and 2 John in some combined form. There are some ancient traditions that suggest there was a person known as "John the elder," not John the disciple, who was specifically responsible for writing 2 and 3 John. Jerome records the commonly held position of his time that "the elder John" was not the apostle who wrote 2 and 3 John: "the last two epistles of John are the work not of the apostle but of the presbyter" (*Lives of Illustrious Men* 9).[1]

From the letter itself, the audience seems to be familiar with the author, because there is no further introduction or elaboration on the author's identity apart from his title "the elder." The encouragement and warning against antichrist characteristic of 2 John might also suggest familiarity. The title *elder* also suggests a degree of authority and is in keeping with the author's address of the audience as children.

Audience. In its letter opening, 2 John addresses its greetings to the "elect lady [*eklektē kyria*] and her children" (2 Jn 1). Throughout the letter this group remains the primary readership, though he sometimes addresses the lady in second-person singular (2 Jn 4-5, 13) and at other times uses the second-person plural (2 Jn 6-12). There have been several suggestions for the meaning of "elect lady." Though a possibility, it is not likely to be a proper name (the lady Electa or "the noble Kyria") or a general term of respect or endearment ("dear lady"), but rather the phrase either refers to the church generally or a specific church and her congregation.[2] That the elder notes "some of your children [are] walking in truth" suggests the author is acquainted with the church but, at the same time, does not necessarily imply that some in the congregation are unfaithful.[3]

The opening of 3 John also names the author as "the elder" who writes to "my dear friend Gaius" (3 Jn 1). Though other individuals named Gaius are mentioned in the New Testament, there is no reason to connect this Gaius with those mentioned in Romans 16:23 or 1 Corinthians 1:14, as this was a very common name (though it is interesting that Paul names Gaius as his host in Rom 16). He is called "dear friend" throughout the

---

[1]*NPNF²* 3:3364.
[2]Raymond E. Brown, *The Epistles of John*, AB (New York: Doubleday, 1982), 655.
[3]C. H. Dodd, *The Johannine Epistles*, MNTC (London: Hodder & Stoughton, 1947), 147.

letter (3 Jn 1, 2, 5, 11), and "the elder" mentions not only his good health but also that "your whole life is going well" (3 Jn 2). Furthermore, the central theme of the letter concerns offering hospitality (3 Jn 5-8) or the lack thereof (3 Jn 9-10), and it seems that Gaius is a clear example of providing hospitality to Christian friends (3 Jn 5-7).

Genre. Both 2 and 3 John fit the genre of a personal letter that follows the typical Greco-Roman letter form, consisting of a letter opening (with the *x* to *y* form of address) followed by a greeting, letter body, and letter conclusion. Second and Third John are the shortest epistles in the New Testament (even shorter than Philemon and Jude). They are almost the same length (2 John at 245 and 3 John at 219 words); also, both letters conform in length to the expectation for an ancient, private letter that would have fit on a single papyrus sheet.

Whereas both texts are clearly personal letters, on account of their content they can be described more specifically. Second John might be classified as a letter of exhortation and advice, where the elder seeks to "advise and dissuade."[4] Third John essentially is a letter of recommendation, where the elder speaks on behalf of traveling evangelists and offers a commendation of Demetrius to Gaius.

The historical context in which the letters of John circulated. The clear connections between the letters of John lead to speculation regarding how they functioned together in their early reception. Were all three letters written at the same time? Were they sent together or separately? Though there is not much in the way of surviving information regarding the circumstances of these letters, we might entertain a few scenarios for the relationship between the three letters of John.

Some have suggested that John wrote to the churches in and around Ephesus and sent all three letters as a packet. In this view, Demetrius carried a letter of introduction to Gaius (3 John), along with a letter to be read in Gaius's church (2 John) as an introduction to the sermon to be delivered (1 John).

---

[4]Duane F. Watson, "A Rhetorical Analysis of 2 John According to Greco-Roman Convention," *New Testament Studies* (1989): 109.

In a slightly different historical reconstruction, it is possible that 1 John was a sermon preached in the elder's home church soon after a schism (see 1 Jn 2:19). But because the secessionists had gone out, taking their false teaching with them potentially to other churches in the area, John sends his sermon (1 John) to churches in the area with a cover letter (2 John) to "the elect lady and her children." For whatever reason, Diotrephes, perhaps a leader at one of the area churches, refuses to receive the bearers of 2 John and the sermon (1 John), and so the elder turns to his friend Gaius for support, sending Demetrius with a letter of introduction in hand (3 John). Both of these scenarios are plausible, but in the end any reconstruction of these events is historical guesswork.

STRUCTURE

Each of the letters follow the same basic pattern of a Greco-Roman letter: a letter opening, followed by the main body of the letter and the letter conclusion.

OUTLINE

2 John

    I. Letter opening (2 Jn 1-3)

    II. Letter body (2 Jn 4-11)

        A. Request concerning the love command (2 Jn 4-6)

        B. Warning against the antichrists and their teaching (2 Jn 7-11)

    III. Promise to visit and letter closing (2 Jn 12-13)

3 John

    I. Letter opening (3 Jn 1-2)

    II. Letter body (3 Jn 3-12)

        A. Joy in faithfulness (3 Jn 3-4)

        B. Request for hospitality and support (3 Jn 5-8)

        C. The opposition of Diotrephes (3 Jn 9-10)

        D. An appeal to do good and the commendation of Demetrius (3 Jn 11-12)

    III. Promise to visit and letter closing (3 Jn 13-15)[5]

[5]Brown, *Epistles of John*, 124.

COMMENTARY | 2 JOHN

Letter opening (2 John 1-3). Second John is a letter from the elder to the "elect lady," most likely a particular church, warning against showing hospitality to those failing to love one another and denying that Jesus Christ will come in the flesh.

The letter opens with a clearly named sender and addressee: "The elder: To the elect lady and her children" (2 Jn 1). Whereas the author calls himself "the elder," for later readers this does not clarify his actual identity. Judith Lieu notes that the "lack of personal name is unparalleled in a private letter and offers no guidance as to his possible identification with known figures from the early church."[6] Whereas the elder is a leading figure for the recipients, due to the fact that he writes with such authority, the office of elder is always designated in the plural form (*presbyteroi*) in the New Testament. The phrase "the elect lady and her children" could either refer to an individual or to a church (or group of churches). It is most likely that this is a figurative way of describing not only the church in general but a specific church or group of churches. Evidence for this view comes in 2 John 4, where the author says that "some of your children" are found walking in the truth. The pronoun *your* here is singular and suggests the "children" or members of a particular church. Further supporting this view, the final verse of the letter closes with, "The children of your elect sister send you greetings" (2 Jn 13), which likely refers to the church and congregation from which the author writes.

The elder writes to the "elect lady . . . whom I love in the truth." The following phrase, "not only I, but also all who know the truth," clarifies that it is not the sincerity of love but that his love is for those who remain in the truth. In light of 1 John, this is a reference to those who believe Jesus Christ is the Son of God come in the flesh and love one another. The secessionists are those who reject both of these claims and thus do not have the truth. In 2 John 2, this truth "remains in us and will be with

---

[6]Judith Lieu, *The Theology of the Johannine Epistles*, NTT (Cambridge: Cambridge University Press, 1991), 8.

us forever." The connection between truth and love continues in the affirmation that grace, mercy, and peace remain with the audience in the next verse. Grace, mercy, and peace, the elder says, "will be with us from God the Father and from Jesus Christ, the Son of the Father, in truth and love" (2 Jn 3). Rather than a wish or hope expressed, the greeting offers an assurance that truth remains in both the author and the readers and again articulates some of the author's central concerns. That grace, mercy, and peace are with "us" rather than the secessionists is a central theme of 1 John. Furthermore, that grace, mercy, and peace are from "God the Father and from Jesus Christ, the Son of the Father" reinforces the relationship between the Father and the Son, articulated throughout 1 John.

Letter body (2 John 4-11). After the letter opening and greeting, the elder expresses his joy over the fact that the audience remains in the truth, specifically in their mutual love for one another.

Request concerning the love command (2 John 4-6). The elder "was very glad to find some of your children walking in truth" (2 Jn 4). Walking in truth is a common way of expressing one's complete pattern of living, and here the children of the elect lady, or the members of the church, are living in accordance with the message of the gospel as it was received in the beginning. Raymond Brown argues that the joy expressed here is not mere sentiment but "indicates that the secession [see 1 Jn 2:19], while a danger, has not yet torn the church apart."[7] Yet, what is the "command we have received from the Father"? The elder equates walking in truth and the command received from the Father. Though there are several options for which scholars have argued, it is most likely that the Father's command is the gospel message itself, which is also suggested by 1 John 3:23: "Now this is his command: that we believe in the name of his Son, Jesus Christ, and love one another as he commanded us."

Following the elder's expression of joy, he turns in 2 John 5 to make a request of the elect lady: "So now I ask you, dear lady . . . that we love one another." This certainly entails mutual fellowship and agreement. The elder

---

[7]Brown, *Epistles of John*, 682.

clarifies that this is not "a new command, but the one we have had from the beginning," a clarification resembling the discussion in 1 John 2:7-8. This command was received from the beginning, that is, when the community first heard the gospel message and the command to love one another that came along with it. The elder continues by clarifying: "This is love: that we walk according to his commands," and his command is "that you walk in love" (2 Jn 6). The elder's request that the church continue in mutual love for one another echoes much of the teaching and concern of 1 John.

Warning against the antichrists and their teaching (2 John 7-11). Moving on from the command to love, the elder articulates the concern to confess Jesus Christ come in the flesh while also warning of the deceivers and antichrists who have gone into the world.

The need to reconfirm the mutual love between the elder and the elect lady is "because" (*hoti*, left out of many English translations) "deceivers have gone out into the world; they do not confess the coming of Jesus Christ in the flesh" (2 Jn 7). Here the elder connects ethics with doctrine— the command to love others is linked with the christological confession of Jesus Christ come in the flesh. As stressed throughout 1 John (especially 1 Jn 3:23), these two doctrines go together: right Christian practice is directly influenced by right Christology—orthopraxy flows from orthodoxy. Colin Kruse notes, "We may say that what the secessionists denied . . . was that Jesus was the Christ, the Son of God come in the flesh, and the reality of his atoning death."[8] Because the deceivers who deny Christ's incarnation are also called antichrist, this all the more associates these individuals with the secessionists of 1 John 2:18-19; 4:1-4. Brown notes that whereas 1 John 4:2 records the right confession as "Jesus Christ has come [*elēlythota*] in the flesh," 2 John 7 says "the coming [*erchomenon*] of Jesus Christ in the flesh." The difference between the perfect and present forms of the verb "to come" suggests that the secessionists not only deny the incarnation (1 Jn 4:2) but also the *parousia*, Jesus' second coming.[9]

---

[8]Colin G. Kruse, *The Letters of John*, PNTC (Grand Rapids, MI: Eerdmans, 2000), 209.
[9]Brown, *Epistles of John*, 670, 686.

In 1 John 4:1-4, the response to the false prophets or antichrists was to test the spirits, yet in response to the deceivers the elder warns the elect lady to "Watch yourselves so that you don't lose what we have worked for, but that you may receive a full reward" (2 Jn 8). That which the readers have worked for must be their faith or the confession that Jesus Christ is coming in the flesh. Perhaps looking to the future coming of Christ explains the reference to reward and loss in 2 John 8. Those who are made children of God through faith in Jesus Christ will receive the reward of eternal life at his coming, while those who deny Christ will suffer the loss of eternal life. The next verse reiterates this same concern another way: "Anyone who does not remain in Christ's teaching but goes beyond [*proagōn*] it does not have God" (2 Jn 9). To "go beyond" or being the one who "runs ahead" (NIV) suggests any way of moving beyond what Christ himself taught as handed down by the faithful, eyewitness testimony of the apostles. On the other hand, the one who remains in Christ's teaching "has both the Father and the Son" (compare with 1 Jn 5:12-13).

In addition to the warning of 2 John 8-9, the elder turns to practical steps the elect lady can take in order to avoid falling into the error of the deceiver and antichrist. The elder says that anyone who does not "bring this teaching" should be denied hospitality ("do not receive him into your home, and do not greet him"). Hospitality in the ancient world was not only a necessity, as often there were no other accommodations, but also a mark of social belonging. Hospitality was much more than merely providing food and lodging; it was a way of turning strangers into family. Thus, offering hospitality was to share in the work of the guest. This is why the elder warns that the "one who greets him shares [*koinōnei*] in his evil works" (2 Jn 11). To share with someone suggests there being fellowship, an indication of a formal relationship. To be clear, this is not a general injunction against showing hospitality to strangers. The elder understood it was likely that members from the secessionist group would be coming to the children of the elect lady in order to influence them. It is only the individuals who did not bring with them the teaching of Christ from whom hospitality was to be withheld.

Thus, the elder writes to warn the elect lady and her children against false teachers who did not confess the teaching of Christ, that is, they denied his coming in the flesh (2 Jn 7-11) and held an aberrant view of love (2 Jn 5-6). These are the same characteristics of the secessionists in 1 John.

Promise to visit and letter closing (2 John 12-13). The elder concludes his short personal letter by conveying the greeting of his own congregation and expresses his desire to visit.

Some have wondered that, if 2 John served as a cover letter for 1 John, why would the elder conclude 2 John by saying, "I have many things to write to you" (2 Jn 12)? Perhaps it was a way of referring to the more that actually could be found in 1 John. Others have argued that this is merely a convention, a way to draw a discourse to a conclusion, and thus is not significant (the phrase is repeated in 3 Jn 13 as well). Regardless, the elder expresses his desire to visit "face to face" (*stoma pros stoma*, literally "mouth to mouth") rather than communicate via "paper and ink." This indicates some of the warmth and affection the elder has for the elect lady. He says the reason for such meeting face to face is "that our joy may be complete" (compare with 1 Jn 1:4 as a reason for writing). The letter concludes with a final greeting in terms of the opening figurative expression of "the elect lady and her children." Here the elder sends the greetings of his home church: "The children of your elect sister send you greetings" (2 Jn 13).

COMMENTARY | 3 JOHN

Letter opening (3 John 1-2). A second letter from the elder is addressed to Gaius, with the instruction to continue showing hospitality to missionaries who confess the truth, particularly to Demetrius. This in light of the fact that Diotrephes, a church leader (where he has "first place"), has refused to offer such hospitality.

Like 2 John, the present letter opens with a clearly named sender and addressee: "The elder: To my dear friend Gaius," and just as in 2 John, the elder describes his addressee as one "whom I love in the truth" (3 Jn 1). Unlike 2 John, 3 John is a proper personal letter written to an individual regarding specific circumstances. Consequently, 3 John is perhaps less theological and more focused on practical and specific circumstances. The letter opening continues in the next verse with a hope or wish for good health, a common feature of Greco-Roman letters of the time. The elder prays "that you are prospering in every way and are in good health" (3 Jn 2). The prayer for good health is expressed with the two words *euodoō* and *hygiainō*, which elsewhere in the New Testament can refer to one being of sound teaching or doctrine (*euodoō* in 1 Tim 1:10; 6:3; 2 Tim 1:13; 4:3; Titus 2:1, 2), but here both terms clearly refer to Gaius's physical health. The final phrase of the greeting extends the prayer for good health to "your whole life" or "your soul" (NIV), indicating the elder's concern for Gaius's physical and spiritual health.

Letter body (3 John 3-12).

Joy in faithfulness (3 John 3-4). Like 2 John, here the elder expresses his joy over Gaius's "walking in truth" (3 Jn 4; see also 2 Jn 4). Fidelity to the truth for Gaius consists in both confession and action. The particular action, as we will see later in the letter, is offering hospitality to those visiting missionaries who, in the elder's estimation, deserve support. In the next verse, the elder continues to express his joy: "I have no greater joy than this: to hear that my children are walking in truth" (3 Jn 4). That repetition of "rejoiced" or "was very glad" (3 Jn 3) and "joy" (3 Jn 4) speaks to the intensity of the elder's joy (perhaps because of Gaius's service of hospitality in light of the lack of hospitality demonstrated by Diotrephes). That the elder calls Gaius one of his children need not imply that he was directly converted by the elder, but rather that Gaius agrees with the elder's teaching that Jesus Christ is the Son of God come in the flesh and that love for one another is his command.

Request for hospitality and support (3 John 5-8). Shifting from the opening greeting and expression of joy, the elder now makes a specific request for continued hospitality from Gaius. Calling Gaius a "dear friend," the elder commends him for "acting faithfully" in what he does for his "brothers and sister, especially when they are strangers" (3 Jn 5). It is possible, as Brown suggests, that these brothers and sisters are traveling missionaries who have turned to Gaius (though strangers to him) because they were refused hospitality by Diotrephes (3 Jn 11-12).[10] These missionaries then "have testified" regarding Gaius's "love before the church" (3 Jn 6). The church (*ekklēsias*) here is the elder's home congregation, where, returning from their travels, brothers and sisters have given a good report of Gaius's care for them. This report is now conveyed back to Gaius as a way of encouraging his further support and ongoing hospitality. The elder encourages Gaius, "You will do well to send them on their journey in a manner worthy of God" (3 Jn 6). Kruse notes that the expression "to send them on their journey" "translates a form of the verb *propempō*, which functioned as a technical term for missionary support in the early church (cf. Acts 15:3; 20:38; 21:5; Rom 15:24; 1 Cor 16:6, 11; 2 Cor 1:16; Tit 3:13)."[11] Both the journey made by the brothers and sisters as well as the hospitality given by Gaius must be in "a manner worthy of God," a phrase that finds further definition in the next verse.

The manner in which the brothers and sisters make their journey, for the purpose of gospel mission, was "for the sake of the Name" while "accepting nothing from pagans" (3 Jn 7). The Name refers to the name Jesus Christ; thus these are missionaries proclaiming the good news of the gospel, which the elder understands as Jesus Christ come in the flesh and as keeping the commandments. That these missionaries received "nothing from pagans [*ethnikōn*]" underlines the degree of sharing implicit in offering hospitality to such travelers. Just as pagans have no part in supporting the efforts of Christian missionaries, in 2 John the elder warned against receiving anyone who "does not bring this teaching" (2 Jn 10). In the next section we will see that Diotrephes's refusal to receive missionaries from the elder is proof of his lack of participation or sharing in the truth of their message. The partnership implicit in hospitality is, again, reinforced in 3 John 8: "Therefore, we ought to support such people

---

[10]Brown, *Epistles of John*, 740-41.
[11]Kruse, *Letters of John*, 223.

so that we can be coworkers with the truth." Of course, "such people" are the brothers and sisters who are missionaries, likely coming from the elder's church. The elder states clearly that supporting them, through offering hospitality, is to be "coworkers" (*synergos*) with them in their mission. Paul specifically uses the term *synergos* to describe those who helped him in spreading the gospel message (Rom 16:3, 9, 21; Phil 2:25; 4:3; 1 Thess 3:2).

The opposition of Diotrephes (3 John 9-10). The appeal to Gaius for continued support and welcome of missionaries from the elder's church (3 Jn 5-8, 11-12) is now somewhat interrupted. In this passage, the elder comments on the hostile actions of Diotrephes toward both himself and the traveling missionaries. This brief passage gives an even more specific, negative example of the high stakes of offering or failing to offer hospitality.

The elder now says "I wrote something to the church, but Diotrephes . . . does not receive our authority" (3 Jn 9). Though some suggest that the reference here to a previous letter could refer to 2 John, this is unlikely because it does not contain any request for hospitality from Diotrephes.[12] The last phrase literally says that Diotrephes "does not receive [*epidechetai*] us," just as in the next verse he "refuses to welcome [or receive, *epidechetai*] fellow believers" (3 Jn 10). The same verb is used in both phrases, the first with a metaphorical sense. It is unlikely that the elder made a visit to Diotrephes's church (though this is technically possible); rather, it is more likely that Diotrephes did not accept or receive the elder's authority or leadership. This is in part because he "loves to have first place among them" (3 Jn 9). Diotrephes seems to have acquired a position of leadership in his church through his own devices, and perhaps implicitly with wrong motives (loving to have first place rather than serve others in hospitality).

The elder then gives more details regarding Diotrephes's deceitful leadership: "he is . . . slandering us with malicious words. . . . He not only refuses to welcome fellow believers, but he even stops those who want to do so and expels them from the church" (3 Jn 10). The elder reports that Diotrephes is guilty of malicious slander. We are not told why Diotrephes

---

[12]See Georg Strecker, *The Johannine Letters: A Commentary on 1, 2, and 3 John*, trans. Linda M. Maloney, Hermeneia (Minneapolis: Fortress, 199), 253-54.

is doing this, only that such claims or accusations by Diotrephes were slanderous. The elder indicates that he intended to visit the city where Gaius and Diotrephes lived in order to "remind him of the works he is doing" (3 Jn 10). More than slander, Diotrephes was also denying fellow believers hospitality and going so far as to expel from the church those who did offer hospitality to them. That Diotrephes failed to offer hospitality means that he has rejected the very request the elder makes in this letter. What does it indicate regarding what Diotrephes believed if he denied hospitality to brothers and sisters (3 Jn 5) who set out for the sake of the Name (3 Jn 7)? His refusal to partner with the elder and the missionaries from his church implicitly indicates that Diotrephes does not hold to the true message, the gospel, articulated by the elder regarding the incarnation of Jesus Christ (2 Jn 7).

An appeal to do good and the commendation of Demetrius (3 John 11-12). Returning to the elder's main flow of thought (3 Jn 5-8), after the digression of the negative example of Diotrephes (3 Jn 9-10), 3 John 11-12 instruct Gaius to imitate what is good and then offers a commendation of Demetrius.

The elder turns his attention once again to Gaius ("dear friend"), instructing him, "Do not imitate what is evil, but what is good" (3 Jn 11). In the context of the letter, Diotrephes's refusal to receive the elder's authority and failure to receive fellow believers are the evil works Gaius is to avoid. This is because the "one who does good is of God; the one who does evil has not seen God" (3 Jn 11). Clearly this is a judgment against Diotrephes because his deeds are evil (refusing respect and hospitality); therefore, he has not seen God.

The elder's appeal to Gaius to show hospitality concludes with the commendation of Demetrius: "Everyone speaks well of Demetrius—even the truth itself" (3 Jn 12). From the context of the letter, the elder is urging Gaius to offer Demetrius hospitality as he visits. It is possible that Demetrius served as the letter carrier and thus could have been present while Gaius read the elder's letter for the first time. It is noteworthy that the elder says the truth itself speaks well of Demetrius. When the elder has spoken of the truth previously, he usually was referring to the gospel, and therefore this is a way of saying that Demetrius agrees with the confession Jesus Christ is the Son of God come in the flesh and with the command to love one another—these are the hallmarks of John's teaching throughout all three letters. In addition to the elder and the truth, Demetrius is spoken well of by others: "And we also speak well of him, and you know that our testimony is true" (3 Jn 12). Here the elder is likely referring to the witness of his local community. The elder's entire church knows of Demetrius's good works, and they send their commendation along with the elder's.

Promise to visit and letter closing (3 John 13-15). In an almost identical letter closing to that of 2 John, the elder once again notes, "I have many things to write to you, but I don't want to write to you with pen and ink" (3 Jn 13; compare with 2 Jn 12). Though the elder has found it necessary to write to Gaius, he expresses his desire to be present with him rather than to use pen and ink. Several English translations combine 3 John 14 and 3 John 15 (KJV, NASB, NIV), whereas several others (ESV, NRSV, CSB) maintain the material in separate verses, following the most recent edition of the edited Greek New Testament.[13] The letter concludes with what is a typical letter closing: "Peace to you. The friends send you greetings. Greet the friends by name" (3 Jn 15). Here the salutation includes a request for mutual greetings among the friends. This is not the typical way to refer to fellow Christians in New Testament letters ("brothers and sisters" or "fellow believers" are both much more common). Kruse suggests that this designation "may have derived from Jesus' description of his disciples as his 'friends' in John 15:13-15."[14] The elder makes the final request that the friends in Gaius's church and community be greeted personally, by name.

FURTHER READING

Lieu, Judith. *The Second and Third Epistles of John*. London: T&T Clark, 1986.

See also the end of the previous chapter for further reading.

---

[13]See *Novum Testamentum Graece*, 28th ed., ed. Barbara Aland, Kurt Aland, Johannes Karavidopoulos, Carlo M. Martini, and Bruce M. Metzger (Stuttgart: Deutsche Bibelgesellschaft, 2012).
[14]Kruse, *Letters of John*, 234.

CHAPTER SIX

The Letter of Jude

As NOTED IN THE INTRODUCTION TO CHAPTER THREE, the degree of overlapping material in Jude 4-18 and 2 Peter 2:1–3:3 motivates many critical scholars to treat 2 Peter as if it were 2 Jude, thus emphasizing the literary-historical connection between Jude and 2 Peter over the canonical connection between 1 and 2 Peter (most modern commentaries treat Jude and 2 Peter in the same volume). Rather than associating 2 Peter with Jude, and thus reordering the Catholic Epistles, the clues in the text suggest that 1 Peter and 2 Peter should be read together, which leads to the question of what connections exist between 2 Peter and 1 John—connections we considered at the beginning of chapter four. Now the following question arises: What kind of connections exist between 1–3 John and Jude? Whereas the theme of warning against false prophets (2 Pet 2:13; 1 Jn 4:1) draws together the letters of John with 2 Peter, in a similar way the theme of false teaching continues in Jude; however, Jude's emphasis is not on the content of the teaching but rather the morally libertine behavior exhibited by the intruders. First John stresses that the denial of Christ come in the flesh is a key false teaching of the secessionists. In a similar fashion, Jude highlights that the intruders are "denying Jesus Christ, our only Master and Lord" (Jude 4). Furthermore, 1 John also shares with Jude a concern for the behavior of the antichrists (1 Jn 2:19) or intruders in Jude; therefore, the theme of false teaching or false living is a common thread drawing together 2 Peter, 1–3 John, and Jude.

A final link connecting 1 John with Jude is that 1 John self-consciously characterizes its message as originating with apostolic eyewitness experience of Jesus (1 Jn 1:1-3). Jude not only calls to mind the teaching of the apostles (Jude 17), but also his opening charge to "contend for the faith that was delivered to the saints once for all" and his closing exhortation to "build yourselves up in your most holy faith" (Jude 20) both refer to the apostolic faith. Thus, the centrality of the apostolic message and the authority of that message are highlighted in both 1 John and Jude.

OCCASION AND SETTING

Jude's letter was written to a community that was being influenced by immoral leaders who had infiltrated the church. Writing with urgency, Jude instructs his readers to stand firm in "the faith that was delivered to the saints once for all" (Jude 3). The bulk of the letter is taken up with the denunciation of these intruders (Jude 5-19), and, as a consequence, the letter has been viewed as largely negative condemnation of these morally bankrupt outsiders. Though the letter, however, does offer a carefully constructed announcement of judgment against the intruders, this denunciation is framed by the positive encouragement to stand firm in the faith, to remain in the love of God, and to wait for the mercy of Jesus Christ (Jude 20-23). Thus, as will be argued more thoroughly below, Jude makes a positive theological contribution to early Christianity and bears an important theological message for today.

Author. The letter claims to have been written by "Jude, a servant of Jesus Christ and a brother of James" (Jude 1). The name "Jude" (or "Judah," *Yəhûdāh*, in Hebrew, or *Ioudas* in Greek) was a common first-century name; however, the Jude here must have been known widely enough for readers to identify him with only the further designation "a brother of James" (Jude 1). One well-known Judas in the early Christian movement

was Judas Barsabbas, who accompanied Silas in delivering the letter composed by the Jerusalem Council (Acts 15:22, 27, 32). Though well known,
however, this Judas is never associated with James. Another possibility is
Judas (son) of James (*Ioudan Iakōbou*, literally "Judas of James"), one of
the Twelve (Lk 6:16; Jn 14:22; Acts 1:13). However, this grammatical construction is a common way of describing the father of the named individual, thus "Judas [son] of James." The majority of scholars conclude that
the Judas mentioned in Jude 1 is almost certainly Judas the brother of
Jesus (Mt 13:55; Mk 6:3), which would also mean that Jude's brother James
is "James the Just," the brother of Jesus and author of the epistle of James.
We know very little about Jude. He was one of four brothers of Jesus, all
of whom did not follow Jesus during his ministry (Mk 3:21, 31; Jn 7:5) but
later joined the Christian movement after the resurrection (Acts 1:14).

Three issues have influenced the discussion regarding when the letter
was written: the identity of the letter's opponents, the rise of "early
Catholicism," and the interpretation of the phrase "remember what was
predicted by the apostles" (Jude 17). The identity of Jude's opponents is
raised below; here we will briefly consider the two remaining issues.

Some have understood clues from the text of Jude to indicate a time
of composition when the early church had formalized its message and
had developed an authoritative church structure, what J. N. D. Kelly
describes as "early Catholicism."[1] The major instruction to the audience
is "to contend for the faith that was delivered to the saints once for all"
(Jude 3) and to "build yourselves up in your most holy faith" (Jude 20).
To some this indicates that this faith is not merely the gospel message
but rather is the fixed body of formal and orthodox church teaching
that developed well after the time of the apostles. Therefore, this perspective insists, the letter was written in a time of "early Catholicism,"
when the teaching and structure of the church was formalized, well
after the early apostolic era. The term *faith*, however, is often used in
other New Testament texts to describe the earliest Christian message,

[1]J. N. D. Kelly, *The Epistles of Peter and of Jude* (London: Black, 1969), 248.

namely, the gospel. Therefore, this argument alone cannot determine the date of composition.

Those following the "early Catholicism" view also point to the chronological implications of Jude 17, where he urges, "But you, dear friends, remember what was predicted by the apostles of our Lord Jesus Christ." The call to remember what the apostles taught, from this perspective, indicates a time well after the apostles have died, and therefore supports a much later date of writing for Jude. However, the phrase does not necessarily indicate that the apostles themselves have died, but only that their predictions belong to the past. Richard Bauckham insists that they are to remember these apostolic teachings, just as they were to remember the instruction they were given at their conversion. He argues, "The most natural meaning of verse 18 is that Jude's readers themselves heard the apostles' preaching," and therefore this verse could imply "that most of the original converts were still living, and thus puts not a lower but an upper limit on the date."[2] The date of the letter cannot be confidently established on its use of *faith* and the reference to the apostles in Jude 17 alone. Though these factors may suggest a late date of composition and thus point away from Jude the brother of Jesus as author, it is just as plausible that the letter originated within the lifetime of Jude the brother of Jesus.

Audience. There are very few clues regarding the intended audience of Jude. The author reminds his readers of the teaching they received from the apostles at their conversion (Jude 17-18), which likely indicates that the author was not the one who founded the Christian community to whom he writes. Because Jude does not offer any further details about his audience beyond "those who are called, loved by God the Father and kept for Jesus Christ" (Jude 1), many conclude that he does not address a specific audience at all. Yet, others think, because of the vivid portrayal of the false teachers and the specific danger they pose for the readers, that there is a specific audience in mind.

[2]Richard J. Bauckham, *Jude and the Relatives of Jesus* (London: T&T Clark, 1990), 171.

We can assume that because the author singles out James as the brother of Jude, these readers both knew and respected James as a leading figure in the early Christian movement. It is also apparent that the author expected the readers to be familiar with the Old Testament and other Jewish documents (1 Enoch and the Testament of Moses), which circulated around Palestine in the early first century. Thus, it may be safe to think that Jude writes to a predominantly Jewish Christian group (or groups), because of the use of these Jewish documents and explicit Jewish exegetical method (see further discussion in genre below). Alongside these sparse indications of audience, we must consider the nature of Jude's opponents. Though it seems apparent that the author never directly addresses the opponents—that is, the author rhetorically condemns the opponents so as to warn the actual readers of the text—the author's description of them does shed light on the situation of the audience.

The "intruders" in Jude. Though Jude and 2 Peter share a significant amount of material, it would be wrong to conclude that the letters confront the same group of opponents. Whereas the opponents in 2 Peter were false teachers who grew up from within the community, Jude addresses a group of intruders who have infiltrated and influenced Jude's audience. Most of the indirect descriptions of the intruders in Jude revolve around their libertinism, that is, their own undisciplined moral living. It seems clear that they have "come in by stealth" from the outside (Jude 4), they influence others by their actions (Jude 11), and they are present at the community's fellowship (likely communion) meal (Jude 12), where they passed along their immoral ideas. They are motivated by greed (Jude 11-12), and their permissive lifestyle helps in winning followers (Jude 16).

Jude focuses his polemic against their rejection of rules for moral living. For example, they reject moral authority in the form of angels (Jude 8), Mosaic law (Jude 8-10), the apostles (Jude 17-18), and that of Christ himself (Jude 4, 8). This rejection of authority seems to be justified by an appeal to their own charismatic inspiration (Jude 8, "relying on their dreams"). In keeping with their rejection of moral authority, Jude characterizes these intruders as indulging in immoral behavior, especially sexual misconduct (Jude 6-8, 10). It is important to note that the intruders are never condemned for any specific doctrinal issue or theological teaching but rather for their immorality and rebellion.

Furthermore, it must be noted that the intruders are never directly addressed in the letter; rather, their denunciation is designed to dissuade Jude's audience from following their example. The rhetoric of the letter contrasts the audience with the intruders. The second-person plural pronoun *you* (Jude 5, 17, 18, 20) marks out the believing readers as holy (Jude 14), beloved (Jude 3, 17, 20), and without blemish (Jude 24). They are the ones who are both "kept for Jesus Christ" (Jude 1) and are to keep themselves "in the love of God" (Jude 21). The intruders, on the other hand, are labeled ungodly (Jude 4, 15 [3×], 18), they turn "the grace of our God into sensuality" (Jude 4), and they live "according to their desires" (Jude 16, 18). This contrast implicitly calls the audience to reject the immoral lifestyle and teaching of the intruders.

Genre. Jude bears the form of a letter, with an opening that includes a named author and the identification of recipients (Jude 1-2). This characteristic opening functions as the essential marker of the letter genre. Though not a regular feature of a Hellenistic letter, Jude also concludes with a doxology (Jude 24-25). Though clearly a letter, the main body of Jude takes the particular shape of an exhortation or sermon.

The structure of the letter indicates that there was a very specific message the author wanted to convey. Various attempts have been made to describe Jude's structure. Earle Ellis argues for understanding Jude 5-19 as a midrash taking up texts from the Old Testament, apostolic teaching, and 1 Enoch for specific commentary.[3] Midrashim (the plural of *midrash*) are rabbinical commentaries on texts from the Old Testament, but in a looser sense, *midrash* refers to Jewish interpretation of a text. Both Ellis and Richard Bauckham argue that the particular type of

---

[3]E. Earle Ellis, *Prophecy and Hermeneutic in Early Christianity*, WUNT 18 (Tübingen: Mohr Siebeck, 1978), 224-26.

midrash Jude represents is a pesher interpretation, which is an exegetical convention observed in the Dead Sea Scrolls.[4] The term "pesher" (*pēšer*) is translated "solution" or "interpretation," and usually appeared after the quotation of an Old Testament text and before its interpretation. Therefore, a pesher interpretation is a "text-plus-interpretation" formula that was common in Jewish exegesis.

The text-plus-interpretation formula appears in Jude throughout the section of condemnation against the intruders (Jude 5-19) and is characterized by three features typical of a pesher. First, the shift from a text (we will need to discuss the kind of texts Jude quotes) to interpretation in Jude is marked by a shift in verbal tense, from past tense in the text to present tense in the interpretation. The texts cast in the past tense are found in Jude 5-7, 9, 11, 14-15, 18, each followed by an interpretation in the present tense in Jude 8, 10, 12-13, 16, and 19. Second, the transition from text to interpretation is also marked by the phrase "these people are" (*houtoi eisin*, Jude 12, 16, 19) or just "these people" (*hytoi*, Jude 8, 10). In using this phrase, Jude takes the example cited in the text and turns to apply it to "these people," or the intruders. Thus, for example in Jude 5-7, Jude argues that the wilderness generation, the fallen angels, and Sodom and Gomorrah are all examples that find their fulfillment in the intruders. Finally, the application of the past example (or type) in the text to the present intruders is a kind of typological interpretation stressing the fulfillment of the text in the author's time and circumstance. Therefore, though framed as a letter, Jude is an exhortation or sermon calling his audience to contend for the faith (Jude 3, 20-23) by staying away from the influence of the intruders, who stand condemned (Jude 4-19).

STRUCTURE

Rather than constituting the focal point of the letter's message, Jude 5-19 prepares "the way for the real purpose of the letter, which is Jude's appeal to his readers to fight for the faith (Jude 20-23)."[5] The structure of the

---

[4]Richard J. Bauckham, *Jude, 2 Peter*, WBC (Nashville: Thomas Nelson, 2003), 4-5.
[5]Bauckham, *Jude, 2 Peter*, 4.

GOING DEEPER: THE LITERARY RELATIONSHIP BETWEEN JUDE AND 2 PETER

Jude and 2 Peter are clearly related on a literary level, but the direction of the literary sharing has been debated. Jude could have used 2 Peter as a source, but that would mean Jude only used the middle part of 2 Peter (specifically, 2 Pet 2:1–3:3), virtually ignoring the first and third chapters. Second Peter's primacy is further doubtful because Jude is the shorter text, and the tendency is for a text borrowing from another to expand in length, not to contract. It is possible that both letters could have followed a third source, whether oral or written; however, then the majority of Jude consists of that third source and thus would not constitute an original composition at all (and there is no manuscript or early patristic evidence of such a text). The modern consensus is that the letter of Jude was composed first, with the author of 2 Peter using Jude to construct his argument.

Though it is likely that 2 Peter uses material from Jude, it would be incorrect to claim that phrases from Jude are simply reused without change in 2 Peter. Rather, the author of 2 Peter has modified and adapted Jude's material and has resituated it in a new argumentative context. Typically, 2 Peter takes passages from Jude and rewrites them using Jude's language and sequence of thought but clearly reconfigures them for a different rhetorical situation.

The new rhetorical situation leads to several differences between the two letters. In 2 Peter, the opponents are called false teachers, and they are characterized as originating from the Christian community itself. In Jude the opponents are intruders coming from the outside (and are never called out for what they actually teach). Whereas Jude uses noncanonical Jewish texts such as 1 Enoch and the Testament of Moses, 2 Peter removes any reference or allusion to these texts when it incorporates this material from Jude. All this is significant because a close study of how 2 Peter used and reshaped the material from Jude sheds light on 2 Peter's purpose. Such study allows us to appreciate what 2 Peter considered most important for its audience and reveals some of the author's theological outlook.

the introduction (Jude 1-2) communicates the circumstances that called forth the writing of the letter. This appears in two parts. First is an initial appeal to Jude's readers "to contend for the faith" (Jude 3). Second is the background to this appeal, namely, a warning against the adversaries who threaten that faith (Jude 4). The body of the letter (Jude 5-19) corresponds to the second element in Jude 4, giving the background to the danger of the intruders and the reason for Jude's central appeal. The central claim of the letter, which appears in Jude 3, comes to a climax in Jude 20-23. This structure is seen clearly in the chiastic formula represented in the outline section below.

OUTLINE

    I. Letter greeting (Jude 1-2)

    II. Letter body (Jude 3-23)

        A. An initial appeal to Jude's readers to carry on the fight for the faith (Jude 3)

           B. Reason for the appeal (Jude 4)

           B'. The background: A commentary on four prophecies of the doom of the false teachers (Jude 5-19)

               1. "Text" 1 (Jude 5-10)

               2. "Text" 2 (Jude 11-13)

               3. "Text" 3 (Jude 14-16)

               4. "Text" 4 (Jude 17-19)

        A'. Climax: Return to the appeal to carry on the fight for the faith (Jude 20-23)

    III. Closing doxology (Jude 24-25)[6]

COMMENTARY | LETTER GREETING | JUDE 1-2

As noted above, the characteristic features of named author, indication of audience, and greeting are the essential markers of the letter genre.

---

[6]Bauckham, *Jude, 2 Peter*, 5-6.

The named author, Jude, and the audience have been discussed above, yet the further description of the recipients is worth noting here.

Rather than specifically naming his audience, Jude addresses his instruction "to those who are called." The placement of the words in Greek suggests that the two phrases, "loved by God the Father" and "kept for Jesus Christ," outline further the audience's calling. The phrase "loved by God" is almost a title for Israel (Deut 32:15; 33:5, 26; 2 Chron 20:7; Ps 28:6; Is 5:1; 44:2), which is here transferred to Christians. Bauckham notes that the phrase has "an eschatological sense: Christians are kept safe by God for the Parousia of Jesus Christ when they will enter into their final salvation."[7] Both verbs, *loved* and *kept*, imply God as the subject of the action and the audience as the object; God loves and keeps believers. Furthermore, both verbs suggest a past action with enduring results into the future. In the original language these two phrases are bracketed by the phrase "to those . . . who are called." "Those called" is another title transferred to Christians from Israel (especially Is 41:9; 42:6; 48:12, 15; 49:1; 54:6), and, in the New Testament, the verb "called" (*kaleō*) becomes a technical term for the process of salvation. Here in Jude 1, the substantival adjective (*klētos*) functions as a technical term for Christians. This rich but general description of the audience is accompanied by a typical Christian greeting: "May mercy, peace, and love be multiplied to you" (Jude 2).

> ## Connections with James
>
> The letter openings of James and Jude are connected in two ways. First, the letter openings are directly connected by means of their self-description as "a servant of Jesus Christ," both using the identical phrase *Iēsou Christou doulos*. A second connection is signaled in Jude 1 by the phrase "brother of James [*adelphos de Iakōbou*]." Richard Bauckham notes that there was just one pair of brothers known as James and Jude in the New Testament (Mk 6:3) and adds, "Jude therefore uses this phrase to identify himself by reference to his more famous brother."[a]
>
> ---
>
> [a]Richard J. Bauckham, *Jude, 2 Peter*, WBC (Nashville: Thomas Nelson, 2003), 24.

---

[7]Bauckham, *Jude, 2 Peter*, 26.

COMMENTARY | LETTER BODY | JUDE 3-23

It is important to remember the structure of the main body of the letter. The initial appeal to contend for the faith (Jude 3) comes to a climax in the instructions of Jude 20-23. The reason for the appeal, the presence of intruders in the community (Jude 4), and the background of their condemnation (Jude 5-19) make up the main body of the letter.

An initial appeal to Jude's readers to carry on the fight for the faith (Jude 3). Whereas Jude originally intended to write a letter "about the salvation we share," circumstances demanded a different kind of letter, one Jude "found . . . necessary to write." The term "necessary" (*anankēn*) often indicates urgency or distress, and in this context the more urgent need was for Jude to write appealing to the audience to contend for the faith rather than to write about their shared salvation. Here he refers to his audience as his "dear friends" and reminds them that the Christian message, the faith, has been definitively delivered to them, the saints.

The letter Jude found it necessary to write urges his audience to "contend" or to "carry on the fight for the faith" (a phrase very much like Paul's "contending together for the faith of the gospel" in Phil 1:27). This effort expended for the faith is not merely a defensive move protecting the gospel; rather, it also includes an offensive move where one promotes and moves the gospel forward through both words and deeds. Finally, the faith here is understood not as the subjective faith of the community but as the central message of salvation through Jesus Christ—the apostolic faith handed down to the community.

Reason for the appeal (Jude 4). Though following on immediately after Jude 3, the reason for the appeal announced in Jude 4 is directly connected to the supporting background context, provided in Jude 5-19. The situation demanding the redirected letter is that "some people" have "come in by stealth" into the community. Their entrance was not secret in the sense that no one knew they were there; rather, their entrance was secret in the way they presented themselves. The initial behavior of the intruders did not alert the church to any obvious problems; therefore, it is through the letter itself that Jude attempts to unmask the danger they pose.

Jude makes a series of four charges about this group. First, the condemnation of this group was announced beforehand ("long ago") in the Scriptures. The condemnation, or "this judgment" announced in the Old Testament, points forward to the future (now present) condemnation of the intruders, outlined in Jude 5-19. Therefore, Jude interprets the Scriptures as referring to the intruders' sins and the condemnation their sins deserve. Second, the intruders are condemned as "ungodly" (*asebeis*, also in Jude 14-15). Rather than disbelief or doctrinal error, the intruders are guilty of moral rebellion against God. Third, they turn or "pervert" (NRSV) God's grace into "sensuality," a term referring to immoral actions, especially sexual immorality. Finally, the intruders deny "Jesus Christ, our only Master and Lord" (Jude 4). This denial does not necessarily take the form of false teaching or public disavowal of Christ, but rather the way the intruders live—they deny Christ through their actions. The intruders constituted an unknown threat to the community, and Jude was compelled to write the letter exposing their dangerous presence.

The background: A commentary on four prophecies of the doom of the false teachers (Jude 5-19). This section of Jude bears the resemblance of a pesher interpretation of the Old Testament and can be broken down into four sections, or texts that are cited and interpreted. As mentioned above, we must consider the kind of texts Jude interprets. Technically there is only one true text cited, from 1 Enoch 1.9, quoted in Jude 14-15. The last text cited is an unknown saying from the apostles. This could have been an actual text; however, it has been lost to time. The two other texts Jude comments on are actually three particular Old Testament groups (Jude 5-7) and three Old Testament individuals (Jude 11), both of which function as scriptural types applied directly to the intruders.

Text one (Jude 5-10). The first text is composed of three Old Testament corporate types: the wilderness generation ("a people out of Egypt," Jude 5), the fallen angels (Jude 6), and Sodom and Gomorrah (Jude 7). Jude insists that his audience already knows these examples and perhaps how they might relate to the intruders.

The first group is the wilderness generation, who perished after being liberated from Egyptian captivity (Ex 12:51; Num 14:29-37). Even though they were saved from Egypt, this generation nonetheless were "later destroyed" in their unbelief. This is a striking reminder that, though the people were once delivered, active faith in God's provision is necessary. The wilderness generation is used elsewhere in the New Testament as a warning against unbelief (1 Cor 10:1-12; Heb 3–4). A second striking feature of this phrase is that Jesus is the one who saved God's people out of Egypt. Some early manuscripts read "Lord" rather than "Jesus"; however, the hardest, and therefore most likely, reading supports "Jesus." Thus, Jesus is both the deliverer and judge of God's people in the past, and, as seems to be Jude's point, Jesus will also be the judge of the apostates in the future. This is a significant example of a christological reading of an Old Testament narrative, which understands God's deliverer (Moses) as a figure of God's ultimate deliverer. Furthermore, this first example is out of chronological order—the rebellious angels came first. Perhaps the wilderness generation is first because it most closely approximates those tempted to apostasy—namely, Jude's audience.

The second group is "the angels who did not keep their own position" (Jude 6), who traditionally have been identified as the fallen angels in Genesis 6:1-4. In the Jewish traditions reflecting on Genesis 6, the angelic beings took human women as wives and procreated with them. Jude shows awareness of the Jewish interpretation of this passage as he describes these angels as "kept in eternal chains in deep darkness," where they await judgment (all these traditions coming from 1 Enoch 6–19). We should note the tradition of the rebellious angels also appears in 1 Peter 2:18-22 and 2 Peter 2:4. The point of using this example is less to stress the Jewish interpretation of Genesis 6 than to highlight that the intruders, like the fallen angels, will be kept for future judgment because of their rebellion against God's order (they "abandoned their proper dwelling").

The third and final example is the immoral cities of Sodom and Gomorrah (Gen 19:4-25). The opening phrase, "likewise," connects the particular sin of the fallen angels with that of Sodom and Gomorrah. Sodom and Gomorrah "and the surrounding towns committed sexual immorality and perversions" (Jude 7). All three examples are associated with rejection of God's order. In the case of the wilderness generation, they rejected God's purposes and order for inhabiting the Promised Land (Num 14:11); the rebellious angels and Sodom and Gomorrah are both extreme cases of sexual perversion marking an outright rejection of God's created order. Jude 7 ends by connecting these as examples of "the punishment of eternal fire." The example of judgment represented by the three examples all point to the judgment awaiting the intruders.

The transition from the text (Jude 5-7) to the interpretation is marked by the shift from past to present tense and the use of "these people" in Jude 8. The phrase "in the same way these people" connects the intruders specifically to the three rebellious Old Testament corporate examples. Jude first describes the intruders as "relying on their dreams," which might be a reference to their claim to prophetic insight gained through their dreams. However, Jude clearly thinks of them as false prophets devoid of the Spirit (Jude 19). Furthermore, the intruders are like these Old Testament types in that they "defile the flesh," which is a reference to their sexual immorality. Finally, they "reject authority" and "slander glorious ones." It is likely the particular authority they reject is that of the Lord (see Jude 4), and the act of slandering glorious ones, most certainly a reference to angels, describes their refusal to speak respectfully about and receive the moral and spiritual order created by God.

Their rejection of spiritual authority and order noted in Jude 8 leads the author to offer a further example highlighting the danger and inappropriateness of such behavior in Jude 9. Here Jude offers the example of Michael's dispute with the devil, which most likely comes from the lost ending of the Testament of Moses. In this story, which the audience most likely knew, the archangel Michael is sent by God to ensure proper burial of Moses' body; however, the devil disputes Moses' worthiness because of his murder of an Egyptian. Even while arguing with the devil, Michael does not presume to condemn the devil for his slanderous accusation. Rather, Michael, leaving judgment in God's hands alone, only responds by saying, "The Lord rebuke you!" (Jude 9).

The point of the story is to demonstrate that even the archangel Michael refused to slander angelic beings, even when they were in the wrong, because Michael respected the given, divine order—something to which the intruders refuse submission. Jude 10 makes this clear by saying the intruders ("these people") blaspheme what they "do not understand." Far from receiving special revelation through their dreams (Jude 8), the intruders demonstrate their ignorance of spiritual authority by speaking against angelic beings (Jude 9) and reject the Lord's authority (Jude 4). In contrast to enlightened understanding, these intruders are like animals; their understanding is limited to instinct. The conclusion is that "by these things they are destroyed." In other words, just like the Old Testament examples received judgment and destruction, so too will the intruders. The scriptural examples thus serve as types "prefiguring the events of the end-times, and pointing specifically to the judgment which the corrupt and corrupting false teachers will receive on the last day."[8]

Text two (Jude 11-13). Jude's second text once again offers three examples from the Old Testament, which serve as types of the intruders. This time he uses the examples of three notorious individuals who typically influenced others to go astray: Cain, Balaam, and Korah. This text is introduced in the form of a woe oracle, common in the Jewish prophets (Is 5:8, 11, 18; Amos 5:18; 6:1). Again, in prophetic and typological fashion, Jude connects the immorality of the Old Testament examples and their judgment to the intruders.

First, a woe is pronounced on the intruders because they "have gone the way of Cain" (Jude 11). Not only the first murderer (Gen 4:1-16), Cain, in Jewish tradition, became the archetypal sinner and the instructor of others in sin.[9] He corrupted the family of Adam and justified lawless

[8]David Horrell, *The Epistles of Peter and Jude* (Peterborough, UK: Epworth, 1998), 123.
[9]See Bauckham, *Jude, 2 Peter*, 79.

behavior by denying divine righteousness and judgment, just like the intruders. Second, they "have plunged into Balaam's error for profit" (Jude 11). In Jewish tradition Balaam is a bad light, one of the great enemies of God's people. Though in the account of Numbers 22–24 Balaam refused to curse Israel, in later tradition he is regarded as greedy for the rewards promised for using his prophetic gift against the people of God. He was a prophet who, in his greed for financial gain, hurried eagerly to give the advice that led Israel into the disastrous apostasy at Beth-peor (Num 25:1-3). Balaam was guilty of leading Israel into immorality and idolatry, just like the intruders. Finally, the intruders "have perished in Korah's rebellion" (Jude 11). Like Cain and Balaam, Korah too was a notorious figure in Jewish tradition. He, along with Dathan and Abiram, led a rebellion against the authority of Moses and Aaron (Num 16:1-35; 26:9-10). Bauckham notes, "Korah's rebellion was against God as much as against Moses and Aaron (Num 16:11; 26:9), and Jude may have seen Moses in this context representing the Law."[10] Korah, Dathan, and Abiram, along with their followers, suffered swift judgment when the earth opened up and swallowed them and then consumed them in fire. Jude's comment that they "have perished in Korah's rebellion" suggests that he views the future judgment to come on the intruders as an event that, though still in the future, has already happened. This is the proleptic use of the verb and is common in prophetic literature.

Once again, the shift from text to interpretation is marked by a shift from past to present tense and by the use of "these people." Applying the scriptural examples in Jude 11 to the intruders, Jude says, "These people are dangerous reefs at your love feasts" (Jude 12). As hidden reefs pose an unseen threat to a ship, so too the intruders are a hidden threat to the Christian community at the most intimate time of fellowship, the communion meal. Bauckham says that this "is the earliest occurrence of the term '*agapē*' in the sense of the Christian fellowship meal" and indicates how deeply the opponents have infiltrated the community and the degree

---

[10]Bauckham, *Jude, 2 Peter*, 83.

to which they exerted their negative influence.[11] The next description similarly marks out the degree of influence the intruders have within the community. They "are shepherds who only look after themselves" (Jude 12). The intruders either claim to be or are acting like leaders in the church, but instead of tending the flock, they only look after themselves. This is clear by Jude's allusion to Ezekiel 34:2, where shepherds (rulers) of Israel are challenged because they feed themselves at the expense of the sheep.

The interpretation section ends with four metaphors from nature, all of which relate to the intruder's claim to be prophets and teachers. They are "waterless clouds," fruitless trees in autumn, "wild waves . . . foaming up their shameful deeds," and "wandering stars." The images relate to the regions of air, land, sea, and heavens (which might be influenced by 1 Enoch 2.1–5.4; 80.2-8). All of these images indicate that their claim to be prophets is empty, worthless, and deceptive.

Text three (Jude 14-16). The third text is the only actual quotation from an existing text. The citation from 1 Enoch 1.9 clearly is a relevant text for Jude as it describes the judgment to come on the "ungodly" (see Jude 4), a term repeated four times in the quotation.

The introduction to the text quotation is remarkable because of its emphasis: "Enoch, in the seventh generation from Adam, prophesied, saying" (Jude 14, my translation). Whereas it is common in the New Testament to introduce a quotation simply "saying" ("it says" or "it is written"), Jude's fourfold introduction of 1 Enoch 1.9 is unusual for its emphasis. He names the writer, Enoch, and then announces his special relationship to Adam (seventh would suggest something special or complete about Enoch). Then Jude names his function, that he prophesied, and finally includes the typical formula for a quotation, "saying" (CSB "prophesied"). The text of 1 Enoch was known in both Jewish and Christian circles, and the way in which Jude introduces the quotation, along with the fact that he offers an interpretation of it, has for some suggested that Jude considered the writing to be inspired (see "Going

---

[11]Bauckham, *Jude, 2 Peter*, 86.

Deeper: Jude's Use of 1 Enoch" following). Whether or not Jude thought of 1 Enoch as inspired, he at least understood that it contained a prophetic word that spoke to the future judgment of the intruders.

In his quotation, Jude has introduced a significant change to the original text. In 1 Enoch 1.9, God is the subject of the sentence, but in Jude 14 it is the Lord who comes in judgment. This reflects a christological interpretation of the passage that stresses hope for the return of Christ. This follows the widespread practice in early Christianity of applying Old Testament passages featuring God appearing to his people to Jesus' coming. Jude understands 1 Enoch 1.9 as a prophetic announcement of future judgment at the Lord's coming. The key word "ungodly" (*asebeias*) appears in Jude 4, 18 and also is a prominent term in 1 Enoch 1.9. The prophetic vision consists of "tens of thousands of his holy ones," who are likely angels, coming to "execute judgment on all . . . the ungodly" (Jude 14-15). The judgment of the ungodly is specifically for their "ungodly acts that they have done" and for the "harsh things ungodly sinners have said against him." The intruders "reject Jesus Christ" (Jude 4), and likely the harsh things said in this context are against Christ.

Again, the interpretation is marked by a shift from past to present tense and the use of "these people." The intruders speak harsh things against the Lord, and they are "discontented grumblers" (a phrase used to describe the wilderness generation, Ex 16:7-12; 1 Cor 10:10) who live "according to their desires" (which, again, may refer to sexual immorality). They "utter arrogant words" and flatter others "for their own advantage."

Text four (Jude 17-19). The final text Jude uses is an allusion to an otherwise unknown saying of the apostles. Because Jude directly addresses his audience in Jude 17 ("dear friends"), some argue that Jude 17-19 is a new section disconnected from the midrash of Jude 5-16 and instead connected to Jude 20-23 (which also addresses "dear friends"). However, it is better to understand Jude 17-19 as the final section of Jude's midrash against the intruders because it bears all the same structural features that

GOING DEEPER: JUDE'S USE OF 1 ENOCH

Jude obviously uses the Old Testament extensively, but he also makes use of significant noncanonical literature. Jude 9 refers to a tradition from the Testament of Moses, Jude 14-15 quotes 1 Enoch 1.9, and there are several allusions to 1 Enoch throughout the letter.[a] Whether this means 1 Enoch was an inspired text in Jude's estimation has perplexed Christian interpreters of the letter. For Tertullian, Jude's use of 1 Enoch indicates that it was an inspired text (*De cultu feminarum* 1.3). Yet for others, such as Jerome, Jude's use of 1 Enoch calls into question the canonicity of Jude (*De viris illustribus* 4). Though we have examples of pagan literature cited in the New Testament (Acts 17:28; Titus 1:12), that the text is introduced in an emphatic way and then is given an interpretation (like other Scripture) might suggest that Jude considers this passage as inspired. In modern scholarship, there are three main views of how Jude viewed 1 Enoch.

1. Richard Bauckham argues that Jude quotes 1 Enoch as inspired but not canonical (very much like the next quotation of apostolic teaching—again, inspired oral teaching from the apostles, yet not canonized)—thus representing the "inspired, yet not canonical" position.[b]

2. J. Darrel Charles argues that Jude quotes 1 Enoch not because he holds it in high regard but because either his audience or the opponents

appear in the other text citations and because the theme of judgment against the intruders continues.

Jude instructs his audience to "remember what was predicted by the apostles" (Jude 17). As noted above, the call to remember apostolic teaching suggests for some that the time of the apostles has passed and thus that the letter was written much later than the life time of Jude, the Lord's brother. However, it is just as likely that Jude looks back not to the apostolic period but back to the apostolic teaching his audience received at their conversion.

The apostles predicted that "in the end time there will be scoffers" and that they will live for "their own ungodly desires" (Jude 18). This echoes the apostolic prediction of scoffers in 2 Peter 3:2. Beyond 2 Peter, this is themselves recognize Enoch as inspired. He used the text not because it is authoritative or edifying but because it is of particular usefulness for the present situation. This forces Charles to minimize that Enoch "prophesied" (Jude 14)—something difficult to do if we take the text seriously.

3. Gene Green picks up an argument, dating at least to the time of Augustine, that Jude quotes 1 Enoch (and the Testament of Moses) just at points where these texts depend on Old Testament passages (Jude 6 // Gen 6:1-4; body of Moses, Jude 9 // Deut 34:5-6, also referencing Zech 3:1-2; citation of 1 Enoch 1.9 in Jude 14-15 // Deut 33:2). But if this is true, why would Jude not just refer to the biblical text?

It is clear that Jude considered the text as an important part of his argument and does not distinguish it from other prophetic texts from the Old Testament—beyond this we can only speculate.

[a]Other allusions to 1 Enoch may be found throughout the epistle. The material regarding the fallen angels in Genesis 6 is a prominent theme found in the Enoch literature. Jude describes the angels "who did not keep their own position" (1 Enoch 12.4; 15.3, 7) and says that the Lord has kept these angels "in eternal chains in deepest darkness" (1 Enoch 10.4-6). The Enoch literature discusses the watchers who fell from heaven as stars, and Jude has here used the traditional material from Genesis as well as the material from Enoch. In general, 1 Enoch 1–5 appears to be at the heart of Jude's exegesis.
[b]Richard J. Bauckham, *Jude and the Relatives of Jesus in the Early Church* (Edinburgh: T&T Clark, 1990), 225-31.

an otherwise unknown apostolic saying. These people are characterized by their mocking of religion and their disregard for morality. Both of these qualities of the intruders are seen throughout Jude.

For a final time, Jude interprets his text as referring directly to the intruders by shifting from the past to the present tense and by using the phrase "these people" (Jude 19). In their mocking attitude they "create divisions" within the community. It is likely that, because Jude 12 mentions the communion meal ("love feasts"), the divisions sown within the community have not yet resulted in a complete split. David Horrell notes, "The highly unusual word Jude uses may imply that they create divisions specifically by 'classifying' some Christians as superior to others, seeing themselves . . . as those who possess the Spirit in some special measure."[12] Perhaps, once again, that they rely on their dreams

[12]Horrell, *Epistles of Peter and Jude*,128.

(Jude 8) supports this overinflated notion of spiritual insight on the part of the intruders. In Jude's final judgment, on the contrary, the intruders "are worldly, not having the Spirit" (Jude 19). The morally bankrupt lives of the intruders nullify any claim they make regarding being led by the Spirit.

Climax: Return to the appeal to carry on the fight for the faith (Jude 20-23). After the carefully constructed announcement of judgment on the intruders, which consisted of scriptural examples and their interpretation, Jude returns to the central instruction of the letter: "to contend for the faith" (Jude 3). In Jude 20-23 Jude comes to the central instruction of the letter.

Once again, as in Jude 17, Jude addresses his audience directly as "dear friends." Though in Jude 20-21 there are four distinct phrases, the passage contains only one command: "keep yourselves in the love of God" (Jude 21). The participles *building, praying,* and *waiting* all relate to this main command. It is worth noting that three of these actions "correspond to a trinitarian formula: Holy Spirit, God, Christ."[13]

As the eschatological temple, Jude's readers are to "build yourselves up in your most holy faith" (Jude 20), in contrast to the intruders creating divisions (Jude 19). The building image makes clear that the early Christian community was viewed as a kind of temple constructed as a whole out of its many members. Keeping with the image, the foundation to the Christian community is "your most holy faith," which is the gospel message they received from the apostles. This, once again, reflects back to the central theme of the letter in Jude 3, to "contend for the faith that was delivered . . . once for all." Throughout Jude, faith is that objective message of the gospel that was first proclaimed and passed on by the apostles.

The second phrase calls the readers to pray "in the Holy Spirit." The preposition "in" (*en*) likely indicates prayer in the control of the Spirit or under the guidance of the Spirit. This is Spirit-empowered prayer where the concerns and even the words are given by the Spirit. Jude contrasts the claim of the intruders, who pass off their dreams as spiritual insights

---

[13]Bauckham, *Jude, 2 Peter,* 112.

("dreams," Jude 8), with what they are in reality, people who "are . . . not having the Spirit" (Jude 19).

The third phrase contains the command proper: "keep yourselves in the love of God." The verb "keep" (*tēreō*) appears at several important points in the letter. Jude's readers are "kept [*tetērēmenois*] for Jesus Christ" (Jude 1), and the angels "who did not keep [*tērēsantas*] their own position" God himself has "kept" (*tetērēken*) for judgment (Jude 6). In Jude 1, 6 the verbs are divine passives, which stress that God is the one who keeps believers for Jesus Christ and the angels for final judgment. In Jude 21, the readers are instructed to "keep [*tērēsate*] yourselves," now stressing the action of believers to remain in the love of God. To keep oneself in the love of God means to remain in God's love for the believer, rather than the believer's love for God; thus, "keep yourselves in the love of God." The concept of keeping or guarding appears one final time in the letter, but with a different verb: "Now to him who is able to keep [*phylaxai*] you from falling" (Jude 24 NRSV). The instruction for believers to keep themselves in God's love for them is couched in the reminder that God has already kept them "for Christ" (Jude 1) and that God is able "to keep" believers from stumbling (Jude 24).

Finally, Jude instructs his readers to wait "expectantly for the mercy of our Lord Jesus Christ," and such waiting is "for eternal life" (Jude 21). Unlike the intruders, who are being kept for judgment, Jude's readers are encouraged to wait in hope and expectation for the coming of Jesus Christ, who will finally bring eternal life to fruition. The expectant waiting for mercy is not an indication that Jude's audience does not already experience Christ's mercy but rather that such mercy will, in the future, come in its fullness.

Mercy forms a connection between Jude 21 and Jude 22-23. The experience and hopeful expectation of mercy on the part of Jude's readers is directly connected to the command to have mercy on others. Though it is clear that Jude 22-23 calls for mercy from Jude's audience, there are several difficulties in this small passage. There is a textual question regarding exactly how many phrases were originally contained in this passage. Most English translations retain three phrases: "have mercy on some who are wavering; save others by snatching them out of the fire; and have mercy on still others with fear" (Jude 22-23 NRSV). Yet some manuscript evidence suggests a shorter, two-phrase passage: "Snatch some from the fire, but on those who dispute have mercy with fear." Another issue is how to translate the second verb in Jude 22: Have mercy on those who "waver" or on those who "dispute"? Finally, to whom are Jude's readers to show mercy?

Jude 22 instructs those who are waiting for the climax of Christ's mercy to "have mercy on those who waver [*diakrinomenous*]." Though several English translations render this term "those who waver," the same term appears in Jude 9, where it is uniformly translated "dispute." There is good reason to argue that Jude is instructing his readers to have mercy on "those who dispute." Or in other words, they are to show mercy to the intruders themselves or those who are following them. The next two phrases in Jude 23 continue to urge the audience to save and again to have mercy. The stress on mercy in the first and third phrases seems to express the central command. After having mercy on "those who waver/dispute," the readers are to save others, "snatching them from the fire," which seems to describe a group of people in danger of judgment. Finally, they are again to "have mercy on others but with fear," the fear likely a reference to fear of God rather than fear of others. The final phrase, "hating even the garment defiled by the flesh," echoes language from Zechariah 3:3-4 and likely refers to the staining or contaminating influence of immoral people within the community. Perhaps the point is that while showing mercy to potentially defiling people (the intruders themselves?), Jude's readers must reverence God alone and reject their contaminating influence on the community. Though the letter announces future judgment on the intruders for their arrogance and immorality, here at the end Jude seems to call his readers to offer mercy and the opportunity to be saved.

COMMENTARY | CLOSING DOXOLOGY | JUDE 24-25

Following the climactic appeal of the letter (Jude 20-23), Jude concludes with a doxology of praise for God's glory and goodness. Usually found at the end of a prayer, such doxologies are only occasionally found at the end of a letter (Rom 16:25-27; 2 Pet 3:18). Though the doxology itself is similar to other doxologies, what is unusual is that Jude's letter does not end like the typical letter, as it fails to conclude with any greetings or final salutation.

In light of the danger posed by the intruders, Jude praises God for his protection and preservation. God alone is the one "who is able to protect [or keep] you from stumbling" (Jude 24) into the error of the intruders. God is the one who is able "to make you stand in the presence of his glory," that is, in the personal presence of God. And Jude's readers are encouraged that they will stand in God's presence "without blemish" or with the purity of the sacrificial animals presented to God in worship in the Old Testament (Ex 29:1; Lev 1:3; Num 6:14). The language of purity is also used in the New Testament to describe those who may stand before God without blame because of Christ (Col 1:22).

Connections with James

In addition to the associations between the letter openings, there are a significant number of parallels between the endings of James and Jude, including shared themes and parallel sequence. First, before their conclusions both letters contain an eschatological section (Jas 5:7-11; Jude 14-19), where the term *kyrios* is used to refer to Jesus Christ as the returning judge. Second, both texts move from a warning of eschatological judgment rendered by the Lord himself to an exhortation to effective prayer (Jas 5:13-18; Jude 20-21). Finally, both letters conclude with an appeal to mercy in the midst of Christ's final judgment (Jas 5:19-20; Jude 22-23).

Jude's closing doxology breaks the succession of parallels between the conclusions of James and Jude and thus signals a unique function. The final doxology of Jude could function as a benediction drawing the entire Catholic Epistles collection to a close. The twofold benediction that God would "protect you from stumbling" and "make you stand in the presence of his glory, without blemish and with great joy" in a general way summarizes themes running throughout the Catholic Epistles.

After expressing God's power to protect and preserve his people in the face of the staining influence of the intruders, Jude concludes his doxology with outright praise of God's glory and power. The author announces the one to be praised, "the only God our Savior" (recalling the Old Testament phrase "the God of our salvation"), and then lists the honors due: "glory, majesty, power, and authority" (Jude 25). This praise and glory to God is offered specifically through Jesus Christ our Lord. The first part of the doxology is a confident expression that God will preserve Jude's readers from the spiritual threats posed by the intruders. The central concern of the letter is expressed in the confident hope that God will cause the readers to stand before him without blemish with great joy. This, of course, leads to a final confession of God's goodness, glory, and power.

The doxology draws Jude's letter to a fitting close while, at the same time, read as the final text in the Catholic Epistles, Jude's doxology also is a fitting conclusion to the entire collection. Jude's primary concerns have been to combat the intruders and their influence (whether in doctrine or ethics) for the sake of the church's health and Christian obedience. The theme of combating false teaching draws together the concern of 2 Peter and 1 John along with Jude. The central theme of obedience (connecting faith and works; Jas 2:14-26; 1 Jn 3:18) especially as articulated in the command to love (Lev 19:18) woven through each of the seven texts also finds a fitting conclusion here in Jude's doxology. That followers of Christ come to wholeness (James) and live out their true identity in Christ (1 Peter) echo Jude's confidence that in the end God himself will keep "you from stumbling" and will "make you stand . . . without blemish" (Jude 24). Finally, the worship and praise of "God our Savior, through Jesus Christ our Lord" (Jude 25) echoes the conviction that Jesus is God the Father's instrument of salvation (1 Pet 1:3; 3:18) who himself is divine ("God and Savior Jesus Christ," 2 Pet 1:1, 11), being the Son of God ("Jesus is the Son of God," 1 Jn 4:15; 5:1, 5). Coupled with James's use of *Lord* to describe the coming of Jesus (Jas 5:8-9), this first phrase of Jude 25 expresses the christological conviction running through the Catholic Epistles.

FURTHER READING | JUDE COMMENTARIES AND MONOGRAPHS

T: technical; ★: recommended; ★★: highly recommended

Bauckham, Richard J. *Jude and the Relatives of Jesus in the Early Church*. Edinburgh: T&T Clark, 1990.

T★★ ———. *Jude, 2 Peter*. WBC. Nashville: Thomas Nelson, 2003.

Charles, J. Daryl. *Literary Strategy in the Epistle of Jude*. Scranton, PA: University of Scranton Press, 1993.

★ Davids, Peter H. *The Letters of 2 Peter and Jude*. PNTC. Grand Rapids, MI: Eerdmans, 2006.

T Green, Gene L. *Jude and 2 Peter*. BECNT. Grand Rapids, MI: Baker, 2008.

Kelly, J. N. D. *A Commentary on the Epistles of Peter and Jude*. Grand Rapids, MI: Baker, 1996.

Moo, Douglas. *2 Peter and Jude*. NIVAC. Grand Rapids, MI: Zondervan, 1996.

Neyrey, Jerome H. *2 Peter, Jude: A New Translation with Introduction and Commentary*. AB. New York: Doubleday, 1993.

Reese, Ruth Ann. *2 Peter and Jude*. THNTC. Grand Rapids, MI: Eerdmans, 2007.

★ Schreiner, Thomas R. *1–2 Peter and Jude*. CSC. Nashville: Holman, 2020.

Conclusion

EACH OF THE PRECEDING CHAPTERS has opened with a brief description of how the letters in the Catholic Epistles are connected. These sections focus on keyword connections that draw together successive letters in the collection. As a complement to these observations, in this concluding chapter I will draw together some of the major thematic connections running through the Catholic Epistles. When set alongside the observations regarding the early church's collection of these particular seven letters outlined in the introduction, the keyword and thematic associations strengthen the view that these letters should be read and interpreted together. Readers will notice text boxes throughout the commentary sections of the previous chapters, which draw attention to the themes outlined in more detail in this chapter. Those themes are summarized in such a way that stresses the internal coherence of the Catholic Epistles as a collection.[1]

THE LOVE COMMAND

The command to love one's neighbor is first announced in the law of Moses in Leviticus 19:18 and is reiterated in Jesus' own teaching (Mt

---

[1]For a fuller discussion of themes in the Catholic Epistles, see Darian R. Lockett, *Letters from the Pillar Apostles: The Formation of the Catholic Epistles as a Canonical Collection* (Eugene, OR: Pickwick, 2017), chap. 6.

22:37-40; Mk 12:29-31; Jn 13:34). Not only is the love command present in both James and 1 Peter, but both letters also refer to its origin in the law of Moses—James cites Leviticus 19:18 (Jas 2:8) and 1 Peter alludes to it (1 Pet 1:22). James couches the command to love the neighbor (Jas 2:8) within a discussion of the incommensurability of showing partiality and faith in Jesus Christ (Jas 2:1). Specifically, preferring the rich at the expense of the poor (Jas 2:2-4) is directly at odds with the command to love. The love command also surfaces in James 4:11-12. Slanderous speech directed toward a brother or sister is tantamount to becoming a judge of God's law. In the climatic phrase of the passage, the inverse of the love commandment is implied: "But who are you to judge your neighbor?" (Jas 4:12). James argues that criticism of a fellow believer contradicts the command to love the neighbor—if one is judging one's neighbor, one is certainly not loving one's neighbor. A final passage in James strongly influenced by the command to love is found in the letter's concluding instruction. James argues, "If any among you strays from the truth, and someone turns him back, let that person know that whoever turns a sinner from the error of his way will save his soul from death and cover a multitude of sins" (Jas 5:19-20). At the end of this passage James alludes to Proverbs 10:12 (which is also cited in 1 Pet 4:8), which says, "love covers a multitude of sins." Though the keyword *love* is missing from James's citation, he focuses on the act of turning a sinner away from the error of his way. The act of recovering and admonishing the neighbor or fellow believer who wanders from the way of truth is an act of love.

In 1 Peter the command to love surfaces as well. After calling his readers to holiness, citing Leviticus 19:2 (1 Pet 1:16), Peter charges his readers to love one another: "so that you show sincere brotherly love for each other, from a pure heart love one another constantly" (1 Pet 1:22). In the context, loving other believers is perhaps the primary way Christians demonstrate the holiness of God. This idea links both references to Leviticus (Lev 19:2, 18) in 1 Peter 1. A similar command appears in 1 Peter 2:17 in the closing series of commands regarding subordination within the civil realm. Peter says: "Honor everyone. Love the brothers and sisters." Rather than loving any neighbor generally, the consistent instruction throughout 1 Peter is to love "brothers," or better, "the family of believers" (NRSV). The command to love one another is also found in 1 Peter 3:8; 4:8. Such love has in view fellow members of the community, who, for 1 Peter, are likely facing suffering and hardship due to their commitment to following in Christ's footsteps (1 Pet 2:21-23). Love specifically for fellow believers is stressed in 1 Peter rather than love for the neighbor generally due to this specific context of suffering in 1 Peter.

Peter opens his second letter with a promise that God gives "divine power" (2 Pet 1:3) and "precious and very great promises" (2 Pet 1:4 NRSV) to enable believers to live a godly life. Peter then gives a list of virtues that should characterize this transformed life. Most importantly, this otherwise Hellenistic virtue list is distinctly Christian in how it begins and ends—the list opens with faith and ends with love. That love is placed last in the list is a way of stressing that it is the crowning virtue of the Christian life. Richard Bauckham argues, "Love is the overriding ethical principle from which the other virtues gain their meaning and validity. Thus, the author of 2 Peter sees that some of the ethical ideals of pagan society should also be Christian ideals, but only if they are subordinated to and reinterpreted by the Christian ideal of love."[2] Therefore, because of the position of this virtue list in the structure of 2 Peter, and the position of love within the list, it is reasonable to highlight the overall significance of the command to love for 2 Peter. There may also be a second reference to the love command in 2 Peter 2:21. Speaking specifically about the false teachers, Peter argues it would have been better for them never to have known the truth than after knowing it "to turn back from the holy command delivered to them" (2 Pet 2:21). The reference to the holy commandment, especially as it appears in the singular, could refer to the command to love the neighbor. Furthermore, the phrase "delivered to them" or "passed on to them" (NIV) suggests an

---

[2]Richard J. Bauckham, *Jude, 2 Peter*, WBC (Nashville: Thomas Nelson, 2003), 193.

official teaching of the early church passed on by the apostles. This is reinforced by the fact that a few verses later Peter exhorts his readers to remember "the commandment of the Lord and Savior spoken through your apostles" (2 Pet 3:2 NRSV). Thus, here we may find a final, implicit reference to the love command in 2 Peter. Both the singular use of *commandment* and the strong indication of passing on of apostolic teaching connect directly to the Johannine epistles.

The love command is pervasive in the Johannine epistles, appearing repeatedly throughout all three letters: 1 John 2:7-11; 3:10-11, 14, 23; 4:7, 11, 20-21; 5:1-2; 2 John 5-6; 3 John 6. In the first of these passages John argues, "I am not writing you a new command but an old command that you have had from the beginning" (1 Jn 2:7). Though he does not specifically say what command is in view, it is likely that John has in mind the command to love the neighbor in Leviticus 19:18 (also compare 1 Jn 3:23; 2 Jn 5-6). That Jesus describes a new command in a very similar way in John 13:34 ("I give you a new command: Love one another. Just as I have loved you, you are also to love one another") further suggests a connection to Leviticus. Perhaps the old law to love the neighbor is new in Christ not because it is disconnected from the original command but because it is a love of neighbor beyond human ability—in Christ, love for neighbor is perfectly displayed and thus is new. Often throughout John's letters the command to love is rendered in the singular, thus again suggesting a reference to *the* love command originating in Leviticus 19:18. Judith Lieu notes, "Although the demand to keep the commands features more than their content, the variation between the plural and the singular (as in 3:22–4) excludes any idea of a developed pattern of rules and instead focuses on the one command. This is ultimately the command to love (3:11; 4:21)."[3]

Whereas the love command along with specific reference to Leviticus 19:18 appears in James through 3 John, it seems to be absent from Jude. The letter twice mentions love, but in reference to love between the

---

[3]Judith Lieu, *The Theology of the Johannine Epistles*, NTT (Cambridge: Cambridge University Press, 1991), 52.

believer and God. Jude 1 addresses "those who are called, loved by God the Father and kept for Jesus Christ." The love of God bestowed on his people here functions as a title and identity marker for Jude's readers. Similarly, Jude instructs his readers to "keep yourselves in the love of God" (Jude 21). This is instruction for believers specifically to keep themselves in God's love for them. Even though these are the only two explicit references to love in Jude, the command to extend mercy to others in Jude 22-23 could be an implicit reference to the love command. The motivation to warn and reclaim those who waver in or stray from the truth is a theme already noted in James 5:19-20. There I stressed that love is what covers a multitude of sin specifically by recovering an erring brother or sister. Here too perhaps is a similar emphasis, namely, that by extending mercy to those who waver or doubt, one might rescue a fellow believer and thus in love cover a multitude of sin. In other words, the concluding instruction to have mercy on the wavering in Jude 22-23 could also be seen as an implicit command to love.

ENDURING TRIAL

After a brief letter opening, James immediately turns to the theme of patient endurance of trials. He encourages his readers, saying, "Consider it a great joy, my brothers and sisters, whenever you experience various trials [*peirasmois . . . poikilois*]" (Jas 1:2). The verb *consider* likely stresses continuation—perhaps "continue urgently to consider" (constative aorist)—which is all the more pressing because "you know that the testing of your faith [*dokimion hymōn tēs pisteōs*] produces endurance" (Jas 1:3). In this context trials refer to a test of devotion or faithfulness, and it is important to note God is the one who tries or tests with the purpose of strengthening the believer's faith. Whereas God is the one who tests, he is never responsible for sending temptation (a test designed for one's failure), because "God is not tempted by evil, and he himself doesn't tempt anyone" (Jas 1:13). The testing or proving is the means by which faith is found to be genuine, or in James's preferred language, "that you may be perfect and complete, lacking in nothing" (Jas 1:4 ESV). Throughout the letter, James argues that such trials are a necessary part of the life of a believer because "the testing of your faith produces endurance [*hypomonēn*]" (Jas 1:3), and this endurance is set within a cosmic framework where the world and the devil (Jas 4:4-5) are at odds with God.

In language almost identical to James, 1 Peter 1:6-9 also commands rejoicing in the midst of trials: "You rejoice in this, even though now for a short time . . . you suffer grief in various trials [*poikilois peirasmois*] so that the proven character of your faith [*dokimion hymōn tēs pisteōs*] . . . may result in praise, glory, and honor" (1 Pet 1:6-8). The specific trial Peter's audience is experiencing consists of suffering and social pressure resulting from their status as aliens and strangers because of their faith in Christ. Peter explains that their suffering is natural and to be expected— they are, after all, followers of Christ, who was himself crucified (1 Pet 1:6; 4:12-13) and who now stands as the ultimate example of innocent suffering (1 Pet 2:21-24; 4:13-19). The trial is bound up in the fact that they should suffer for doing what is right, not for doing what is wrong (1 Pet 3:14-17; 4:14-15). Though the present suffering at the hands of nonbelievers causes hardship, Peter insists that even in their present circumstances his readers can rejoice because of the resulting glorious reality of their salvation, the result of enduring trials.

Though 2 Peter does not directly address suffering, persecution, or testing, in the list of virtues in 2 Peter 1:5-7 Peter urges his readers "to supplement your faith with goodness, goodness with . . . endurance [*hypomonēn*], endurance with godliness" (2 Pet 1:5-6). Endurance in early Christianity was associated with persevering in trust toward God and with enduring hope that God would fulfill his promises. In 2 Peter there was a special need to endure in the face of false teachers who threatened the church. These teachers threatened the community in their challenge to apostolic traditions. Robert Wall notes,

> When 1 Peter and 2 Peter are studied together as integral parts of the [Catholic Epistles'] Petrine witness, the biblical reader is reminded that the spiritual failure most often provoked by suffering is to com-promise or attenuate the community's core beliefs as a strategy for

avoiding the very hostility generative of suffering. Typically, orthodoxy is the first casualty of hardship (see Jas 1:13-16).[4]

As 1 and 2 Peter are read together—and along with the rest of the Catholic Epistles—the connection between trials and compromise is clearly seen.

First John continues to strengthen the connection between trials and orthodoxy. John instructs his readers, "Dear friends, do not believe every spirit, but test the spirits" (1 Jn 4:1). Beyond this command to test the spirits, Lieu argues that "the structure of the letter itself reproduces the process of self-analysis and testing."[5] The letter opens with eyewitness claims about the word of life, and throughout the letter the community must test these claims as to whether they have fellowship with God (1 Jn 1:3). The theme of self-examination or testing continues later in the letter: "This is how we know that we know him: if we keep his commands" (1 Jn 2:3). Again and again John challenges his readers to examine themselves, specifically their conduct and theology, especially in light of those who have left the believing community (1 Jn 2:19) because of a deficient confession of Christology (2 Jn 7). Unlike James and 1 Peter, where trials are external, enduring the test or trial in 1 John is an exercise in self-assessment. The tests that may verify or falsify a claim to knowing God and keeping his commandments appear throughout 1 John:

Table 8.1[1]

Walking in the darkness vs. walking in the light	1 John 1:6
(Not) keeping his commands or his word	1 John 2:3-6; 3:24; 5:2
Hating vs. loving one's brother	1 John 2:9-11; 3:14-15; 4:7-8, 20
Doing sin or sinning vs. not sinning	1 John 3:4, 7-10

[1]Adapted from Judith Lieu, *The Theology of the Johannine Epistles*, NTT (Cambridge: Cambridge University Press, 1991), 52.

Whereas John does speak of commands in the plural, as mentioned above, he most often refers to *the* command as singular; therefore, the overarching test that might verify the claim to know God in 1 John is the test of loving one another.

---

[4]Robert W. Wall, "A Unifying Theology of the Catholic Epistles," in *The Catholic Epistles and Apostolic Tradition*, ed. Karl-Wilhelm Niebuhr and Robert W. Wall (Waco, TX: Baylor University Press, 2009), 32.

[5]Lieu, *Theology of the Johannine Epistles*, 50.

Jude does not use specific language to identify testing or trials; however, in keeping with the literary relationship with 2 Peter, the author notes the concern to "contend for the faith" (Jude 3). This faith, like in 1 John and 2 Peter, is the apostolic tradition, which is under threat by a group of libertines who have secretly infiltrated the community. Whereas the longest section of Jude is devoted to offering the background of the intruders (Jude 5-19)—their condemnation that was foretold (Jude 4)—the central exhortation of the letter is to guard and keep apostolic orthodoxy in the face of such pressure or trial. Thus, the overall concern to defend the apostolic faith in the face of external threat can be seen as a trial the church must overcome.

GOD AND THE WORLD AS INCOMPATIBLE ALLEGIANCES

James uses the word "world" (*kosmos*) five times in his letter (Jas 1:27; 2:5; 3:6; 4:4 [2×]), each time with a negative connotation. In the first occurrence of the term, James implicitly contrasts "pure and undefiled religion before God the Father" with the staining influence of the world (Jas 1:27). Here there is clear opposition between God and the world. James 2 asks, "Has not God chosen the poor in the world to be rich in faith?" (Jas 2:5 ESV). The phrase "poor in the world" should be read as poor in the eyes of or in the estimation of the world. The grammar of the passage emphasizes that it is from the perspective or valuation of the world that these people are counted poor. In other words, here again is a contrast between God and the world—God chooses those that the world esteems as worthless. Furthermore, in James 3:13-18 James contrasts "wisdom from above" (Jas 3:17) with wisdom that is "earthly, unspiritual, demonic" (Jas 3:15). Though using a different term (*epigeios* rather than *kosmos*), once again God (or wisdom from God) is set in opposition to the world. Finally, in James 4:4 James uses *kosmos* twice in conjunction with friendship: "You adulteresses! Don't you know that friendship with the world is hostility toward God? Therefore, whoever wants to be a friend of the world becomes an enemy of God" (my translation). Friendship in the ancient world was a way of referring to loyalty (politically, economically, and militarily), and thus here we find a sharp opposition between God and the world. One cannot be loyal both to God and the world at the same time.

In 1 Peter, Christians are called to do right in the face of suffering— Peter calls his readers to be holy (1 Pet 1:14-16; 2:5, 9; 3:5) and pure (1 Pet 1:22; 2:2; 3:2). This purity is to be lived out in the midst of the non-believing world, yet as those separate from that world (1 Pet 1:14-18; 4:1-4). Peter instructs his readers to live out their new identity in Christ before nonbelievers, which inevitably leads to suffering. In this context the audience is to maintain cultural contact with the world, while at the same time remaining distinct. Thus, there are elements of both resistance and conformity in 1 Peter. Maintaining separation from the world by doing good while suffering will be a witness to that same watching world (1 Pet 2:11-12). Thus, the relationship between God and the world in 1 Peter is complex—neither completely conforming or rejecting, but in contact for the purpose of witness.

Whereas the relationship between the Christian community and the world is nuanced in 1 Peter, in 2 Peter it is much clearer. Throughout 2 Peter there is a clear contrast between the truth of apostolic teaching and the deception of the false teachers (2 Pet 2:1-3; 3:3). Though he does not directly connect the deceptive doctrine of the false teachers with the world specifically, Peter refers to "corruption that is in the world because of evil desire" (2 Pet 1:4). Here the world is the realm in which both moral and physical decay and corruption takes place. Furthermore, Peter describes the destruction or judgment of the "ancient world" (2 Pet 2:5) and the world of that time, referring to the event of the flood (2 Pet 3:6). In both cases the world not only is the location of human corruption but also by association is a negative entity worthy of judgment. This is an implicit opposition between the God who judges and the world.

Even more poignantly, the contrast between God and the world is strikingly black and white in 1 John. Like James, the world in 1 John marks out everything that is opposed to God: "Do not love the world or the things in the world. If anyone loves the world, the love of the Father is not in him" (1 Jn 2:15). Love for the world and love for God are completely incompatible, such that the person attempting to nurture both loves is either a hypocrite or self-deceived. David Nienhuis continues, "Indeed the [things of God and the things of the world] represent opposing and exclusive realms wherein beings 'abide': faithful believers abide in God and the things of God (1 John 2:10, 14, 24-28; 3:6, 9, 24; 4:12-16), but the world is the abode of the antichrists (4:3), false prophets who propagate a heterodox Christology (4:1), and even the devil himself."[6] By one's actions, it is clear one is either a child of God (1 Jn 3:9-10) or a child of the devil (1 Jn 3:8); there are no other options.

Finally, much like in 2 Peter, the opposition between God and the world is implicit in Jude. The word *world* does not appear in Jude's short letter, yet the implicit contrast between the truth of apostolic teaching and living is cast in direct opposition to the intruders who expose Jude's readers to immoral ways of living. As the apostles are God's messengers of the gospel of Jesus Christ, and the intruders those who reject and resist the apostles, we see the implicit contrast between God and the world in Jude.

FAITH AND WORKS

James specifically argues for the necessary connection between confession and a transformed life—the connection between faith and works (Jas 2:14-26). Abraham was "justified by works in offering Isaac" (Jas 2:21), and Rahab was "justified by works in receiving the messengers and sending them out by a different route" (Jas 2:25), both illustrating James's central claim that "a person is justified by works and not by faith alone" (Jas 2:24). It is important to stress that James is not contrasting faith and works as if they are separable elements; rather, James is keen to contrast faith with works and a counterfeit faith that has no works. This concern for the connection between faith and works should be understood in the context of James's emphasis on wholeness or perfection before God (Jas 1:2-4). It is the double-minded person (Jas

---

[6]David R. Nienhuis, *Not by Paul Alone: The Formation of the Catholic Epistle Collection and the Christian Canon* (Waco, TX: Baylor University Press, 2007), 205.

1:8; 4:8) and the one who is not a doer of the word (Jas 1:22-25) who are guilty of not uniting faith and works. Those who unite faith and works in James renounce partiality (Jas 2:1-7), control the tongue (Jas 1:26; 3:1-12), and are animated by wisdom from above (Jas 3:13-18). James's concern for wholeness, the proper integration of confession and action, permeates the entire letter.

The concern for integration of faith and works in 1 Peter manifests more generally in the concern to live well in the eyes of a watching world: "Conduct yourselves honorably among the Gentiles, so . . . they will observe your good works" (1 Pet 2:12). In the letter's opening section clarifying the reader's new identity in Christ (1 Pet 1:3–2:10), Peter directs their attention to God the Father, who "has given us new birth into a living hope" (1 Pet 1:3). Though Peter speaks about faith on its own (1 Pet 1:5, 7, 9, 21; 5:9), faith and hope are overlapping ideas in the letter (1 Pet 1:21). The new life of living hope (or faith) is one characterized by a new identity in Christ. Peter instructs his readers that this new identity must be lived out and demonstrated by means of good works. The concern for exhibiting good conduct, especially manifested in suffering well, is expressly for the purpose of offering a witness to nonbelievers (1 Pet 2:12). The connection between faith and works is crucial for the argument of 1 Peter.

The relationship between faith and works is much more prominent in 1 John. As noted above, the test in 1 John extends beyond testing "the spirits" (1 Jn 4:1) and includes the more comprehensive testing whether one's claim of faithfulness to God is true or false. The claims enumerated in 1 John 1:6–2:10 are examined in the light of one's action. The test is whether one does God's commandments (1 Jn 1:6; 2:17, 29; 3:4, 22; 5:2). Unlike James, who speaks directly about faith and works (Jas 2:14-26), 1 John prefers to speak of believing (*pisteuō*, 1 Jn 3:23; 4:1, 16; 5:1, 5, 10, 13) rather than faith (*pistis*). Despite these differences, James and 1 John are strikingly similar in how they relate faith and works, as seen in the following passages:

Table 8.2

James 2:14-17	1 John 3:16-18
What good is it, my brothers and sisters, if someone claims to have faith but does not have works? Can such faith save him? If a brother or sister is without clothes and lacks daily food, and one of you says to them, "Go in peace, stay warm and be well fed," but you don't give them what the body needs, what good is it? In the same way faith, if it doesn't have works, is dead by itself.	This is how we have come to know love: He laid down his life for us. We should also lay down our lives for our brothers and sisters. If anyone has this world's goods and sees a fellow believer in need but withholds compassion from him—how does God's love reside in him? Little children, let us not love in word or speech, but in action and in truth.

Both letters describe a similar scenario, where the believer encounters a fellow Christian in need. Yet what is given in both situations is mere words rather than tangible care. This is the prime example that works must accompany faith if it is to be genuine saving faith. First John aptly summarizes the need for integration of faith and works, which is true of the entire Catholic Epistles collection while echoing back to the love command: "Let us not love in word or speech, but in action and in truth" (1 Jn 3:18).

PROTECTING THE CHURCH FROM FALSE TEACHING

Whereas the defense and support of true apostolic teaching is implicit in James and 1 Peter, this is a special emphasis in 2 Peter, 1 John, and Jude. Both 2 Peter and Jude are explicitly concerned with either false teachers (2 Pet 2:1-3; 3:3) or intruders living in an immoral way (Jude 4). Peter confronts the content of the false teachers directly offering a rebuttal for each of the false claims. Jude, on the other hand, wrestles against a group of intruders who are notorious for their denial of the gospel through immoral living and pursuit of ethical freedom. John, in a similar way, confronts the actions and false christological claims of the secessionists who have separated from the Christian community yet continue to exert a negative influence on John's believing audience. Second Peter and 1 John both directly address doctrinal issues—the return of Christ and final judgment for 2 Peter, and false christological claims for 1 John. First John and Jude confront groups of so-called Christians who have abandoned the authority of apostolic teaching and have denied the Lord Jesus Christ by how they live. Though responding to different concerns, all three letters hold together in their concern for correct doctrine and living, and more importantly in their concern for the peace and purity of the church.

CONCLUSION

Because the Catholic Epistles were written by different authors, to different audiences, addressing different topics, many conclude that the letters should be read and interpreted in isolation from one another. This is the typical conclusion most scholars draw. Yet, because of the successive connections between each of the letters, noted at the beginning of each chapter, and the themes traced through the letters of James, Peter, John, and Jude, there is reason to argue, along with the early church, that the Catholic Epistles should be read and interpreted together. The insights offered throughout this book, especially in the commentary sections, do not depend on reading the Catholic Epistles together. The observations from the early church, however, along with the connections and themes running through the Catholic Epistles, suggest reading and interpreting them together as a coherent collection.

Author Index

Achtemeier, Paul J., 54, 62, 78
Allison, Dale C., 52
Athanasius, 3
Bauckham, Richard, 11-15, 18, 25-26, 35, 51, 98-102, 104, 106, 110, 113, 118-19, 189, 191-92, 194-95, 200-201, 204-6, 214
Brown, Raymond E., 124-25, 127-28, 131, 147, 149, 156, 160, 162, 165, 168, 173, 175, 177-78, 182
Carson, D. A., 13
Chester, Andrew, 34
Cicero, 98
Clement of Alexandria, 55, 125, 172
Cyril of Jerusalem, 3
Dibelius, Martin, 11, 14
Dionysius of Alexandria, 126
Dionysius of Corinth, 54
Dodd, C. H., 173
Doering, Lutz, 56
Elliott, John H., 54-55, 60
Ellis, E. Earl, 191
Eusebius, 3, 9, 12, 53, 55-56, 97, 127, 172
Gallagher, E. L., 3
Green, Joel B., 74
Grudem, Wayne, 84-85
Harris, W. Hall, 151
Horrell, David, 65, 78-79, 104-5, 119, 200, 205
Hort, F. J. A., 23

Irenaeus, 125, 172
Jerome, 11, 56, 98, 173, 204
Jobes, Karen, 56, 69, 71-72, 75, 83-84, 90
Johnson, Luke Timothy, 11, 27
Josephus, 12, 150
Kamell, Mariam J., 25
Kelly, J. N. D., 188
Kovalishyn, Mariam. *See* Kamell, Mariam
Kruse, Colin G., 130, 136, 158, 165, 178, 182, 185
Lieu, Judith, 176, 215, 218
Lockett, Darian, 10, 52, 212
Martin, Ralph P., 34
McKnight, Scot, 22
Moo, Douglas, 13, 24, 30, 33, 47, 99-100
Nienhuis, David R., 123-24, 221
Origen, 11, 97
Painter, John, 9, 172
Penner, Todd C., 11
Philo, 150
Pliny, 58
Schutter, William, 57
Strecker, Georg, 183
Suetonius, 58-59
Tacitus, 58-59
Tertullian, 125, 204
Wall, Robert W., 123-24, 217-18
Ward, Tim, 167
Watson, Duane, 99-100, 174

Scripture Index

Finding the Textbook You Need

The IVP Academic Textbook Selector
is an online tool for instantly finding the IVP books
suitable for over 250 courses across 24 disciplines.

---

ivpacademic.com